Authority, Unity and Freedom of Conscience

Copyright 2017 Remains with authors

Avondale Academic Press
PO Box 19
Cooranbong NSW 2265
Australia

and

Oak & Acorn Publishing
PO Box 5005
Westlake Village
CA 91359
United States of America

Cover design & Layout: Glenda McClintock and Ken McClintock
Copy editor: Howard Fisher
Cover Image: Shutterstock.com

Cataloguing in publication data may be found at:
http://catalogue.nla.gov.au/

ISBN:
978-0-9599337-1-0 Paperback
978-0-9599337-3-4 Kindle eBook

Authority, Unity and Freedom of Conscience

Edited by
David Thiele and Brad Kemp

Contents

List of Contributors	7
Introduction *Bradley R. Kemp*	9
UNITY	13
1. What Is Jesus Saying in John 17? *Roy Adams*	15
2. Toward a Theology of Unity *John C. Brunt*	31
FREEDOM	47
3. Liberty in Messiah: The Steep and Narrow Path to Unity *Olive J. Hemmings*	49
4. Religious Freedom: Some Historical Perspectives and Present Applications *Reinder Bruinsma*	65
5. Justice and Equality: Is God Interested? *Ray C. W. Roennfeldt*	85
ELLEN WHITE'S PERSPECTIVES	105
6. Unity in the Writings of Ellen G. White *Wendy A. Jackson*	107

7. "Circumstances Change the Relation of Things"
Rolf J. Pöhler 133

ORGANIZATIONAL ISSUES 153

8. Reorganization of Church Structure, 1901–03:
Some Observations
Barry Oliver 155

9. General Conference Working Policy: The Challenge of Enforcement and the Opportunity for Development
Lowell C. Cooper 185

10. Catholic or Adventist? The Ongoing Struggle Over Authority (and 9.5 Theses)
George R. Knight 211

List of Contributors

Barry Oliver, retired in 2015 from the South Pacific Division of Seventh-day Adventists (Secretary 1997-2007 President 2007-2015).

Bradley R. Kemp, President, New Zealand Pacific Union Conference.

David Thiele, New Testament Lecturer, Avondale College of Higher Education.

George R. Knight, Emeritus Professor of Church History, Andrews University.

John C. Brunt, retired pastor (Azure Hills Church in California) and university professor/administrator (Walla Walla University).

Lowell C. Cooper, retired from 21 years as an officer of the General Conference (four years as an Associate Secretary and 17 years as a General Vice-President).

Olive J. Hemming, Professor of New Testament and Ethics at Washington Adventist University.

Ray C. W. Roennfeldt, President, Avondale College of Higher Education.

Reinder Bruinsma, formerly President, Netherlands Union of SDA Churches

Rolf J. Pöhler, Theological Advisor of the North German Union Conference, Germany.

Roy Adams, retired in 2010, after serving as an associate editor of the Adventist Review for 22 years.

Wendy A. Jackson, Lecturer in Systematic Theology at Avondale College of Higher Education.

Introduction

Bradley R. Kemp

New Zealand Pacific Union Conference

The history of the Christian Church testifies to its willingness to engage in dialogue over difficult issues. Acts 6 and 15 record early conflicts that show how the church worked to resolve them through a process of meetings and discussion. In the following centuries the church engaged in serious debate over the composition of the canon of scripture and such doctrines as the nature of God (Trinity), the nature of Christ, and the Mother of Jesus (*Theotokos*), to name a few. So serious were some of these controversies that bishops from the different religious centers would bring their armies for protection. Dialogue, debate and discussion were hallmarks of the early centuries of the church until doctrine was set and papal authority was introduced. Until this time religious freedom prevailed.

The Protestant movement began as a reaction to the doctrinal and social failures of the Roman Catholic Church. As a result of careful study of the Scriptures, questions concerning certain doctrinal matters began to be asked. Again, debate, dialogue and discussion ensued until the church stepped in and tried to squash such freedom of discussion, thought and conscience. It was during this time that the organised church tried to maintain unity at the cost of conscience. Many of these reformers were persecuted and killed for daring to raise a voice of dissent. It is instructive that Ellen White attributes the following statement on the importance of conscience over policy to the dissenting German princes during the time of the reformation: "Protestantism sets the power of conscience above the magistrate, and the authority of the word of God above the visible church."[1] The right to disagree on issues of conscience was seen as an inalienable right

---

1 Ellen White, The Great Controversy (Nampa, ID: Pacific Press, 2005), 203.

by the early leaders of the Protestant movement. This was also an important value held in the early Seventh-day Adventist church.

In the early days of the development of the Adventist faith, believers who had been convicted by the Holy Spirit came together in the Sabbath Conferences of 1848 to pray, to read, to discuss and to deliberate the great issues surrounding the seventh-day Sabbath. Here we see from the outset that the Adventist movement was characterised by its willingness to engage in dialogue over important issues. The Adventist pioneers were not afraid to tackle tough questions. They worked through issues that were both theological and structural. These meetings were not characterised by a top-down process. Rather, they were characterised by intense Bible study, prayer and open dialogue with a view to reaching consensus in the given area of study. From these conferences there emerged a people more vitally connected to God's word, to one another, and to the distinctive messages that still resonate as the core of the Seventh-day Adventist church.

During the Annual Council of the General Conference of 2016, the question of unity was discussed, particularly in the context of the 2015 General Conference Session's negative vote on allowing Divisions to make their own decision on conferring ordination without regard to gender. However, little time was available for any in-depth study to be done during the decision-making process at this meeting. Debate was restricted to three minutes for any one speaker which limited the development of a meaningful discussion that had depth and maturity, which in turn affected the quality of the decisions that were made. Given the importance of this subject a number of unions felt that more time needed to be devoted to studying this issue, and to engage in open dialogue and prayer. The "Unity 2017" conference was organised to provide such an opportunity. At this conference there were presentations and discussion on structure and authority in the church, the nature and practice of unity, and how as an organisation we practice and respect freedom of conscience around non-core issues. A good understanding of these issues can only be helpful in the current debate and is important for an improved understanding of ecclesiology.

What follows are the papers that were presented at the "Unity 2017" conference. In chapters one and two a biblical study on unity is provided. The first, by Roy Adams, explores Jesus' message to his disciples as recorded in John 17. Here Jesus prays that the church may be one as he and his Father are one. The second, by John Brunt, takes a broader scope and attempts to provide the reader with a basic theology of unity.

The subject in section two is the theme of freedom. Olive Hemmings undertakes a biblical study on the theme of freedom of conscience. Here she explores the contrast between the New Testament ethic of love and liberty and its alternative—conformity to rituals and regulations that have no spiritual value in and of themselves, but serve only to enslave. Reinder Bruinsma provides a history of the church's involvement with religious freedom. This is followed by Ray Roennfeldt's exploration of the nature of God, particularly with respect to the characteristics of justice and equality.

Section three includes two studies on Ellen White's perspective on unity. First, Wendy Jackson provides a detailed review of how Ellen White understood and used the idea of unity in her writings. Then Rolf Pöhler explores how Ellen White related to development and change and how this contributed to her understanding of changes in structure, authority and policies of the Adventist church.

In the concluding chapters issues relating to church organisation, structure and authority are examined. Barry Oliver provides a detailed study on the reasons for organisation change in 1901 and 1903. Lowell Cooper addresses the importance of policy for the church and the role that it can play in mediating a resolution in the current situation through policy development rather than policy enforcement. George Knight brings the book to its conclusion with a study on Adventism's approach to biblical authority, Ellen White's thoughts on authority, and the development of authoritative structures in the Seventh-day Adventist Church. He concludes with a challenge for the church with his 9.5 theses.

These papers are published here in the hope that they make a meaningful contribution to the current dialogue on unity and gender equality in ministry.

UNITY

1. What Is Jesus Saying in John 17?

Roy Adams
Adventist Review – Retired

This chapter is an attempt to break through the static and the noise, and get at the heart of Jesus' burden in his strategic prayer, recorded in John 17. An attempt has been made to set aside personal presuppositions about the passage, not relying on the views of theological or biblical experts, or on the positions of dictionaries and commentaries, but to try to listen to what the text itself is saying—to read the passage as if for the first time, asking how the ordinary person would understand Jesus' words if they happened upon them in some deserted place, away from commentaries, sermons, or notes of any kind. Reading the chapter in the original language (an exercise which forces a slower pace for this writer) also contributed to this listening process.

This as-if-for-the-first-time reading of the text quickly changes a long-standing common conception of the chapter—namely, that the subject of unity is its dominant theme. The subject of unity, while very present, *does not* dominate the passage and in fact the prayer covers a variety of themes.

John does not record Jesus' Gethsemane supplication mentioned in the Synoptics. In John, the event in chapter 17 is Jesus' final prayer before the cross.[1] In this prayer Jesus unburdens Himself before God in a manner unprecedented in the other gospels. Six themes come to the fore: *glorification, revelation, protection, sanctification, unity, and reunion.*

---

1 In the words of Andreas J Köstenberger, the prayer is "strategically placed immediately prior to his arrest, which would trigger in rapid succession the various events surrounding [His] crucifixion." *A Theology of John's Gospel and Letters* (Grand Rapids: Zondervan, 2009), 246.

Glorification

Evidently Jesus' prayer was offered while He was still at the location of the Passover meal, where John, together with the other disciples, would have heard it. Jesus presumably would have wanted them to witness this unvarnished unburdening of His soul to His Heavenly Father. And now, more than half a century later, and facing the crosswinds of events in the church and in the world around him, John returns to the famous prayer, the Holy Spirit guiding his mind toward its most salient features. Jesus began His supplication in a way that is alien to modern readers, with a focus on the idea of glorification. "Father, the hour has come. Glorify your Son (δόξασόν σου τὸν υἱόν), that your Son may glorify you" (17:1).[2]

What did Jesus have in mind here? What's behind this idea of glorification? What form was it to take?

John places considerable emphasis on the notion of glorification in his gospel. His opening pronouncement is on this theme: "The Word became flesh and lived among us. *We have seen his glory* (τὴν δόξαν αὐτοῦ), *the glory of the one and only Son*, who came from the Father, full of grace and truth" (1:14). Even without fully understanding all that John had in mind here, the mere reading of those words transports the mind to a sublime place, filled with excitement and wonder. It was a glory "shining through the veil of his flesh."[3]

Other passages pick up the theme. By changing water into wine at a wedding celebration in Galilee, John says, Jesus "revealed his glory, and his disciples put their faith in him" (2:11). Lazarus' resurrection, Jesus Himself observed, was "for *God's glory,* so that the son of God may be glorified through it" (11:4, NRSV). In vision, John says, Isaiah "saw Jesus' glory and spoke about him" (12:41).

"Bringing glory" is what children do to their parents when they perform well in school, excel in sports, or stand out in some other praiseworthy endeavor. Humans glorify (or bring glory to) God when we do God's work, when we obey God's word, when we act in such a way as to enhance the divine values or mission in the world. Jesus echoes this notion in John 17:4 Addressing his Father, he said: "I've

---

2 Unless otherwise noted the scriptural citations in this paper are taken from the NIV.

3 R. C. H. Lenski, The Interpretation of St. John's Gospel (Minneapolis, MN: Augsburg, 1961), p. 1159.

brought you glory on earth by completing the work you gave me to do."

The glorification idea intensifies in John's gospel as Jesus gets closer and closer to the cross. This is seen in Jesus' response to certain God-fearing Greeks who appeared in the crowd around Him during Passion Week, asking for an audience. Apparently he saw in their request a broader yearning for the salvation He had come to bring, a salvation possible only through the cross, now merely days away. As if oblivious to the specific request (and the passage leaves the reader wondering whether the desired audience ever materialized), images of that impending cosmic moment flashed upon his mind, evoking those somber words recorded in John 12:23 that anticipated the great prayer of chapter 17: "The hour has come for the Son of Man to be glorified."

That glorification would involve (for Jesus) the ghastly experience of the cross. But, as he described it, the seed, if it is to multiply and feed the multitude, must first die (12:24). And (mixing metaphors) only as the Son of Man is lifted on a tree, experiencing the death of a planted seed, would he have the power to "draw all people" to Himself, including the multitude represented by those enquiring Greeks in His audience that day (12:32, NRSV). And thus he braced Himself for that dreadful moment: "Now my soul is troubled, and what shall I say? 'Father, save me from this hour'? No, it was for this very reason I came to this hour. Father, *glorify* your name!" (12:27, 28a). God's answer was immediate, like rumbling thunder above the din and hubbub of the crowd: "I have *glorified* it, and will *glorify* it again" (12:28b).

Buttressed by this assurance, and inching ever closer to the cross after Judas, bent on his dark mission, left the supper room that Thursday evening, Jesus intensified his focus on glorification. According to John, "…when [Judas] was gone, Jesus said, 'Now the Son of Man is *glorified* and God is *glorified* in him. If God is *glorified* in him, God will *glorify* the Son in himself, and will *glorify* him at once" (13:31–32).

As he comes to the opening sentences of his prayer in chapter 17, Jesus picks up this running theme a final time. The fact that he refers again to the idea of "the hour" having come (verse 1) gives further evidence that he was looking ahead to the cross and that glorification had something to do with his impending death and the resurrection to follow (although the resurrection is never explicitly mentioned in the chapter).

A prominent theme "of Johannine high Christology," says Paul N. Anderson,

> is *the glorification of the Son of Man*.... Such passages as 1:51; 3:14; 6:62; 8:28; 12:23–36; 13:1, 13a all refer to some aspect of the Son of Man ... ascending, being lifted up or being glorified. This is in keeping with the descent/ascent schemas of the christological hymns (Phil. 2:5–11; Col 1:15–20; Heb 1:1–4). But in John, glorification is paradoxically connected with the cross.[4]

Perhaps Jesus' most intriguing statement about glorification comes in 17: 5, when he asked God to "glorify me in your presence with the glory I had with you before the world began." Here he takes the idea of glorification to a different level. How is παρὰ σεαυτῷ, translated by the NIV and other modern translations as "in your presence" or "in your own presence," to be understood? If the reflexive pronoun σεαυτω means "thyself" or "yourself," where does the idea of "in your presence" come from—especially when it is linked to παρὰ, a complicated preposition, requiring more than two pages of fine-print explanation in Arndt's and Gingrich's *Greek-English Lexicon of the New Testament?*[5]

The situation is analogous to that of historians who, when studying the mysteries of religion, sometimes have to realize that their methodological "instruments are too clumsy to handle the evidence" in front of them.[6] Perhaps biblical interpreters face the same difficulty from time to time. For here one gets the sense that Jesus probably meant something much deeper than the translators are able to manage—that he was probably asking God to glorify Him (Jesus) *with God Himself*, in a way too complex for human words. Suffice it to say that at the very least it was a plea for the reinstatement before the heavenly intelligences of Jesus' divine honor and prerogatives, voluntarily relinquished for the sake of His incarnation.

---

4 Paul N. Anderson, *The Christology of the Fourth Gospel* (Valley Forge, PA: Trinity Press International), p. 266.

5 Walter Bauer, William F. Arndt and Frederick W. Gingrich, *Greek-English Lexicon of the NT and Other Early Christian Literature* (Chicago, IL & London: University of Chicago Press, 1979), .s.v. παρά.

6 John McManners, "Introduction," In *The Oxford Illustrated History of Christianity,* ed. John McManners (Oxford & New York: Oxford University Press, 1990), 6.

Finally, it would appear that that relinquishment occurred not when Jesus entered Mary's womb, but "before the world existed" (17:5, NRSV). This is a mind-blowing thought, if correct, because it shows that the provisions of divine grace anticipated the fall, predating the creation of the planet itself.

So the idea of glory, introduced by John at the beginning of his gospel ("the Word became flesh ... (and) ... we have seen his glory") reaches its climax in the major burden with which Jesus begins his prayer. Notwithstanding the darkness involved, it was a note of triumph, but filled with pathos and paradox.

Revelation

Following his emphasis on glorification, Jesus' burden shifts to *revelation*—that is, making God known in the world, and Jesus Christ whom God has sent (17: 3–9, 25, 26). He declares, "I *have revealed you* to those whom you gave me out of the world" (17: 6). Lenski notes that "the aorist [Ἐφανέρωσά, 'I have revealed'] records the accomplished fact," and ultimately means "more than 'to teach.'" It has "the sense of '*to reveal.*'"[7] In other words, "Jesus is the emissary of God ... who through his words and deeds brings revelation."[8]

As John remembered Jesus' prayer in the closing years of the first century, he would have done so in dynamic relation to the contemporary context, a context shaped by a number of contrarian philosophies inimical to the Christian faith. The presence of Gnosticism, for example, with its esoteric approach to the whole concept of knowledge and revelation,[9] with its claim to "secret revelation," was combined with "a dualism of spirit and matter, mind and body," and all this linked with ideas of "determinism or predestinarianism."[10]

Perhaps not all these ideas were fully developed when John wrote his gospel late in the first century. But it seems evident that he was writing with a distinct consciousness of this and other aberrant

---

7 Lenski, *Interpretation*, 1128, 1129.

8 Rudolf Bultmann, paraphrased in John Ashton, *Understanding the Fourth Gospel* (Oxford: Clarendon Press, 1991), 53.

9 Alfred R. C. Leaney, "Gnosticism," in *A Dictionary of Christian Theology*, ed. Allan Richardson (Philadelphia: Westminster / London: SCM, 1969), 133., s.v. "Gnosticism."

10 Henry Chadwick, "The Early Christian Community," in *The Oxford Illustrated History*, ed. John McManners (Oxford & New York: Oxford University Press, 1990), 26.

philosophies. The use of expressions such as "word" and "knowledge" in the Synoptics is generally ordinary and pedestrian (except perhaps for Matt. 13:11 and Luke 8:10, where Jesus talks about the "knowledge of the secrets of the kingdom of heaven" as having been given to His disciples; or Mk 12:24, where he charges Jewish leaders with "not knowing the Scriptures or the power of God").

But in the Gospel of John, the "word," the *logos,* seems to take on heightened significance. One gets the sense that something in the air, something in the culture, is jogging John's memory in the direction of highlighting a certain kind of knowledge, a special focus on the concept of *logos,* as if conscious of confronting an alien species of these ideas in the culture. Note how he begins his first epistle, for example:

> "That which was from the beginning, which we have heard, which we have seen with our eyes, which we have looked at and our hands have touched—this we proclaim concerning the Word of life. The life appeared; we have seen it and testify to it, and we proclaim to you the eternal life, which was with the Father and has appeared to us" (1 John 1:1, 2).

The knowledge John recalled Jesus enunciating in his prayer, unlike that promoted by the Gnostics, was based on the revelation of God—not detached or esoteric, but connected to a person, the Person of God and the Man, Jesus Christ—the *logos* who "became flesh and made his dwelling among us" (John 1:14).

As his farewell discourse was coming to an end, Jesus spoke about his impending departure, stressing God's love for those who had left all to follow him: "[T]he Father himself loves you," He said to them, "because you have loved me and have believed that I came from God. I came from the Father and entered the world; now I am leaving the world and going back to the Father" (16:27, 28).

Impressed, the disciples offered their own confession. "Now we can see," they said, "that you know all things…This makes us believe that you came from God" (16: 30). *"Yes!"* Jesus thought, and he could not hold it back: "You believe at last!" (16:31). Moments later, Jesus would refer to that shining confession in His prayer: "I gave them the words you gave me and they accepted them. They knew with certainty that I came from you, and they believed that you sent me" (17:8).

The revelation had been successful and that was critical because of what Jesus had spelled out with unmistakable gravity near the beginning of His prayer: "Now this is eternal life: that they may know you, the only true God, and Jesus Christ whom you have sent" (17: 3).

So important is this revelation, this knowledge of God, Jesus returns to it as he ends the prayer: "Righteous Father, though the world does not know you, I know you, and they know that you have sent me. I have made you known to them, and will continue to make you known in order that the love you have for me may be in them and that I myself may be in them" (17:25, 26).

One cannot "listen" to Jesus' prayer without coming to the conclusion that He wanted that revelation (of God and God's Son) to spread to the entire οἰκουμένη, the entire world. And if (as is logical to believe) he anticipated that the laborers would always be few (see Matt 9:37; Luke 10:2), then it would be theologically irrational for Him to envision any curtailment of the workforce of his followers by a blanket disqualification of one gender that, in every age, has constituted more than half of the church.

Protection

The picture Matthew draws of Jesus' followers in the world is that of "sheep among wolves" (Matt 10:16). Paul invoked the same metaphor when he warned the elders of the Ephesus church that, after he was gone, "savage wolves will come in among you and will not spare the flock" (Acts 20:29). Jesus does not use that language in his prayer (nor does the gospel of John carry the particular metaphor), but it is clear that the believers' need for protection features prominently in the sentiments of John 17. So that even in the absence of that specific language, one can sense Jesus' burden for the protection of the followers he was leaving behind, followers he repeatedly refers to as sheep in his discourse in John 10.

With more than one quarter of the verses of John 17 devoted to this theme, the intensity and solicitude with which Jesus commences the segment in verse 9 should be noted: "I pray for them. I am not praying for the world, but for those you have given me, for they are yours….I will remain in the world no longer, but they are still in the world, and I am coming to you. Holy Father, *protect them by the power of your name* ... "(17: 9–11).

The verb in 17:11 is the imperative τήρησον, from τηρέω, translated "keep" in the KJV, which is accurate, but Jesus' meaning is understood more clearly when other possible meanings of the term are examined; namely, *to " keep watch over, [to] guard,"*[11] or, as I am interpreting it here: *"to protect."*

The pain of leaving a flock of vulnerable sheep behind in the world comes through as Jesus unburdens Himself on this point: "While I was with them, I protected them and kept them safe ..." (17:12). But because of the work still needing to be done after he was gone, Jesus prayed not that God would "take them out of the world but that [He would] protect them from the evil one" (17: 15), who had dogged His footsteps all His life.

In this plea for protection, one hears echoes of His assurance-laden promise in chapter 10: "My sheep listen to my voice; I know them, and they follow me. I give them eternal life, and they shall never perish; no one will snatch them out of my hand" (10: 27 28). What he promises in chapter 10 forms a huge portion of the burden of his prayer in chapter 17. And after more than 2000 years, one can still hear the pathos, the urgency, in Jesus' voice as He pleads for the security of his followers: "Holy Father, protect them by the power of your name ... " (7:11).

Here Jesus draws from his extensive knowledge of Old Testament Scripture, where "the name" stands, among other things, for the person himself or herself—and where God's name, in particular, is a force to reckon with. The psalmist knew this when he wrote: "May the Lord answer you when you are in distress; may *the name of the God of Jacob* protect you" (Ps 20:1). The writer of Proverbs says that "*the name of the Lord* is a strong tower; the righteous run to it and are safe" (Prov 18:10).

Listening to the prayer, the disciples would have received enormous comfort in knowing that as they would live and operate in a dangerous world, they could count on the protection of the highest power in the universe. Christians today, who currently see the church in grave danger, may also plead for that divine protection to shield them.

Sanctification

The idea of sanctification appears in 17:17–19, occupying a place in the prayer that cannot be ignored: "Sanctify them in the truth; your word is truth. As you have sent me into the world, so I have sent them into the world. And for their sakes I sanctify myself, so that they also may be sanctified in truth" (NRSV). The word translated

---

11 Bauer, Arndt and Gingrich, *Lexicon,* s.v. τηρέω.

"sanctify" is ἁγιάζω, which means "to make holy, to consecrate, to purify, to sanctify." When used of persons, the word usually means to "*consecrate, dedicate, sanctify*, i.e., [to] include in the inner circle of what is holy ... "[12]

With reference to people, this is not a common word in the gospels—or, indeed, in the New Testament. Its only uses in the gospels with reference to people are the two uses in John 17:17–19. However, it is used elsewhere in the New Testament. Paul speaks of Christ loving the church and giving "himself up for her to make her holy [the verb is ἁγιάζω], cleansing her by the washing with water through the word" (Eph 5:25, 26). In 1 Thessalonians 5:23, he offers a prayer that "God himself [would] ... sanctify [ἁγιάζω] [the recipients of his letter] through and through", and that their "whole spirit, soul and body [might] be kept blameless at the coming of our Lord Jesus Christ." Furthermore, the apostle Peter admonished believers to "set apart [ἁγιάζω] Christ as Lord" in their hearts (1 Pet 3:15), and the author of Hebrews intimates that "Jesus ... suffered outside the city gate in order to sanctify (ἁγιάζω) the people by his own blood" (Heb 13:12, NRSV).

Given the absence of any elaboration in John of the meaning of the experience requested in Jesus' prayer, the usage by these other NT writers seems wholly in keeping with the sense of Jesus' request in John 17. "Sanctify them in the truth; your *word* is truth" (17:17) matches perfectly Paul's idea of sanctifying the church "by the washing with water *through the word*" (Eph. 5:25, 26).

To move from being sanctified "by his blood" (Hebrews) to being sanctified "in the truth" (John 17) represents an intriguing shift in perspective which cannot be followed up here. But here again, as John recalls Jesus' prayer, echoes of philosophical ferment in the culture of the late first century can be detected. John represents Jesus as saying, "Sanctify them in the truth." He follows up with a definition meant for the listening disciples—and, from John's perspective, meant to stabilize his potentially restive readers: "Thy word is truth."

In a critical development, in front of Pilate Jesus said, "My kingdom is not of this world. If it were, my servants would fight to prevent my arrest by the Jewish leaders. But now my kingdom is from another place.' 'You are a king, then!' said Pilate. Jesus answered,

---

12 Bauer, Arndt and Gingrich. *Lexicon,* s.v. ἁγιάζω.

'You are right in saying that I am a king. In fact, the reason I was born and came into the world is to testify to *the truth*" (John 18:36–38).

Pilate responds: "What is truth?" (18:38), and then, without waiting for a response, he returns to the anxious Jews gathered outside the judgment place. But John answers the question—in his Gospel and epistles. He remembered Jesus saying in His prayer: "[God's] word is truth." It applies to the written word, but even more to the living λόγος "who came from the Father, full of grace and truth" (1:14), and who said with all appropriate arrogance: "I am the way and the truth and the life. No one comes to the Father except through me" (John 14:6).

Much more could be written on all of this, but a couple of insightful observations from John Ashton suffice to conclude this section. He notes that "Jesus' determination to consecrate himself on behalf of his disciples (17:19), unquestionably [is] an allusion to his approaching death ... "[13] And as he encourages their own sanctification, He expresses His intention to send them into the world, just as he himself had been sent." The implications are momentous," Ashton says: "The role of the community is plainly the same as that of Jesus himself."[14]

Unity

The subject of unity first surfaces in 17:11, where it is connected to the idea of protection: "I will remain in the world no longer," Jesus said, "but they are still in the world, and I am coming to you. Holy Father, protect them by the power of your name, the name you gave me, *so that they may be one as we are one.*" Not protect them so they might be physically safe, as would be the natural inference; but protect them "that they may be one as we are one."

Having uttered those sentiments, Jesus seems to drop the subject. But as he transitions from His concern for those original followers to deal with "those who will believe in me through their message" (17: 20) (that is, believers through to the end of time),[15] he returns to the subject of unity with full vigor, mentioning it four times in 17: 21–23. His language is concentrated and focused, conveying the weight of the burden He carried on this issue. For his followers in succeeding decades and centuries, he prayed "that they may all be one. As you,

---

13 Ashton, *Understanding*, 491.
14 Ashton, *Understanding*, 510.
15 "This reflects Jesus' vision of spiritual multiplication and reproduction" (Köstenberger, *Theology*, 248).

Father, are in me and I am in you, may they also be in us, so that the world may believe that you have sent me" (17: 21 NRSV).

Perhaps the fundamental thing to notice here is that the unity Jesus envisioned is patterned after the unity of the deity— "as you, Father, are in me and I in you." This places Jesus' expectation on a level far above that conceived in names like, say, "the United States" or "the United Kingdom." In a way of speaking, these are human-made enterprises and confederations. Jesus, however, described His vision of unity in language meant to disabuse us of the notion of any human origination.

Four times in the short passage this divine orientation is repeated. The initial statement in 17:21 has already been noted. In the same verse, Jesus indicates that this unity is possible only when His followers are "in us" (ἐν ἡμῖν ὦσιν). The third iteration of the idea comes in 17: 22: "… that they may be one as we are one." Then, for good measure, Jesus repeats the idea a fourth time in 17: 23: "I in them and you in me, that they may become completely one…" (NRSV).

So the model for this unity is Deity itself, the Godhead. This suggests that it is not an artificial or humanly-engendered reality; not something created by committee actions, council resolutions, or church pronouncements; not something that can be administratively manufactured or contrived. Nor is it a condition to be controlled or enforced. Divinely construed and deep, it comes by each of us, and all of us together, submitting to the infilling of God, through Jesus Christ. *"I in them, and you in me."* In this sense, it is a mystery—the mystery of the divine indwelling in God's followers, individually and corporately.

Lenski is correct in regarding this unity as a "mystical oneness," resembling "the essential oneness of the divine Persons … absolutely the highest type of oneness known."[16] "Our oneness is not merely placed beside the oneness of the divine Persons as though all that exists between them is a likeness." No, Lenski argues, "the two are vitally connected … We believers can be one with each other only by each of us and all of us being one with the Father and Jesus."[17] And although that divine unity "cannot be duplicated" in the human sphere, says Lenski, "yet it can be imitated."[18]

---

16 Lenski, *Interpretation,* 1155.
17 Lenski, *Interpretation,* 1165.
18 Lenski, *Interpretation,* 1137.

So how is this unity to be visualized? What shape is it to take? How is it to be manifested? On these questions, opinions diverge. "Being spiritual and mystical," says Lenski, surprisingly, "this unity is of necessity invisible and does not consist in any form of outward organization."[19] Another scholar, Wayne Grudem, believes "that such unity does not actually require one worldwide church government over all Christians." "In fact," he says, "the unity of believers is often demonstrated quite effectively through voluntary cooperation and affiliation among Christian groups..."[20]

However, in John 17 Jesus seemed to be speaking about a unity visible enough to be noticed, and strong and attractive enough to bring conviction to an observing world. It would be hard to make the case that the world could be persuaded by something it could not see. Jesus said, "... may they also be in us *so that the world may believe* that you have sent me" (17:21); and "may they be brought to complete unity *to let the world know* that you sent me" (17: 23).

Unity was a critical burden of Jesus' strategic prayer in the upper room that night, two thousand years ago.

So what are some of the implications of Jesus' prayer for the state of unity in the church at large and in the Seventh-day Adventist Church, specifically?

As some Christian thinkers see it, notwithstanding a host of theological, ecclesiological, and regional issues and tensions over the centuries, the Christian Church, with all its spiritual flaws and shortcomings, stayed generally (though imperfectly) united for centuries, the first major break coming in A.D. 1054 over the *filioque* controversy, when the Eastern (now Orthodox) church broke away from the Western (Roman Catholic) church.

Then came the Reformation of the 16th century, leading to the splintering of the Western church into a multitude of denominations as an unintended consequence. Describing the denominational divisions in his own country, the United States, theologian Martin Marty, citing statistics from the late 1980s, referred to "... well over 200 separate contending denominations, most of them Christian, each of them somehow suggesting that they possessed the truth."[21]

---

19 Lenski, *Interpretation,* 1157.

20 Wayne Grudem, *Systematic Theology: An Introduction to Biblical Doctrine* (Leicester: Inter-Varsity Press; Grand Rapids, MI: Zondervan; 1994), 877.

21 Martin Marty, "North America," in *The Oxford Illustrated History,*

Somewhere in this global denominational maelstrom are Seventh-day Adventists, some 20 million strong. They constitute 0.7% of the world's 2.8 billion Christians, and a miniscule 0.3% of the world's 7.5 billion population.

Yet Adventists have a deep-seated belief that they have been commissioned with a special, end-time message for the entire planet, including brothers and sisters in other Christian communions. It is a staggering and, from a human standpoint, insurmountable task, notwithstanding clichéd reports about the message spreading by "leaps and bounds." If Adventists really believe in the imminence of the parousia, and have even a partial understanding of the magnitude and complexity of the mission, then there could be no question about the need to engage every able-bodied person, every willing talent in the task. To understand the magnitude and complexity of the mission, and at the same time try to erect theological or ideological barriers to full participation in the church's mission, whether on the basis of class, or race, or age, or gender is nothing short of theological malpractice.

As Jesus prayed, he was looking down the future to dangers facing His followers. With prophetic vision, he would have seen the immediate crisis that they would face in the period surrounding his death and immediately following his departure, the crisis in Jerusalem, that led to the initial scattering of believers, mentioned in Acts 8:1. He would have seen the doctrinal and theological tensions, as his followers passed through the period of theological transition from the Old Testament period to the New, with problems involving a multitude of Jewish practices and observances that would need sorting out to determine their continuing validity. There would be problems involving salvation (the role of circumcision and the law); problems involving race (the status of Gentiles); problems involving class (the status of slaves); and problems involving gender (the standing of women).

In regard to gender and other illegitimate causes of tension within the church, the apostle Paul could not be more in keeping with the oneness Jesus called for in his prayer: "There is neither Jew nor Gentile, neither slave nor free, nor is there male and female, for you are all one in Christ Jesus" (Gal 3:27, 28). And as a church, we will be judged by what we allow to divide us.

---

ed. John McManners (Oxford & New York: Oxford University Press, 1990), 387.

For most of His earthly ministry, Jesus was surrounded by a close-knit group of twelve followers. But as He spoke that critical prayer in the upper room that evening, only eleven were present to hear it. The departure of Judas on his dark mission represented the first rift in the unity of the group, a development that had to be uppermost in Jesus' mind as He prayed in the hour that followed. Decades later, John still remembered how it felt. "It was night," he said (13:30), cryptically describing the darkness apostasy brings.

Consider the enormity of Judas's act that fateful night in Jerusalem and compare that with what we allow to divide us today—the role of women in ministry, for example. What we have here, after all, is a group of people simply wanting to join their male counterparts *in the mission of God's church*, and, in all fairness—and in keeping with common human decency—to be fully and equally recognized for it. To allow *THAT* to divide us is obscene.

One more thought on Jesus' prayer for unity:

In 13:35 Jesus points to love as the critical identifying mark of His followers. Everyone will know that you are My disciples, He said, "if you love one another." In John 17, He gives another critical identifier. Not one by which to recognize His disciples this time, but one that would identify Him before the world, one that would tell the world who He is. "May they also be in us so that the world may believe that you have sent me" (verse 21).

We probably should not see these two markers as standing in competition. In essence, they're complementary. Yet theologically, within the confines of John's gospel, we may say that one precedes the other. For as important as it is for the world to recognize us as Christ's disciples by our love for one another, that in the end carries no intrinsic significance if people don't know who Jesus is, if they have no saving knowledge of the Master. So in this sense, this first identifier (the world recognizing us as disciples) can function on the theoretical level, as an intellectual curiosity even. But the second one (knowing Jesus as Messiah, as the One sent from God, in the biblical sense of "knowing") is personal, experiential, and carries with it eternal consequences.

That, in fact, was one of the most critical assertions of Jesus' prayer: "And this is eternal life, that they may know you, the only true God, and Jesus Christ, whom you have sent" (verse 3, NRSV).

And if the unity of believers is a marker that points to Jesus as the One sent from God--the Messiah, the Redeemer, the Savior of the world--then one might almost say that unity in the gospel of John (and in the prayer of Jesus) supersedes even love itself.

Except that in his second reference to this idea, Jesus skillfully inserts love into the equation. "I in them and you in me—so that they may be brought to complete unity. Then the world will know that you sent me and have loved them even as you have loved me" (verse 23). Capping and extending that theme in the final verse of the chapter, He says: "I have made you known to them, and will continue to make you known in order that the love you have for me may be in them and I myself may be in them".

What we see here, in other words, is a prayer that God's love may inhabit the disciples--love for God and for one another, the very thing that identifies them as Jesus' disciples; and a prayer that Jesus might be in them, the very thing that produces unity, which in turn identifies Jesus to the world as the Messiah, the One sent from God.

This means that the two identifiers have come together; that unity and love have kissed each other. Love is still "the greatest" (1 Cor. 13:13); but unity, a natural fruit of love, does not lag far behind. And in the context of Jesus' prayer, it carries a weight seen nowhere else in Scripture.

Reunion

Throughout his gospel, John stresses Jesus' close affinity with his followers. When, while speaking plain truth to the multitude, he saw large sectors of the people deserting Him, Jesus turned to the twelve, his closest earthly companions, with the plaintive query: "Do you also wish to go away?" (6:67, NRSV), or, as the New International Version puts it: "You do not want to leave too, do you?" An answer in the affirmative would have devastated him.

What a relief it must have been to hear Peter's response on behalf of the twelve: "Lord, to whom can we go? You have the words of eternal life. We have come to believe and know that you are the Holy One of God" (John 6:68, 69).

In John 10:11 Jesus describes himself as "the good shepherd [who] lays down his life for the sheep" he loves. And in chapter 13 John says of Jesus that "having loved his own who were in the world, he loved them to the end" (13:1, NRSV).

Although we cannot speak of Jesus' farewell discourse as "his final words" in the common sense (as if he would die and remain deceased), it is probably correct to say that Jesus' words in chapters 13–17 (even beginning as early as chapter 12) carry a distinctive note of finality about them. They represent Christ's last concerns before the cross—concerns for his followers and for the progress of his work in the world.

As John sets up the scene in chapter 13, for example, he indicates that as Jesus faced the upcoming Passover Festival, it was with a sense "that the hour had come," the hour "for him to depart from this world and go to the Father" (13:1, NRSV). "Jesus knew," John said, "that the Father had put all things under his power, and that he had come from God and was returning to God . . ." (13:3). It was for him the end of a journey and he made it clear to the little company gathered in the upper room, that He would be with them "only a little longer" (13:33). This prompted Peter to put the question, "Lord, where are you going?", to which Jesus was pleased to point out that Peter and the others "will follow later"(13:36).

In chapter 14 the going-away theme continues. Jesus intimates that he is going to God's house "to prepare a place" for them, but "will come again and will take you to myself, so that where I am, there you may be also" (14:2, 3). The same sentiment continues in chapter 16: "…now I'm going to him who sent me … " (16:5) and "I came from the Father and entered the world; now I am leaving the world and going back to the Father" (16:28). Reluctantly, he was going to leave them so that the Spirit might come (16:7), but not even the coming of the Spirit could squelch his insatiable desire to be with them again.

So, as recorded in John 17, Jesus comes to the closing lines of his supplication and prays for what he had promised in chapter 14: "Father, I want those you have given me to be with me where I am, and to see my glory . . ." (17:24).

This is the great reunion Jesus has always longed for. That hope and that promise are not conditional. It's a date He *will* keep. And what a reunion that will be!

2. Toward a Theology of Unity

John C. Brunt
Walla Walla University – Retired

The Basis for Unity

If you go to a synagogue service you will be sure to hear the following words sung, probably more than once: *Shema Yisrael adonai elohenu, adonai echad.* "Hear O Israel, the Lord our God, the Lord is One." This is the central affirmation of the Jewish faith, recorded in Deuteronomy 6:4.[1]

The "oneness" of Yahweh is the basis for unity, for unlike other ancient religions in which the national god was seen as one of many gods, each of whom ruled over its own nation, the Hebrew Scriptures teach that Yahweh is not only Israel's God, but that he is the God of all and the Creator of all. If God is one, and the creation is one, God's universe should be a perfect unity.

According to the Scripture, however, the unity of God's creation was disrupted by human failure and rebellion against God. Human sin led to alienation and violence, as seen when Cain murdered Abel. The disruption of unity is portrayed in the account of the Tower of Babel in Genesis 11. In their pride and arrogance the people tried to build a great tower to make a name for themselves. God chose to scatter them, as Genesis 11:5-9 declares:

> But the Lord came down to see the city and the tower the people were building. The Lord said, "If as one people speaking the same language they have begun to do this, then nothing they plan to do will be impossible for them. Come, let us go down and confuse their language so they will not understand each other."
> So the Lord scattered them from there over all the earth, and they stopped building the city. That is why it was called

---

1 Scripture quotations in this chapter are from the *New International Version* unless otherwise noted.

Babel—because there the Lord confused the language of the whole world. From there the Lord scattered them over the face of the whole earth.

The Hebrew Scriptures are in large part the story of God's faithfulness in the face of human failure. God formed a special covenant with the descendants of Abraham, yet there was no question that the whole world was still in God's view. Notice Exodus 19:4–6 in which God instructs Moses to tell the people:

You yourselves have seen what I did to Egypt, and how I carried you on eagles' wings and brought you to myself. Now if you obey me fully and keep my covenant, then out of all nations you will be my treasured possession. **Although the whole earth is mine**, you will be for me a kingdom of priests and a holy nation.

God is God of the whole earth, but Israel was chosen to be a kingdom of priests who would mediate God's love and will to the rest of the world. God's goal was the reunification of all people and of all things so that the entire creation would again express the oneness of God and the harmony of creation. Over and over again, human failure got in the way of this purpose. Throughout the history of God's dealing with Israel the vision continues to reappear. God wants to restore the unity of creation.

The Mystery of Reunification

When it appeared that God's plan would never come to fruition, for the people of God were ruled by Rome and were in disarray, Jesus Christ, God's only Son, came to unveil the "mystery" or "secret" of God's plan. In the language of the New Testament the term "mystery" is not something that cannot be known, but is known only to those who are in on the secret. In Ephesians 1:8–10 Paul lets the world in on God's secret, revealed in Jesus Christ:

With all wisdom and insight he has made known to us the mystery of his will, according to his good pleasure that he set forth in Christ, as a plan for the fullness of time, to gather up all things in him, things in heaven and things on earth (NRSV).

The word translated "to gather up" is one of the longest words in the Greek New Testament (eight syllables) and is difficult to translate in a way that captures the full beauty of the term. The Greek word is ἀνακεφαλαιώσασθαι. It is a combination of the preposition ἀνά, which in combination means "up" or "again," and κεφαλή, the word for "head." Literally it means to sum things up under one head. The word's only other occurrence in the New Testament comes in Romans 13:9, where Paul says that all the commandments are "summed up" under the one word, "Love your neighbor as yourself." God's secret plan, now made known in Christ, is to unify all things in the universe, both in heaven and on earth, in Jesus Christ. This includes both the human world and the natural world, as Paul emphasizes in Romans 8:20–23:

> For the creation was subjected to frustration, not by its own choice, but by the will of the one who subjected it, in hope that the creation itself will be liberated from its bondage to decay and brought into the freedom and glory of the children of God. We know that the whole creation has been groaning as in the pains of childbirth right up to the present time. Not only so, but we ourselves, who have the firstfruits of the Spirit, groan inwardly as we wait eagerly for our adoption to sonship, the redemption of our bodies.[2]

The statement in Ephesian 1:8–10 is by no means an isolated one. On the contrary, the rest of the book of Ephesians gives witness and detail to this plan of unification. In the early part of chapter two it is revealed that not only is Jesus Christ seated in the heavenly realms, but believers too are there with Him. In the latter part of chapter two the writer proclaims that the walls that stood between peoples, especially Jew and Gentile, are now shattered in Christ, who has become the "peace" that brings both groups together (2:11–14).

In chapter three Paul prays that all Christians will be able to grasp the seemingly incredible dimensions of God's love in Christ.

Chapter four begins with the admonition that Christians live a life worthy of this amazing good news, which means being humble, gentle and patient with each other. Then Paul tells Christians to make "every effort to maintain the unity of the Spirit in the bond peace" (4:3). The word translated "unity" (ἑνότης) is only used twice in the New Testament—here and ten verses later in 4:13. It comes from the word for "one" and simply means "oneness." In verse 13 Paul explains that it is in coming into unity that believers reach maturity, which is nothing less than the full stature of Christ.

---

2 For a comprehensive and insightful treatment of the theme of the significance of the natural world in Paul's thought, see Sigve K. Tonstad, *The Letter to the Romans: Paul among the Ecologists* (Sheffield Phoenix, 2016) in the Earth Bible Commentary series.

In Ephesians 4:4–6 the essential elements of unity in the church are set forth: one hope, one Lord, one faith, one baptism, and one God over all. Here it is made clear that theological unity is an aspect of this oneness. The New Testament presents different perspectives. Witness the difference between Paul's and John's use of the term "flesh," or James' and Paul's use of the word "faith." Yet a core of beliefs is essential to Christian faith. For example, Paul speaks of how dangerous it is to deny the resurrection of Christ and of the believers (1 Corinthians 15), and John shows the danger of denying that Christ has come in the flesh (2 John 7). Theology is important because ideas have consequences. The declaration, "one hope, one Lord, one faith, one baptism, one God over all", draws the church to theological unity in these essentials.

In Ephesians five and six Paul outlines implications of this unity for how Christians should live in individual households. They are to be mutually subject to each other out of reverence for Christ (5:21). This mutual subjection includes husbands and wives, parents and children, slaves and masters.

Throughout Ephesians numerous metaphors and images that help communicate the shape of this unity are found.[3] In Ephesians 2:19–22 the church is compared to a family or household, to a building, built on the foundation of the apostles and prophets with Christ as the chief cornerstone, and to a temple in which God comes to dwell and in which members are the individual stones in the structure. All these images imply unity. Unity is also the focus in the metaphor of the body of Christ in which each member constitutes an indispensable part of an organism whose head is Christ (Ephesians 4). (This image is worked out in more detail in Romans 12 and 1 Corinthians 12.)

It might appear from a reading of Ephesians that this idyllic portrait of unity in Christ came easily and naturally in the early church. However, Ephesians is one of the least "occasional" letters in the New Testament. The book of Acts and the letters that are more specific in

---

[3] For an exhaustive study of the metaphors and images used for the church in the New Testament see: Paul S. Minear, *Images of the Church in the New Testament*, foreword, Leander E. Keck (Louisville, KY: Westminster John Knox, 2004). For an excellent Adventist treatment of the subject see: John K. McVay, "Biblical Metaphors for the Church and Adventist Ecclesiology," *Andrews University Seminary Studies*, Vol. 44, No. 2, (2006), 285–315.

addressing real-life problems within individual churches reveal that unity came through struggle. It was forged amid conflict, controversy and compromise at both the local and church-wide scale.

The Struggle for Unity: The Church at Large

The post-resurrection experience of the early church begins with the outpouring of the Holy Spirit at Pentecost described in Acts 2. In a sense this is the great "un-Babel." The Spirit works to undo the disunity of Babel. As God confused the languages in Genesis 11, the Spirit now allowed the message of good news to transcend the various languages so that all could understand, whatever their language might be. The Spirit brings unity to a diverse collection of people speaking different languages gathered in Jerusalem.

This unity, however, was not easily achieved in the new church. It would have been quite possible for early Christianity to divide into two totally separate communities, one of Jewish Christians and the other of Gentile Christians. No one was more committed to holding these two together than the apostle Paul, as is clearly shown both in his letters and in Luke's account of his ministry in the book of Acts.

Paul's fundraising activity provides a particularly vivid example of his work to hold the Jewish and Gentile Christians together in unity. Over a period of years he took up a collection throughout the Gentile churches to help the financially disadvantaged church in Jerusalem. He collected funds in Galatia, Macedonia and Achaia, and was not above using the example of giving in one place to encourage Christians in another place not to be outdone (See 1 Cor 16:1–4 and 2 Cor 8).

In Romans 15 we discover what this collection represented to Paul. According to 15:23–26 Paul's plan when he wrote from Corinth was to travel to Spain, via Rome. But first he was taking a little detour to Jerusalem to deliver personally the money he had collected. In other words, he was planning to travel 780 air miles in the opposite direction (and he was not flying) for the sake of this collection. That's how important it was to him. And it was important not only because Jerusalem needed the money. It was important as a theological symbol of the unity of the church, as shown in 15: 25–27:

> At present, however, I am going to Jerusalem in a ministry to the saints; for Macedonia and Achaia have been pleased to share their resources with the poor among the saints at Jerusalem. They were pleased to do this, and indeed they owe it to them; for if the Gentiles have come to share in their

spiritual blessings, they ought also to be of service to them in material things (NRSV).

Through a kind of financial interdependence, Paul sought to hold the Jewish and Gentile Christians together in one body. This is evidence that for Paul unity meant more than local fellowship. He envisioned a worldwide unity that embraced all Christians from Jerusalem to Asia Minor to Greece to Rome and, as he hoped, even on to Spain. The financial collection provided a tangible symbol of this worldwide unity.

Earlier in this same chapter Paul reveals the clue to the origin of this vision for unity. It goes back to his reading of the Scriptures. Through the patriarchs, prophets and psalmists, God revealed the plan for unifying all creation by including the Gentiles. Within the flow of this passage Paul quotes from 2 Samuel 22:50, Psalm 18:49, Deuteronomy 32:43, Psalm 117:1 and Isaiah 11:10, all of which shout to him that God's plan for unity was not a recent novelty, but was revealed through the Scriptures to anyone who read with eyes of faith. Paul says (Rom 15:7–13):

> Welcome one another, therefore, just as Christ has welcomed you, for the glory of God. For I tell you that Christ has become a servant of the circumcised on behalf of the truth of God in order that he might confirm the promises given to the patriarchs, and in order that the Gentiles might glorify God for his mercy. As it is written, "Therefore I will confess you among the Gentiles, and sing praises to your name"; and again he says, "Rejoice, O Gentiles, with his people"; and again, "Praise the Lord, all you Gentiles, and let all the peoples praise him"; and again Isaiah says, "The root of Jesse shall come, the one who rises to rule the Gentiles; in him the Gentiles shall hope." May the God of hope fill you with all joy and peace in believing, so that you may abound in hope by the power of the Holy Spirit (NRSV).

This vision of unity between Jew and Gentile drove Paul in his evangelistic activity, his theological reflection, and his practical action. Unity between Jew and Gentile was so vital that Paul was willing to travel close to 3,200 kilometres (2000 miles) out of his way for it. He was willing to stand up and refuse to allow Titus to be circumcised for it (Gal 2:3–5). He was willing to rebuke no less than the apostle Peter face to face to preserve it (Gal 2:11–14). He was willing to endure the hardships of beatings, stonings, shipwrecks and prisons for it (2 Cor 11). He was even willing to accept the suggestion of James and the elders that he go to the temple and sponsor a vow when he went to Jerusalem, even though he knew the danger (he was arrested and spent the next five years as a prisoner (Acts 21:24)).

The Struggle for Unity: Local

Although Paul's vision of unity in Christ had a worldwide perspective, it took particular shape in the nitty-gritty of daily life at the local level where Christians of diverse backgrounds welcomed each other by worshiping together, praying together, and eating together in peace and joyful fellowship. Unity in Christ broke down all the barrier walls that separated people and inhibited the joy of mutual fellowship. Christ brought a new equality that sought to include all people in one new reality in Christ, the ἀνακεφαλαιώσασθαι (gather up) of Ephesians 1. It included Jews and Greeks, men and women, slave and free (Gal 3:28) as well as Scythian and barbarian (Col 3:11). It was for "all" who believed (Rom 1:16). Each one cared for the other so that when one suffered all mourned and when one was honored all rejoiced (1 Cor 12:26; Rom 12:15).

This fellowship was important from the very beginning of the church. According to Acts 2 the first believers met in the temple daily, not only for prayer and worship, but also for fellowship (κοινωνία). Paul uses this word no less than a dozen times in his letters. This unified fellowship is directly tied to mission as well. In Acts 2:47 it is apparent that as believers met in unified fellowship their numbers grew and many were added to their number daily. Unity is vital for mission.

Diversity within Unity

Some, if not many, in the early church believed that the only way to hold the church together and achieve this unity was to have complete uniformity of practice in all areas of Christian life for the entire diverse body of early Christians. If some Christians were circumcised, for example, all had to be circumcised. Peter, Paul and James opposed this view at the Jerusalem Council, as recorded in both Acts 15 and Galatians 2.[4] The Council agreed there could be

---

4 Some scholars hold that Acts 15 and Galatians 2 refer to different events. This is unlikely, but such a position would not detract from the point we are making if we (and I do) accept Acts 15 as a reliable account. There is one intriguing question, however. In Acts 21:25, why does James seem to tell Paul about the Council as if he had never heard of it?

one church that embraced both Jew and Gentile, but allowed Jews to continue practicing circumcision and Gentiles to become Christians without circumcision or becoming Jews first. In the modern world it is hard to comprehend what a huge decision this was and what far-reaching implications it brought. **It achieved unity by allowing for diversity.** It maintained unity of purpose by allowing for diversity of practice. In other words, it achieved the unity of inclusive fellowship by allowing for diverse practices that took into account the ethnic, cultural and geographical diversity of the early church. Had the early church demanded unity in all practices and policies, it probably would have meant at least two different Christian churches, separate from, if not at odds with each other.

However for Paul this allowance for diversity was not merely a pragmatic decision. It was a well-thought-out theological conviction. It had to do both with his ecclesiology and his theology of mission. He sets it forth in 1 Corinthians 9:19–23 in the middle of a discussion about food offered to idols which will be dealt with in more detail later.

> For though I am free with respect to all, I have made myself a slave to all, so that I might win more of them. To the Jews I became as a Jew, in order to win Jews. To those under the law I became as one under the law (though I myself am not under the law) so that I might win those under the law. To those outside the law I became as one outside the law (though I am not free from God's law but am under Christ's law) so that I might win those outside the law. To the weak I became weak, so that I might win the weak. I have become all things to all people, that I might by all means save some. I do it all for the sake of the gospel, so that I may share in its blessings (NRSV).

Paul is not saying, "Anything goes." What comes in the parentheses is vital. Allowance for diversity does not mean really being under the law, on the one hand, or being lawless toward Christ, on the other. Diversity does not mean that all is relative.

One way to give shape to this interplay between unity and diversity is to look at several case studies within the New Testament where Paul and Peter deal with controversies and threats to unity. How do they come to grips with them? What does this teach us about unity and diversity?

Threats to Unity—Case Studies

Inclusive, egalitarian fellowship was then, as it is now, a fragile thing. Threats raised their ugly heads whenever Christians acted in ways that failed to embrace fully inclusive fellowship in Christ. Inclusiveness and egalitarian fellowship were absolutely essential ingredients in God's vision for unity. Whenever they were threatened, globally or locally, Paul was stirred to action. He could not stand idly by whenever real life fellowship, acceptance and welcoming of each other gave way to a prejudice that made any Christian, in any way, a second-class citizen, and that included women.

Perhaps the most obvious example of this is the occasion in Antioch when Peter was eating with Gentiles, but then withdrew when certain people came from James, the brother of Jesus and leader of the church in Jerusalem. Paul says they did this for fear of the "circumcision." Eating with Gentiles could have made life difficult for Jewish Christians who might find it awkward to continue table fellowship with their non-Christian relatives. It was probably a complex situation for many of them. For Paul, however, the issue was clear. Peter's refusal to eat with Gentiles, and Barnabas' decision to follow suit was, for Paul, "hypocrisy" (Gal 2:13) and Peter "stood condemned" (Gal 2:11).

Peter's actions went against the important "all" of Romans 1:16. The exclusion of any from that "all" threatened the very heart of the gospel. That is why Paul was willing to say that anyone who preached a different gospel, even if it were an angel from heaven, was "anathema" (Gal 1:8,9). The "different gospel" was condemned because of its existential implications, namely the disruption of inclusiveness and egalitarian fellowship.

We see the same kind of concern in Paul's treatment of divisions in the church in Corinth. In the first chapter of 1 Corinthians he speaks of the various factions that divided the church, and in chapter 11 he gives us a hint as to what this factionalism meant in the lived experience of the community. Again it involved a lack of table fellowship. Each faction ate separately and refused to share their food, so that some had plenty and others were hungry (1 Corinthians 11:21). This breakdown in Christian unity was so abhorrent that Paul calls it "contempt for the church of God" (1 Corinthians 11:22).

That this unity did not mean uniformity of all practices is demonstrated when Paul tackles a question put to him by the Corinthians (1 Corinthians 8–10). What about eating food offered to idols? In the first century world meat-markets were generally adjacent to pagan temples and portions of most of the meat had been a part of pagan sacrifice. Paul's answer to their question is neither a "yes" nor a "no," but an "it depends." He takes three chapters to work out the factors upon which "it depends".[5] Only at the end of 1 Corinthians 10 does he get down to the specifics.

In the first part of this chapter Paul makes an important caveat. Christians are never to participate in the idolatry or the sexual immorality of pagan worship (1 Cor 10:1–23). This would violate God's law. No amount of "it depends" would ever justify such behavior. However, Christians don't need to worry about what was sold in the meat-market. They could eat it. If invited to a non-Christian's house for dinner, they do not need to ask questions about whether the food had been offered to an idol, but if a sensitive host pointed out that they might not want to eat certain food because it has been offered to an idol, out of sensitivity to the host, one should avoid it. If eating would be a stumbling block and hurt another person for whom Christ died, the Christian with knowledge, in the position of power, should be willing to give up even legitimate rights for the sake of that more vulnerable person who might be injured.

Paul's allowance for diversity on this issue is especially remarkable because according to Acts 15 the Jerusalem Council, in which he participated, voted to forbid eating food that had been offered to idols, without offering any exceptions (Acts 15:20, 29). Surprisingly, Paul never mentions the Council or its decision in this three-chapter discussion, even though 1 Corinthians was definitely written after the Council. The issue is complicated, but is appears that Paul was willing to go against the action voted by the Council. Perhaps he felt that this policy was not necessary for all time or for all places or for all situations. In this case, for Paul, good sense appears to trump adherence to voted policy.

---

5 This nuanced approach to the question about food offered to idols showing that the answer "depends" on various factors that influence its moral significance seems to have been lost completely in the early church. See John Brunt, "Rejected, Ignored, or Misunderstood? The Fate of Paul's Approach to the Problem of Food Offered to Idols in Early Christianity," *New Testament Studies*, Vol. 31, No. 1 (January 1985), p. 113–124.

When Peter followed the prompting of the Holy Spirit in Acts 10 and baptized the uncircumcised Cornelius and his household, Peter also had to know that this was hardly within the established practice of the early church at that time. This event took place before the Jerusalem Council. Therefore it is hardly surprising that Peter received criticism: "So when Peter went up to Jerusalem, the circumcised believers criticized him and said, 'You went into the house of uncircumcised men and ate with them'" (Acts 11:2,3).Peter seemed to convince the critics, however, that his actions were justified when he told them (Acts 11:17), "Who was I to think that I could stand in God's way?" He heard the Spirit speaking and felt compelled to follow, in spite of the current practice of the church.

Paul's viewpoint is apparent in another discussion involving food in Romans 14 and15. Here there is no reference to food offered to idols, but to the fact that some eat only vegetables and some eat meat.[6] There is also some kind of dispute involving days, perhaps fast days.[7] In Rome people seem to be arguing about what to eat and when to eat it.[8]

Paul refused to give a single "right answer" to these Christians, but allowed for diversity of practice. He says that believers should be fully convinced in their own minds (Rom 14:5). Probably some would have been concerned that this was precisely the problem. The Roman house churches needed Paul to tell them what practice was correct. They needed him to give them the "right" answer; to get them all doing the same thing; to bring them into "unity." But he didn't do it. He did not consider controlling everyone else's behavior to be a part

---

6 Several factors seem to preclude the idea that Paul is again addressing the question of food offered to idols as he did in 1 Corinthians 8–10. None of the specific words for food offered to idols occurs in Romans. There is also no warning about the problem of idolatry or the sexual immorality of pagan worship. Nor do the Corinthian slogans such as "all things are lawful" and "we have knowledge" appear.

7 For evidence that Paul is referring to fast days rather than worship days see Raoul Dederen, "On Esteeming One Day Better Than Another," *Andrews University Seminary Studies* 9:1 (1971) p. 16–35, and Max Rauer, *Die "Schwachen" in Korinth und Rom nach den Paulusbriefen. Biblische Studien.* Freiburg: Herder, 1923.

8 For a series of articles on whether or not Paul is addressing a specific situation in Rome see Karl P. Donfried, Ed., *The Romans Debate: Revised and Expanded Edition* (Peabody, MA: Hendrickson, 1991). I am convinced that Donfried is correct and Paul is addressing a specific situation.

of his apostolic job description. He told those who were "more strict" (probably the meaning of "weak" in his context)[9] to stop judging the "less strict," and he told the "less strict" not to look down with scorn on the "more strict." Each could continue their own practice. In fact, those who were "more strict" were not to violate their convictions and do what they did not believe was right, while the less strict were not to act in a way that hurt the "more strict." But this diversity of practice was not to be a deterrent to unity, for unity did not mean everyone doing it the same way, but it did mean welcoming each other even when they acted differently.

Paul's commitment to freedom of conscience was too great for him simply to give a "right answer" for everyone. Convictions were important and Christians needed to be free to follow them. It was wrong for Christians to violate their convictions or to force another person to violate their convictions. The key word in the discussion is "welcome" (προσλαμβάνω). Paul begins in 14:1 by commanding, "Welcome each other." In 14:3 he proclaims that God has welcomed them. At the end of the discussion in 15:7 he concludes, "Welcome each other as Christ has welcomed you." They need not have all the same convictions. They need not have the same practice. But it was vitally important that they have the same welcoming spirit of fellowship and mutual caring.

According to Paul, Christians must be free to follow their convictions, as long as those convictions are within the framework of God's will. Idolatry, adultery, bigotry and prejudice are never within that framework. But the framework could include a significant diversity of practice as long as love, mutual respect, and reverence for each other prevailed. As he says in the middle of this discussion: "For the kingdom of God is not a matter of eating and drinking, but of righteousness, peace and joy in the Holy Spirit, because anyone who serves Christ in this way is pleasing to God and receives human approval" (Rom 14:17, 18).

Of course, there were limits to inclusiveness within the community as well. If a person stubbornly and willfully flouted God's law and even the standards of the pagan world, such as the man who was co-habiting with his father's wife (1 Corinthians 5:1), the community

---

9 There is a story in Horace, *Sermones* 1:9:60–78, in which the phrase, "somewhat weaker brother", seems to be synonymous with "more scrupulous."

needed to cut off fellowship. But this was an extreme exception, and was for the purpose of awakening the individual and bringing him back to his senses. In the normal experience of the church, however, the mystery of God's plan for unity was actualized and became reality when Christians welcomed each other, respected each other, and ate with each other, even when practice, policy and preference differed.

Conclusion—Toward a Theology of Unity

The elucidation of a full theology of unity is beyond the scope of this chapter, but I have touched on several elements that must be part of any theology of unity.

First, a theology of unity must give witness to the unity of God and all of the creation. God created a unified world filled with diverse lifeforms that lived harmoniously within one ecosystem, and although this unified world was disrupted by human failure, the story of God's continuing faithfulness that permeates all of Scripture, both Old and New Testaments, must be at the heart of any theology of unity.

Second, a theology of unity must take into account the teaching of the New Testament about God's mysterious plan to unite all things in Christ, as well as Jesus' desire to see his disciples united as one.

Third, a theology of unity must attempt to understand Paul's principled conviction, outlined in 1 Corinthians 9, that true unity could only be achieved by allowing for diversity. This is a great irony. Paul knew that trying to force all Christians, both Jew and Gentile, into one mold would ultimately destroy any real chance for unity. It would cause separation. A theology of unity will maintain this ironic tension.

Fourth, a theology of unity must take account of the actual, lived experience of the early church. How were these early Christians able to live together even when policies and practices differed so widely? What were the kinds of issues that threatened to destroy their living together in peace? How were these threats overcome? Good theology is never merely theoretical. It learns from real experience.

Fifth, a theology of unity needs to include the analysis of life together in Christ in the contemporary context. What are the elements that threaten this unity? What elements in contemporary culture are analogous to issues like idolatry and adultery in which Paul does not allow for diversity, and what elements are analogous to issues such as circumcision and food where he vigorously defends diversity?

Sixth, a theology of unity must explore the concept of freedom in Christ. Paul admonishes the believers in Rome who have different behavioral standards not only to welcome each other, but also to allow each to follow their own convictions. He teaches that it is wrong to violate one's convictions or to attempt to force others to violate their convictions. A sound theology of unity will also include a theology of respect for freedom of conscience.

Seventh, a theology of unity will struggle with the tension between individual integrity and communal identity. How does a Christian community live together in unity, uphold its identity, and maintain the integrity of individuals within it? Perhaps stories from Adventist history can help in reflections on this dilemma.[10]

Eighth, a theology of unity should explore the relationship of financial interdependence to unity in the church. Paul gave high value to the collection of funds from the Gentile world for the poor in Jerusalem. Is financial interdependence still important today, and if so what forms should it take?

Finally, a theology of unity will benefit from exploring the many metaphors for the church found within the New Testament. These rich images speak to a part of us that goes deeper than words and should help us intuit the depths of Christian unity.

Each of these issues would warrant a paper in itself (if not a book). They are presented in the hope that this paper will be a catalyst for future study.

As we reflect on all these elements, we must always remember two verses: "Hear O Israel, the Lord our God, the Lord is One" (Deut 6:4); and "With all wisdom and insight he has made known to us the mystery of his will, according to his good pleasure that he set forth in Christ, as a plan for the fullness of time, to ἀνακεφαλαιώσασθαι (to gather up) all things in him, things in heaven and things on earth" (Eph 1:8-10).

---

10 Numerous examples of interesting stories can be found in Gilbert M. Valentine, *The Prophet and the Presidents: Ellen White's Influence on the Leadership of the Early Seventh-day Adventist Church* (Nampa Idaho: Pacific Press Publishing Association, 2011).

A Final Story

Since I'm a preacher, I have a hard time concluding without a story. Please indulge me this pastoral quirk.

When I pastored the Azure Hills Church in California we had the largest Adventurer Club in the North American Division. It had more than two hundred children aged from 4 to 9 years. Can you imagine taking all of them along camping with their parents? Our leaders did it twice every year. One annual weekend trip was to a beautiful campground on the beach about three and a half hours' drive from the church. A group of 300 to 400 would camp from Friday through Sunday.

I couldn't go for the weekend, but when I finished preaching on Sabbath morning, I would hop in the car with a sack lunch, drive in time to be there for supper, sundown worship, and marshmallows around the campfire.

Families in the group had quite different convictions about Sabbath activities for the kids. Before I came to the church they had worked out a plan. They decided that everyone should be able to follow their convictions, and no one should be judged, scorned, or pressured. They agreed that there would be options on Sabbath afternoon, and parents would decide which option their family would follow. Some would go down to the beach and let their kids go into the water. (The beach was down a cliff from the camp and not immediately visible.) Others would go on a hike. Others would play active Bible games. Every family could choose its option. No one would criticize anyone for the option they chose. And at the end of the afternoon, they all came together for supper, and ate together in joyful fellowship.

The people worked all this out among themselves. They did it without pastoral involvement. And it worked. It has continued to work over a period of almost twenty years. I can't help but wonder, might the broader church organization learn from the wisdom of these faithful people in the local church?

FREEDOM

3. Liberty in Messiah: The Steep and Narrow Path to Unity

Olive J. Hemmings
Washington Adventist University

The early church was multi-ethnic and multi-convictional, steeped in a Greco-Roman religious-philosophical milieu. This mix worked powerfully against any efforts to obtain uniformity of practice. So strong were the convictions of some that not even the ruling of the church's Jerusalem Council was able to establish uniformity of practice. The Council ruled that Gentiles did not need to be circumcised, but this continued to be a factious issue. The Council ruled that Gentiles should not eat meat offered to idols as they had done before their conversion, but this too remained a factious issue.

Similarly, the Seventh-day Adventist church in a General Conference session has voted against permitting any region of the world church to have autonomy in the matter of ordaining women to ministry, but it still remains a factious issue.

The apostle Paul addresses such divisive issues not by appealing to the ruling of the Jerusalem Council, but by appealing to the Abrahamic Covenant through which God brings liberty. He strongly opposes enforcement of uniform practice on matters that have no spiritual virtue in and of themselves. He refers to these issues as τὰ ἀσθενῆ καὶ πτωχὰ στοιχεῖα (weak and beggarly rudiments) (Gal 4:9), describing them as enslavement to the flesh (Gal 4:21–31; 1 Corinthians 3:3) or capitulation to a "weak" conscience (1 Cor 8:7). Paul explains that to live in covenant is not about rituals and traditions, but about love for one's neighbor, i.e., fair and equitable relations in community fostering the bond of faith (Gal. 3:28; Rom 13:8–14). Like Jesus of Nazareth, Paul's purpose is to reinforce this fundamental ethic of the kingdom of God *vis a vis* rituals and traditional practices. By careful ethical instruction of factious communities such as those in Galatia,

Corinth and Rome, he calls the church to a liberty in Messiah that enables it to embrace diverse practices in the faith without rancor.

In Galatians Paul writes: "For freedom Christ has set you free. Stand firm therefore and do not submit again to a yoke of slavery." This statement is a climactic point in the letter to the Galatians which is in effect a conversation about freedom of conscience. The question of liberty of conscience can be discussed profitably in the context of this statement as it addresses factious issues in the early church and reinforces the fundamental ethic of the Kingdom of God as the only path to unity.

The argument of this chapter is that the New Testament's teaching on unity is a call to enter the new covenant experience of liberty that frees the community from the need for conformity to rituals and regulations that have no spiritual value in and of themselves, but which serve to keep it enslaved.

In many places the term "Messiah" is used instead of "Christ". Both terms mean the same, i.e., one anointed specifically to mediate God's liberating justice. However, general Christian consciousness tends to recognize "Christ" as a name rather than as a title with a messianic function.

Furthermore, it becomes necessary to explain clearly the use of the term "love" (*agapē*) in this chapter. It is used synonymously with "justice"—liberating or delivering justice. *Agapē* is not at all rooted in emotion; but neither is it "sacrificial" as many denote it. The renowned ethicist, the late Glen Stassen, calls it "delivering love" that creates a just community.[1] According to him, the label "sacrificial" "seems to misunderstand the significance of Jesus' death. Jesus did not sacrifice himself on the cross for the sake of self-sacrifice. He died for the sake of delivering us from the bondage of sin into community"[2] so that we too may practice delivering love.[3] Love is the theme of the Sermon on the Mount which Jesus identifies as doing to others as you would have them do to you (Matt 7:12)—the very demonstration of love for God (Matt 22:39; 1 John 4: 20–21)). It is the outworking of justice towards community well-being—shalom—the focus of Hebrew prophecy. It is that which makes the believing community perfect as

---

1 See, Glen H. Stassen and David P. Gushee, *Kingdom Ethics* (Downers Grove, Illinois: IVP Academic, 2003), 327–334.

2 Ibid, 330.

3 Ibid, 327–334.

God is perfect (Matthew 5:48). In the Johannine writings, it is the new commandment (John 13:34–35; 1 John 2:7–11) that makes believers one, and demonstrates who God is—nothing else. In the context of the Sermon on the Mount, it is the narrow road that leads to life, and the central theme of Jesus' call for unity.

For Freedom Messiah Has Set You Free—Righteousness, Faith, and Works of Law

Paul's declaration, "For freedom Christ has set you free. Stand firm therefore and do not submit again to a yoke of slavery" is the response call to Paul's thesis, "a person is not justified by works of law, but through faith in Jesus Messiah" (Gal 2:15). His teaching on "righteousness" or "justification" in Galatians (and Romans) is his radical assertion that Gentiles who do not subscribe to Jewish rituals and traditions have a right to membership in the covenant community— the community of the righteous. The term "righteousness by faith" is often used when speaking of Paul's soteriology and is contrasted to "works of the law", with particular reference to personal sins. However Paul's message is to a community—about how it conducts itself inter-relationally as people of the covenant. It is a message of inclusion and freedom of conscience. Five hundred years of Reformation have silenced this conversation. However, the late 1970s saw the rise of the New Perspective on Paul (NPP), inspired by the publication of E.P. Sanders' *Paul and Palestinian Judaism*.[4] The NPP has heralded a new look at Paul's conversation on "justification" through the lens of scripture, rather than through the lens of the Reformation. It thereby reads Paul's argument in the context of Second Temple Judaism, the nature of the Jesus Movement, and the actual issue he addresses. In light of this context, key terms such as righteousness, faith, and works of the law—terms so often misunderstood in Paul's conversation— need to be defined.

Righteousness

The Greek terms rendered into English as righteous (δίκαιος), righteousness (δικαιοσύνη), and justify (δικαιόω) actually mean,

---

4   E.P. Sanders, *Paul and Palestinian Judaism* (Minneapolis, MN: Augsburg Fortress, 1977). Sanders' work is more correctly described as a "new perspective on Judaism." The term "new perspective on Paul" has its origin with James D. G. Dunn, "The New Perspective on Paul," *Bulletin of the John Rylands Library* 65 (1983): 95–122.

respectively, "just", "justice", and "give justice", with the sense of "liberating justice." Δικαιοσύνη (righteousness) is the Greek equivalent of the Hebrew *tsedakah* (צְדָקָה). *Tsedakah* is the Hebrew prophetic plea against oppressive structures such as corruption, greed and the exploitation of the vulnerable. It is a call for right relations in community as in doing to others so that all may live in peace and freedom. It is the focus of Jesus' Sermon on the Mount, summed up in the golden rule (Mat 7:12); hence his call, "seek first the kingdom of God and his justice" (Mat 6: 33). This is how Paul uses the term in his discussion of what many understand as "righteousness by faith".

Faith

The term translations render faith (πίστις) actually means "faithfulness". (In Greek argumentation the πίστις [faith] is the proof of, or faithfulness to one's claim). The phrase "faith in Jesus Christ" (πίστις Ἰησοῦ Χριστοῦ), both in the Greek and in the context of Paul's discussion, literally reads "faithfulness of Jesus Messiah." God's people receive justice through the faithful mediation of Messiah. This is the actual meaning of the Abrahamic covenant in the context of Jewish Messianic expectation.

Works of Law

Jews believed that only practicing Jews were heirs of the Abrahamic promise and, as the covenant community, they were inherently free (John 8:31). To gain access to that freedom one had to become a practicing Jew—signified by the ritual purity of circumcision with its accompanying rituals and regulations. Paul calls these ἔργα νόμου (works of law). The conviction about circumcision remained entrenched among Jewish Jesus-followers, including Peter, who was confronted by God in a radical vision to convince him to enter the house of an uncircumcised Gentile (Acts 10). (In fact, even after the Council of the Church at Jerusalem ruled that Gentiles did not have to receive circumcision, Peter was still so intimidated by the seemingly influential "circumcision faction" that upon their arrival in Antioch where he used to eat with the Gentiles, he led other Jews, including Paul's ally Barnabas, to withdraw from eating with Gentiles, perhaps for fear of losing his own influence. Paul calls him out for his hypocrisy on this issue (Gal 3:11–14). One may understand this entrenchment even more in light of the fact that the early church was a Judaic community: it was not a different religion. The Jesus

Movement was another rabbinic school, and Paul a rabbi doing his work of instruction.

Unity in Diversity—the Path to Liberty

Paul does not dismiss the validity of his own Jewish tradition: "Do we then overthrow the law, by this faith? By no means!" (Romans 3:31a). Rather, he advocates the right of Gentiles to the Abrahamic promise without having to conform to Judaic tradition: "... he will justify the circumcised on the ground of faith and the uncircumcised through that same faith" (Rom 3:30). Gentiles who resist the very ritual that ratifies the Abrahamic Covenant have a right to that Covenant, because it is not ritual and legal regulations but a spiritual experience, "circumcision of the heart" (Rom 2:29), that produce just relations within a diverse community. If they were to coerce the consciences of these new believers, that would prevent the community from entering into the covenant experience of liberty. Both the coerced and the coercer are enslaved to the flesh—the rudimentary elements of this world—and that cannot bring true liberty.

Liberty

A close examination of the context of the use of the term "liberty" will demonstrate the extent to which Paul (as with Jesus before him) opposed the coercion of conscience in the interest of "unity". The term ἐλευθερία (freedom or liberty) goes back as far as the Ancient Greek city-state Athens[5] around the 8th century B.C.E. Its fundamental significance rests in whether one is living free (ἐλεύθερος) as opposed to being a slave (δοῦλος).[6]The δοῦλος (slave) is someone else's

---

5 Ancient Athens distinguished itself among the Greek city-states in its quest for ἐλευθερία—democratic freedom—vis a vis the total enslavement of the people to the state as was the case in its neighbor city-state, Sparta. Athens became a center of free thinking, the hub of Greek philosophy, and the birthplace of modern democracy. The great philosophers Socrates, Plato and Aristotle lived in Athens. But it is significant to note that the Athenians voted to kill Socrates in 399 B.C.E. because Socrates sided with Spartan oligarchy, placing law over the individual, and opposed freedom of thought in defense of what he regards as unchangeable truth. (See Michel Foucault, "The Ethics of the Concern of the Self as a Practice of Freedom," in *Ethics Subjectivity and Truth* [New York: The New Press, 1999], 281–301).

6 Mogens Herman Hansen "Democratic Freedom and the Concept of Freedom in Plato and Aristotle," https://vitruvianman.wikispaces.com/file/view/greek+freedom.pdf, 2, retrieved 6 June 2017.

possession and lives according to the dictates of someone else's will and conscience, while the ἐλεύθερος (free) is his or her own person.[7]

Freedom (ἐλευθερία) was a major issue in the Hellenistic Roman age and fundamental to the religious and philosophical zeitgeist of the era. First-century Apocalyptic Judaism asserted freedom through the Abrahamic Covenant, and looked to a future Messianic age in which this liberty would come to full realization. Greeks sought liberation of the spirit from the corruptible material world—the flesh—through the pursuit of knowledge. Unlike this Greek usage, Paul uses the term "flesh" to indicate slavery to rules and regulations that have no inherent spiritual virtue. The use of the term in Greek philosophy[8] heralded an era that sought an alternative to authoritarian government and compulsory and ethically bankrupt religious traditions and rituals. First-century Jewish rabbis—Jesus of Nazareth, the great scholar/professor Gamaliel, and Paul of Tarsus, for example—all drew upon both the Hebrew prophetic and the Greek philosophical traditions.

In a certain sense, ἐλευθερία (liberty) in Greek philosophy goes hand in hand with justice (הַצְּדָקָה /δικαιοσύνη) in Hebrew prophecy. Both Jesus and Paul sought to reform the tyrannical legalistic and ritual-centric element of their own religious tradition by drawing upon these two traditions. In their use of the terms ἐλευθερία (liberty) and δικαιοσύνη (justice) one observes the confluence of Greek philosophical and Hebrew prophetic traditions in the quest for liberty.

So in this context, liberty does not stand alone. It is inextricably connected to this very important concept in the Hebrew scripture—justice.

Liberty and Justice

The statement, "For freedom Messiah has set you free …" is a declaration of God's justice through Messiah. Paul uses the allegory of Sarah and Hagar (4:21–31) to indicate the extent to which obsession

---

7 Ibid.

8 In the Hellenistic and Roman periods, philosophy functioned as religion, "especially among the educated." It "provided a criticism or re-interpretation of traditional religion, and offered moral and spiritual direction" generally absent from ritualistic and cult-centered religion. See, Everett Ferguson, *Backgrounds of Early Christianity* (Grand Rapids, MI: Wm. B. Eerdmans, 1993), 300. In general, Greek philosophy functioned in the same way as Hebrew prophetic tradition.

with rituals and legal regulations enslaves the community, and the extent to which unconditional acceptance for the other believer of different conviction liberates it.

Hagar represents the Old-Covenant experience that marks off boundaries, and assumes that God's vindication comes only to a specific group identified by their traditions. Sarah on the other hand represents the New-Covenant experience that frees the non-Jew to stand before God with the assurance of God's faithfulness to the Abrahamic Covenant. Here is an important understanding: Paul depicts Sarah as ἡ ἐλευθερία (the free woman) by quoting the Septuagint version of Genesis 21:10 in which Sarah says to Abraham, "Cast out the slave and her child; for the child of the slave will not inherit with my son Isaac." But the passage he quotes in Genesis contains neither of the two terms at play in the conversation—δοῦλος (slave) and ἐλεύθερος (free). In fact the word the Septuagint passage uses for slave is παιδίσκη ("slave girl" or "maid"). Paul maintains παιδίσκη (slave girl) in the allegory. However, he omits the phrase "my son Isaac" (Genesis 21:10) and he replaces it with the phrase "the child of the free woman" (Gal 4:30). Here he inserts the term ἡ ἐλευθερία (the free woman) which is not present in the text from which he quotes.

This is a pivotal point in Paul's application of the Greek philosophical concept of ἐλευθερία (free). Hellenistic consciousness personifies ἐλευθερία as "lady liberty", epitomized in the Goddess Artemis. Artemis is "lady liberty" who resists conventional boundaries—roles and rules that restrict her power—and roams the forest with her aides protecting the vulnerable from the tyranny of the powerful.

In this allegory Paul inserts the Greek idea of ἐλευθερία (free), making Sarah "lady liberty", the representative of the Abrahamic Covenant.[9] By this skillful rhetoric, the Greek idea of ἐλευθερία—liberation from tyrannical rule—becomes the most important element in his conversation about justification. It is important to understand that this conversation is not merely about liberty. It is actually about justice. This point is crucial to this study.

---

9 One even wonders whether the correspondence between the Hebrew Heroine Sarah and the Greek Goddess Artemis in Paul's use of Isaiah 51: 1:4 *("... the children of the desolate woman will be more than the children of her that is married ... ")* is merely co-incidental. According to the myth, Artemis, who chooses to remain an unmarried virgin, is the goddess of childbirth.

Liberating Justice

Thus Paul's defense of radical diversity in Galatians makes the case that the Abrahamic covenant is a covenant of liberating justice, specifically with regard to the conscience, not only for practicing Jews, but for everyone who accepts its Messianic fulfilment through Jesus of Nazareth. One can understand this covenantal quest for liberty through the most significant historical event in Israel's history, the Exodus.

When Israel cried out under Egyptian slavery, God heard their groaning and remembered the covenant with Abraham (Ex 2:23–24): "And God said to Moses 'Go to Pharaoh and say to him, "thus says the Lord: Let my people go, *so that they may worship me*" … '" (Ex 8:1, emphasis added). This is to say God's covenant is a covenant of justice—liberation from slavery and oppression—and specifically the release of the conscience from those who assume ownership of it.

When Paul, an apocalyptic Jew[10], encountered the gospel in the embodiment of the risen Messiah, he became convinced (through an unbiased revisit of the scriptures) that this liberation was not only for practicing Jews. The Sarah–Hagar allegory demonstrates the irony that the very people God sets free by the promise of the Abrahamic covenant are now in slavery (Gal 4:25), because some believe that enforcing and or conforming to a uniformity of religious tradition and regulation is what defines them as members of the community of the free.

The poignant message in Galatians is that certain practices rest entirely upon the personal convictions of believers, and enforcement of these upon the church nurtures a state of enslavement rather than liberty in Messiah. Paul develops this idea in explicit terms of liberty of conscience in 1 Corinthians and Romans in regard to meat offered to idols.

Freedom of Conscience

The key text in Paul's writing on this topic is, perhaps, 1 Corinthians 10:29: "For why should my liberty be subject to the judgement of someone else's conscience?" This powerful rhetorical

---

10 Foundational to Jewish apocalyptic understanding especially in the period of the second temple was the coming in of a new age of God's reign through Messiah the arbiter of justice who liberates God's people from oppressive principalities and powers.

question is directed to the Corinthian enforcers of the Jerusalem Council's regulation to abstain from meat offered to idols. It suggests that the church's ruling on a matter that should be left entirely up to the conscience may be more divisive than unifying. What Paul calls for is not conformity to the rule. Rather he appeals to a conscience that transcends the factious convictions on the issue by invoking the Covenant ethic as he does in Galatians—that is, liberating justice and love.

It is, therefore, important at this point to clarify the meaning of conscience in Paul's conversation about liberty.

Conscience

In eight of the thirty occurrences of the term συνείδησις (conscience) in the New Testament, it is used in connection with the issue of meats sacrificed to idols. While the word in ancient Greek philosophical understanding denotes an internal guide or judge, this internal guide receives instruction from the external factors that form the totality of one's experience in the world.

We have a tendency to think of conscience as a personal thing, the little angel that sits on your shoulder and whispers to you what is right and what is wrong. But in fact, conscience arises from the socio-historical experience that shapes one's consciousness. Friedrich Nietzsche, in The Genealogy of Morals[11], traces its origin to the promise between autonomous individuals in the interest of their survival. Sigmund Freud calls it the "superego" which develops from the ethical restraint placed on the individual by its social/cultural/religious upbringing. The conscience arises from what Thomas Hobbes, John Locke and Jean-Jacques Rousseau discuss as the "Social Contract" that allows communities or groups to regulate relationship and behavior for the welfare and protection of all.[12] These definitions coincide with the compound structure of the Greek συνείδησις (conscience): σύν (together) and εἰδήσις (knowing) literally meaning "knowing together" or "common idea". In this sense, appropriate synonyms for "conscience" are "consciousness" or "conviction".

---

11 Friedrich Nietzsche, *On The Genealogy of Morals: a Polemic* (*Zur Genealogie der Moral: Eine Streitschrift*, 1887), trans, Walter Kaufmann and R.J. Hollingdale (New York: Vintage Press, 1967).

12 https://en.wikipedia.org/wiki/Social_contract, retrieved 12 June, 2017.

In the case of the believing community, the conscience informs as to what constitutes right conduct before God. The conscience is not necessarily an automatic judge of what is absolutely right or wrong; rather it judges one's decision based on what one understands to be right or wrong given one's exposure in the world of knowledge and experience. This is why Paul acknowledges both the "weak" conscience (1 Cor 8:7) and the knowledgeable (I Cor 8:9) in the issue of meat offered to idols.

The Weak Conscience and the Knowledgeable

The weak conscience lacks knowledge and remains bound to its native pagan culture, unable to liberate itself from it in spite of the gospel teaching that "there is no God but one" (1 Cor 8:4). Paul notes that "It is not everyone who has this knowledge. Since some have become accustomed to idols until now, they still think of the food they eat as food offered to an idol; and their conscience being weak is defiled. (1 Cor 8:4–8). Such a conscience is unreflective, lacking the will to examine whether a particular custom "brings us close to God (1 Cor 8:8). Paul says that such people are condemned if they eat because they do not act from faith (Rom 14:23). The knowledgeable conscience disassociates meat from the non-existent idol to which it was offered, (1 Cor 8:8, 9). Paul says: "I know and am persuaded in the Lord Jesus that nothing is unclean in itself: but it is unclean for anyone who thinks it unclean" (Rom 14:14).

Contrary to popular preaching on this issue, Paul does not favor the weak conscience over the knowledgeable. While he asks the knowledgeable to defer to the weak, he also asks the weak not to trample the liberty of those who eat (1 Cor 10:29). In Romans 14: 2–4 he states it even more forcefully: "Some believe in eating anything, while the weak eat only vegetables,"[13] but whether one eats or abstain, or observes or not observes a day above another, as long as they do it "in honor of the Lord" no one should judge them (Rom 14:1–6). Both the knowledgeable who disregard the sensibility of the weak and the weak who impose their conscience on the knowledgeable lack spiritual maturity and remain bound to the flesh (1 Cor 3:2–3). It is this spiritual immaturity and not the diversity of conviction that creates the disunity and keeps the church in a state of spiritual bondage.

---

13 Paul is not speaking of eating in terms of health, but in terms of cultic superstition.

The Free Conscience: Knowledge and Love

Regarding the conscience, one can identify two levels of liberty in the conversation about meat offered to idols. The first level is the level of knowledge or awareness. The second level is love. According to Paul, knowledge without love is destructive to the body: "knowledge puffs up, but love builds up" (1 Cor 8:2). However, Paul believes that knowledge is an important gateway to spiritual growth and liberty of conscience. Those who lack knowledge he describes as "infants in Christ" who are "not ready for solid food" because they "are still of the flesh" (1 Cor 3:2–3). In Galatians, those of the flesh are both the "circumcision faction" and those who comply. These are "in slavery" to rituals and regulations, so that they will not accept diversity in the faith. Paul aims to give such believers "solid food" when he considers them ready for it (1 Cor 3:1–3) and, as can be seen in his epistles, Paul does deliver the "solid food": "If you let yourself be circumcised, Christ is of no benefit to you" (Gal 5:2); "If I partake with thankfulness, why should I be denounced, because of that for which I give thanks?" (1 Cor 10:30); "In the Lord, nothing is unclean in itself; but it is unclean for anyone who thinks it unclean" (Rom 14:14); "In the Lord, man is not independent of woman nor woman of man ... everything comes from God" (1 Cor 11:11–12). God is the only head. Headship is flesh. Solid food, indeed!

As Paul notes, not everyone "has ... knowledge", and not everyone is at the same stage in their spiritual development (Rom 14:1). There will always be diverse practices and convictions in the faith. Therefore Paul calls the deeply divided Corinthian community to a "more excellent way"—the way of love (1 Cor 12:31–13:13). Based on all that Paul has been saying, this love is not conformity to the loudest voice. Rather, it is respect for all the voices of faith. In Romans he prefaces his appeal to accept the conviction of the other thus: "Owe no one anything except to love one another ... love your neighbor as yourself ... love is the fulfillment of the law" (Rom 13: 8–10). This is the context of Romans 2: 13–15, where Paul says that the conscience of the Gentiles who do not possess the law "bears witness" to "what the law requires," that is, to "love your neighbor as yourself." As noted above, the well-being and safety of every person is the root of the conscience. That is why, as Paul succinctly states it, one does not have to have the Torah to understand this timeless ethic. This reflects Jesus' teaching on the ten commands that they are really about love, i.e., liberating justice. And this defines the love of God: " ... the second commandment is like the first: love your neighbor as yourself" (Matt 22:39; cf. 1 John 4: 20–21). Interestingly, the ancient Greco-Roman world is renowned for its great piety[14] and its love for the gods, as demonstrated by elaborate rituals, but its culture was ethically bankrupt.[15] The great philosophers arose to address this ethical void. This same empty piety also existed in ancient Israel; hence prophetic oracles such as: "I hate and despise your festivals, and take no delight in your solemn assemblies" (Amos 5:21); " ... who asked this from you? ... New moon and Sabbath and calling of convocation ... my soul hates; they have become a burden to me" (Isa 1: 12–14); "But let justice roll down like waters and righteousness like an ever flowing stream" (Amos 12–14). Love for God depends not on ritual purity but upon the extent to which the faith community accepts and regards each other with respect in serving God through Messiah. This is true liberty of conscience and the only path to unity.

It is important to understand that the issues of conscience discussed here are not issues of moral rectitude, but issues of ritual purity. It is instructive to examine these in light of the issue that now threatens to divide the Seventh-day Adventist church.

Rituals, Conscience and the Case of Women's Ordination

Paul believes and teaches that some stipulations in scripture may be entirely a matter of conscience, and therefore factious, and especially so because of their purely ritualistic function: "Some judge one day to be better than another, while others judge all days to be alike. Let all be fully convinced in their own mind ... I know and am persuaded in the Lord that nothing is unclean in itself ..." (Rom 14:5,14). Nothing in the Old Testament indicates that circumcision is not necessary. But the church came to terms with the reality of a faith-community that was no longer purely Jewish. This makes the case against a literalistic application of scriptures. To Paul such an approach constitutes a fixation of the flesh, a constant diet of milk that impedes spiritual maturity.

Paul's arguments suggest that a ruling of the church may not produce spiritual fruit because of the factious nature of the issue. When that

---

14 Ferguson, *Backgrounds*, 300.

15 Bart D. Ehrman, *A Brief Introduction to the New Testament* (New York: Oxford University Press, 2013), 22–24.

ruling is factious, i.e., when it violates the conscience of some, the church must appeal to a higher conscience, which allows everyone to practice the faith according to the dictates of their conscience. Thus Paul's admonition: "let all be fully convinced in their own minds" (Rom 14:5b). This is the fulfilment of the law: "love your neighbor as yourself" (Rom 13:8).

It is vitally important to point out here that the question of women's ordination, like the question of circumcision, is rooted in ritual purity. One is about the foreskin and the other about blood (Lev 12). The latter has bred an age-long misogynous culture that remains consciously and unconsciously entrenched, especially in religion. It is Old-Covenant consciousness. This is why Paul states in Galatians 3:28: "There is no longer Jew or Greek ... male or female ... " This is New-Covenant liberty in Messiah.

In light of this, the case of the current issue over women's ordination is clearly a question of conscience, and that on two levels. First, if one approaches the scripture from a truly literalistic standpoint, then it seems that the early church in different regions acted according to conscience regarding the function of women. For example, women in Corinth and Rome functioned as prophets, teachers, and apostles (1 Cor 11:1–16; Rom 16:1–8), while "brethren" in Ephesus wanted them to shut up and go home to their rightful roles as child-bearers (1Tim 2:9–15). This is one major reason why after years of study of the Bible by the Seventh-day Adventist Church, there is still no conclusive consensus to prohibit the ordination of women. Some side with the "brethren" in Ephesus and some with the sisters and brothers in Rome, but both groups' convictions are based on their cultural inclinations.

If all the lengthy studies commissioned by the church conclude that the Bible does not prohibit the ordination of women, the current issue as it stands need not divide the church. If the early church judged the ritual act of circumcision—for which there was a clear scriptural mandate—to have no sanctifying value in and of itself, then this applies even more to the question of women's ordination, one that has no clear scriptural mandate. The compulsion to conform to the conscience of one faction in the church indicates that the community as a whole has yet to achieve freedom of conscience toward spiritual maturity. In the context of Galatians, this inability to accept differences in this matter of conscience, leaves us in slavery, bound to flesh and unable to access fully the freedom that comes through Messiah. There can be no unity if the conscience of one group is allowed to coerce that of another.

Liberty and Unity in Christ

Paul's positon coheres with that of Jesus, especially with Jesus' prayer for oneness among believers (John 17:21), which comes in a context of liberty similar to that seen in Paul's writings.

According to John, Jesus states, *"If you continue in my word you are truly my disciples, and you will know the truth, and the truth will set you free"* (John 8:31). This proclamation emerges from the overarching theme of love in the Johannine writings (John, 1, 2 and 3 John). John couches all the Jesus sayings about truth and love in the context of the Abrahamic Covenant. It is in this context that we get a true understanding of Jesus' prayer that the believing community "be one" (John 17:21). What makes them one is their love for one another.

In John, the audience listening to Jesus' statement on truth and freedom is comprised of Jews "who had believed in him." Their response is to defend their inherent freedom through the Abrahamic Covenant (John 8:33) but Jesus replies that their actions do not demonstrate that they really grasp the freedom that the Covenant offers: "If you were Abraham's children, you would be doing what Abraham did, but you are trying to kill me (8:40) … because there is no place in your heart for my word" (8:37). The central passage in John's writings reflects Paul's interpretation of the Abrahamic covenant in Galatians and *Romans*: "For God so loved the world that he gave his only Son, so that anyone who believes … may have eternal life" (John 3:16). God's covenant of justice is one of love for all who accept the promise through Messiah, not just for a particular group who live according to certain rules and regulations. According to John, the truth Jesus speaks of is this truth of God's love and the believer's faith (-fullness)[16] to it, namely, to love one another. Jesus declares: "I give you a new commandment, that you love one another … By this everyone will know that you are my disciples, if you have love for one another" (John 13:34; cf. 1 John 4:21). John's mature theological reflection echoes this: "This is the message that we have

---

16 As explained on page 52.

heard from him and we proclaim to you, that God is light ...Whoever loves a brother or sister lives in the light" (1 John 1: 5; 2:10).

Love brings the believing community into liberating justice and thereby, it lives out the very faith (-fullness) of Messiah. Love is the truth that sets us free.

Jesus prays that the believing community "be one" (John 17:21) as a testimony to the world of the love of God: "... so that the world may know that you have sent me and have loved them as you have loved me" John 17:23). In the light of the Abrahamic Covenant, the oneness for which he prays is not conformity to rules that do not even reflect love. Jesus was killed because, rather than conforming to the letter of the law, he taught and lived its spirit, namely love.

Love is the truth that brings true freedom and unites all believers in Christ. Jesus invites the believing community into a deeply spiritual experience—the very Christ experience. According to John, to love is to abide in God (1 John 4:16), to be "begotten from God" (1 John 4:7), and to pass from death into life (1 John 3:14). This is to say that the believing community may also become one with God as Jesus and God are one. This is the "in Christ" experience of true liberty into which Paul invites the church. Thus Paul can declare that in Christ "there is no longer Jew or Greek ... slave or free ... male or female (Gal 3:28) and "In Christ, woman is not independent of man or man ... of woman ... all things come from God" (1 Cor 11:11–12). God is the only head. In Christ "nothing is unclean in itself" (Rom 14:14).

The tendency to strive over these temporal things stems from our earthly limitations. Paul shows the factious community in Corinth a "more excellent way" and that is *love* (see 1 Cor. 12:31–13:13), because it is the only thing that outlasts our partial earthly understanding: "For now we see in a mirror dimly ... now I know only in part ..." In Christ, fear of uncertainty subsides and we rest in the mystery of God's being: "... I put an end to childish ways." Such an experience cannot be voted, legislated, or coerced. It requires spiritual discipline and instruction in the true spirit of scriptures through responsible, Christ-filled, exemplary discipleship. It requires a focus on growing members that is at least equal to that of growing membership. This is hard, much harder than enforcing conformity to the "elementary rudiments" of our individual consciences.

It is, nevertheless, the road on which Jesus Messiah invites the church to travel: "Enter through the narrow gate; for the gate is wide and the road is easy that leads to destruction, and there are many who take it. For the gate is narrow and the road is hard that leads to life, and there are few who find it" (Mat 7:13).

4. Religious Freedom: Some Historical Perspectives and Present Applications[1]

Reinder Bruinsma
Formerly President, Netherlands Union of SDA Churches

Introductory Remarks

Freedom is a precious commodity. It is at the heart of the Christian message and is the basis for a Christian way of life. Jesus stressed that freedom is a vital aspect of discipleship. *He is the Truth* (John 14:6). His followers are assured that as they follow him, "the Truth [i.e. Jesus Christ] will set you free" (John 8:31). But what is this true freedom that people can experience through their relationship with Christ? It clearly has an important spiritual component, but must also have practical implications. How does the freedom that Christ gives translate in how people live out their faith and in how they relate to others who practice their faith differently from them?

The modern understanding of religious freedom is embedded in the conviction that all human beings share some basic, inalienable rights. These have been codified in the *United Nations Declaration of Human Rights* (1948). It was agreed by most nations on earth that all men, women and children have these universal rights, regardless of where they live, and irrespective of their gender, sexual orientation, ethnicity, and political or religious persuasion. Since then, several other pieces of international legislation have been added, dealing more specifically with certain individual rights.

These human rights documents cover a wide spectrum. There are security rights that stress the sanctity of the human body and protect people against such crimes as murder, massacre, genocide, torture

---

[1] Major parts of this chapter are adapted from a presentation, entitled "Religious Freedom in the Lutheran Tradition and for the Adventist Christian in 2017," given at the European Theology Teachers Convention held at Friedensau Adventist University on April 21, 2017.

and rape. Political rights guarantee the liberty to participate freely in political activities, the right to express oneself freely and the right to take part in protests.

Other rights ensure that each person is entitled to due legal process and cannot be imprisoned without trial or be subjected to abuses of the legal system. In addition, the welfare rights (or economic rights) stipulate that every person must have access to education and be protected against severe poverty or starvation. The rights that guarantee equal citizenship for all, emphasizing total equality before the law and forbidding every form of discrimination, have come increasingly to the forefront in recent years, especially in Western countries which have experienced an influx of large numbers of immigrants.[2]

In the context of the present discussion, article 18 of the *Universal Declaration* is of prime importance:

> Everyone has the right to freedom of thought, conscience and religion; this right includes freedom to change his religion or belief, and freedom, either alone or in community with others and in public or private, to manifest his religion or belief in teaching, practice, worship and observance.[3]

When dealing with freedom of conscience and freedom of religion, a few aspects stand out.

1. The inner freedom that the Christian can experience when he or she lives 'in Christ'.

2. The freedom to believe and worship as one chooses.

3. The issue of separation between church and state.

4. The absence of coercive measures by the church.

5. The absence of coercive measures by the state.

Great progress has been made in ensuring a greater degree of freedom of religion and conscience in most parts of the world. A major step forward was made during the Second Vatican Council when the Roman Catholic Church formally accepted the right to religious freedom of all people.[4] But much remains to be done.

---

2 Reinder Bruinsma, "Sorgen um die Religionsfreiheit in einer postmodernen Welt," *Gewissen und Freiheit*, 62 (2008): 18–35.

3 The various human rights instruments can be found in many sources. For an easily accessible web-version, see http://lib.law.washington.edu/_archive/humanright.html.

4 The text of the 'Declaration on Religious Liberty', is found in

In the present discussion of various aspects of religious freedom it must first of all be recognized that the contemporary concept of religious liberty is of relatively recent origin. In ancient times, in particular, areas of the world were mostly ruled by a system of theocratic absolutism, in which the rulers were often venerated as divine figures. And it tragically must also be accepted that ever since Christianity came on the scene "religion and freedom have not been natural allies."[5] In most of Christian history we see a serious lack of religious freedom. Although through the ages the church regularly insisted that it should be free from all control of temporary rulers, the reality was usually rather different. Freedom of the church from the control by the state may be an important part of the modern view of religious freedom, but it was long in the making. Scholars disagree whether political philosophers or theologians were the primary movers in the process of establishing a theoretical framework to undergird freedom of conscience and religion.[6] The fact is that some religious thinkers did underline the primacy of the individual conscience and this certainly had a major impact on the theories of religious rights that gradually developed.

Often the church's demand of freedom from coercion by the state was not accompanied by a generosity to grant full freedom to individuals to follow their own conscience and to make their own religious choices. For many centuries the church was frequently inclined to organize the suppression and even the persecution of its own dissident members.[7] In theory, the church usually upheld the notion that non-Christians could not be forced to convert to Christianity, but in actual practice this principle was often ignored. The official policy of the medieval church was that Jews should be free to exercise their own religion but the practice was often quite different.

Although a lot has been achieved in defending and safeguarding religious freedom around the world, several organizations—such as

---

Austin Flannery, ed., *Vatican Council II: The Conciliar and Postconciliar Documents* (Northport, NY: Costello, 1987), 799–812.

5 James Wood, 'Editorial: Religion and Religious Liberty,' *Journal of Church and State*, 33 (1991), 226, as cited in Brian Tierney, "Religious Rights: A Historical Perspective," in *Religious Liberty in Western Thought*, eds. Noel B. Reynolds and W. Cole Durhum (Atlanta, GA: Scholars Press, 1996), p. 29.

6 Tierney, "Religious Rights," 38–42.

7 Tierney, "Religious Rights," 36.

the United States Commission on International Religious Freedom—still regularly report the numerous infringements and point to dozens of countries where religious freedom remains an illusion.[8] Even in the "free" Western world there is good reason to remain alert, as individuals and organizations may still ride roughshod over the religious rights of individuals or unpopular groups.

In these introductory remarks it must also be noted that religious freedom is more than *indifference* as to what people believe and goes beyond mere *tolerance*. This is an important point to remember in the twenty-first century world in which the attitude of many people towards other religions is, at best, one of tolerance, rather than one of genuine respect for their religious freedom. In many areas in the world the relationship between Christians and Muslims is at best one of toleration, often state-enforced. But, as Dr. Bert B. Beach, a well-known Adventist champion of religious freedom, once stated: "Tolerance implies that freedom of religion and belief is not really an intrinsic right, but that society, in a spirit of beneficence may grant a privilege, to that which is not wholly approved of, or possibly even suspect."[9]

The Reformation and Religious Freedom

In this year in which the world commemorates Luther's first public step on the path of the Reformation, it is more than fitting to ask the question: *How does the modern view of religious freedom compare with the understanding of the magisterial sixteenth century Reformers?* To answer this question it is necessary first to look briefly at Luther's thinking about religious freedom.

In 1520 Martin Luther wrote his foundational treatise about man's freedom—*On the Freedom of a Christian*.[10] Although it is clear that Luther felt strongly about the need for freedom from the papal yoke and from the non-biblical teachings of the Roman Catholic Church—which is especially clear in his dedicatory letter to Pope Leo X that

---

8 See eg. http://www.uscirf.gov/sites/default/files/Overview%20USICRF%202016%20Annual%20Report.pdf.

9 B. B. Beach, *Bright Candle of Courage* (Boise, ID: Pacific Press, 1989), 13.

10 The Latin title is: *De Libertate Christiana*; in German: *Von der Freiheit eines Christenmenschen.*: http://www.jmstanton.com/Docs/Martin%20Luther%20-%20On%20the%20Freedom %20of%20a%20Christian%20with%20lines.pdf

introduces his pamphlet—*On the Freedom of a Christian* is mainly about the *inner* freedom of the Christian. He states two propositions as his point of departure: "A Christian man is the most free lord of all, and subject to none; a Christian man is the most dutiful servant of all, and subject to everyone." Two paragraphs later he clarifies this as follows: "We first approach the subject of the inner man, that we may see by what means a man becomes justified, free, and a true Christian; that is, a spiritual, new, and inward man."

For Martin Luther the freedom of the Christian is fundamentally *freedom from the law*. The person who is really free "… has no need of works, neither has he need of the law, and, if he has no need of the law, he is certainly free from the law … no one should need the law or works for justification and salvation." That does not mean that the Christian has a license to do "bad" things, but "his works are to be done freely, with the sole object of pleasing God." A modern Lutheran author commented: "Here is an early Lutheran document . . . filled, nay, rather bursting at the seams with the universal, law-free gospel of God's mercy and therefore of justification by grace through faith on account of Christ alone."[11]

With regard to the relationship between church and state, Luther built on Augustine's doctrine of the two kingdoms—both of which God created, albeit with different roles. Both church and state have their own spheres, but Luther did not want total separation. The state should provide protection for the believers, while Luther also allowed civil rulers a degree of control over ecclesiastical matters. [Luther himself was provided protection after the Diet of Worms by Elector Frederick, and remained for some time under an assumed name (Squire George) in the Wartburg Castle.] There is considerable justification for these words: "Defenders of the free-church principle have, with some fairness, concluded that eventually this doctrine of the two realms created a persecuting Lutheran state church."[12]

Lutheranism spread widely in parts of Europe, but not uniformly so, and whether or not one became a Lutheran Christian was in many cases not the individual's free decision. Much depended on whether or not the ruler in a particular area had converted to Lutheranism.

---

11 Timothy J. Wengert, 'Luther's Freedom of a Christian for Today's Church,' *Lutheran Quarterly*, XXVIII (2014): 9.

12 Alister E. McGrath, *Historical Theology: An Introduction to the History of Christian Thought* (Malden, MA; Blackwell, 1998), 202.

The Peace of Augsburg in 1531 was concluded between the Emperor Charles V and the Schmalkaldic League (an alliance of German Lutheran princes). Rulers could choose whether their region would be Roman Catholic or Lutheran. This settlement is summarized in the formula, *Cuius Regio, Eius Religio* ["whose realm, his religion"]. Calvinism was not legally recognized until the Peace of Westphalia in 1648.[13]

In Germany Lutheranism had achieved a position of equality alongside Catholicism. However in the Scandinavian countries Lutheranism came to replace Catholicism fully as the established church. Until recently almost the entire populations of the Scandinavian countries belonged to the Lutheran State Church.[14] In recent decades the Lutheran church in the Nordic countries lost this privileged status.

In Calvin's thinking church and state were also closely connected. The state, Calvin argued, must be subjected to the church and Christian statesmen are to defend true doctrine.[15] However, only in a few countries did Calvinism become the "established" religion, Scotland being the most prominent example.

A Free Will

Both Luther and Calvin were opposed to the concept of a free will. When Desiderius Erasmus published his booklet entitled *On the Freedom of the Will* (1524), Martin Luther responded with *On the Bondage of the Will* (1525).[16] Luther denied that human beings have a free will and that they can freely choose either good or evil, since sin incapacitates human beings from taking any step towards salvation. It is often not sufficiently recognized that not only Calvin, but also Luther believed in double predestination, even though Luther did not emphasize it quite as much as Calvin did.[17] Calvin refuted the idea of a free will at length in the second book of his monumental *Institutes of the Christian Religion*.[18] [Adventists, of course, feel much more akin

---

13 Kenneth Scott Latourette, *A History of Christianity, vol. 2: Reformation to the Present* (San Francisco: Harper Collins, 1975 edition), 726–729.

14 Roland H. Bainton, *The Reformation of the Sixteenth Century* (Boston, MA: Beacon, 1952), 141–159.

15 Bruinsma, "–Sorgen um die Religionsfreiheit, 133–138.

16 http://www.chapellibrary.org/files/4913/7643/2893/botw.pdf.

17 Louis Berkhof, *The History of Christian Doctrines* (Edinburgh: Banner of Truth, 1969), 148.

18 John Calvin, *Institutes of the Christian Religion*, transl. by Henry

to the views about the human free will of the Radical Reformation[19] and of what would later be called the Arminian tradition.]

The rather intolerant attitude of the Reformers towards the "mother church" that they had left is well known, but the harsh disciplinary measures against those in their own ranks who held theological positions they deemed heretical should also be noted. Calvin's approval of the execution of Michael Servetus in 1553 because of his, in Calvin's view, erroneous teachings on the doctrine of the Trinity and on the doctrine of baptism is a sad example,[20] and his refusal to extend freedom of religion to those who preached or practiced "heresies" is likewise well-known. Luther's relationship with the more radical reformer (and his former friend) Andreas Carlstadt, who was to be banished from Saxony by Frederick the Wise, is a clear illustration of Luther's intolerance of alternative theological views.[21] Luther's unrelenting anti-Semitism is also well documented.[22] Thus Luther manifested a regrettable inconsistency in his approach to freedom. This is, after all, the man who in 1521 stated before the Diet of Worms: "To act against our conscience is neither safe for us or open to us. On this I take my stand. I can do no other. God help me."[23]

Mixed Feelings About the Reformers

Seventh-day Adventists are very positive with regard to many aspects of the work of the sixteenth-century Reformers. But Martin Luther, by and large, receives a much more positive press in the Adventist Church than John Calvin, even though Calvinism was a much stronger force in American nineteenth-century religion than Lutheranism. Perhaps the clearest illustration of this is found in the way the two Reformers are treated in Ellen G. White's book *The Great*

Beveridge (Peabody, MA: Hendrickson, 2008), 145–216.

19 George H. Williams, *The Radical Reformation* (Philadelphia, PN: Westminster, 1962), passim.

20 See, e.g. T.H.L. Parker, *John Calvin: A Biography* (Oxford: Lion Hudson, 2006 ed.), 146–154.

21 Roland Bainton, *Here I Stand: A Life of Martin Luther* (New York/Nashville: Abingdon, 1950), 263.

22 See Martin Luther, *Von den Jüden und iren Lügen* (1545). A recent English version is: *On the Jews and their Lies* (Austin, TX: River Crest, 2014).

23 V. Norskov Olsen, *Papal Supremacy and American Democracy* (Loma Linda, CA: Loma Linda University Press, 1987), 130.

Controversy.[24] Not only did she devote many more pages to Luther than to Calvin, but she also appeared to be much more positive about Luther than about the Reformer from Geneva.

With regard to Calvin, Ellen White states:

> For nearly thirty years Calvin labored at Geneva, first to establish there a church adhering to the morality of the Bible, and then for the advancement of the Reformation throughout Europe. His course as a public leader was not faultless, nor were his doctrines free from error.[25]

A little further in the same book she spoke in no uncertain terms about the 'monstrous' Calvinist doctrine of predestination.[26]

Compare this with the glowing accolade accorded to Martin Luther:

> Foremost among those called to lead the church from the darkness of popery into the light of a purer faith stood Martin Luther. Knowing no fear but the fear of God, and acknowledging no foundation for faith but the Holy Scriptures, Luther was the man for his time.[27]

And when referring to Luther's appearance before the Diet of Worms, Ellen White comments:

> Thus stood this righteous man upon the sure foundation of the word of God. The light of heaven illuminated his countenance. His greatness and purity of character, his peace and joy of heart, were manifest to all as he testified against the power of error and witnessed to the superiority of the faith that overcomes the world.[28]

Nevertheless Adventists are critical with respect to a number of the positions of the Reformers. For instance they do not support the views of the Reformers with regard to various aspects of freedom. They agree with Luther that we are "free from the law" in the sense that salvation is *sola gratia*, but they would be hesitant to talk about freedom from the law in the way Luther does. Adventists stress the limitations of the law, but also underline that the law, in Paul's words, is "holy, righteous and good", and still plays an important role in the Christian life.[29]

---

24 Ellen G. White, *The Great Controversy* (Nampa, ID: Pacific Press, 2005 [1911]).

25 White, *Great Controversy*, 236.

26 White, *Great Controversy*, 261.

27 White, *Great Controversy*, 120.

28 White, *Great Controversy*, 160.

29 For example, John C. Brunt, *Romans* (series: *The Abundant Life Bible*

Another area where Adventists find it difficult to appreciate these magisterial Reformers is in the area of their understanding of man's free will, as already noted.

Likewise, when the modern concept of freedom of conscience and religion is used as the standard for measuring the approach of the Reformers, they must be deemed to have fallen far short of these ideals. Some have maintained that Luther replaced Catholic religious persecution with Protestant oppression and persecution. Reference has already been made to the classic example of Calvin's intolerance—the case of Servetus—but his harsh enforcement of very strict discipline in Geneva is also a far cry from what we would call religious freedom.

The Radical Reformation and Its Abiding Influence

Adventists disagree with both Luther and Calvin (as well as Zwingli) with respect to the relationship between church and state. On this issue Adventists are also much closer to the Radical Reformation tradition, which would be the dominant philosophy of the so-called "free" Protestant churches, and became the basis of the American principle of full separation between church and state.[30] Some groups in Reformation times were more "radical" than the "magisterial" Reformers and their associates. The Anabaptists were the most important branch of the so-called "Radical Reformation."[31] They rejected the kind of close association between church and state that would lead to the establishment of "state churches" or "established churches" in a number of European countries. They were opposed to the territorial system of the Lutherans and were also opposed to any participation in warfare and the swearing of oaths.

The Radical Reformation provided the immediate roots for movements such as the Mennonites, the Quakers and the Baptists. In many ways modern evangelicalism—and, indirectly, Seventh-day Adventism—can trace some of its major ideas to the Radical Reformation. The Anabaptists insisted that baptism of believers was the only valid mode of entrance into the church, which they

---

Amplifier (Boise, ID: Pacific Press, 1996), 143–162.

30 Reinder Bruinsma, *The Body of Christ: A Biblical Understanding of the Church* (Hagerstown, MD: Review and Herald, 2009), 106.

31 George H. Williams, *The Radical Reformation* (Philadelphia: Westminster, 1962) is still a good guide to the Radical Reformation. See also William R. Estep, *The Anabaptist Story: An Introduction to Sixteenth-Century Anabaptism* 3rd ed. (Grand Rapids, MI: Eerdmans, 1996).

conceived as a visible community of committed Christians. They were staunch defenders of the individual's free will as the basis for accepting or rejecting the salvation that Christ offers. They interpreted the communion service in purely symbolic terms, and in some cases reintroduced foot-washing as a rite that precedes the communion.

Several positions adopted in this Radical Reformation also became part and parcel of Adventist beliefs and practices, to a large extent through the early Methodist connections.[32]

Adventist Interest in Freedom of Religion

Seventh-day Adventism originated and developed in a nineteenth century North-American context. It is important to remember that from its inception American Protestantism had a distinctly Calvinist flavor. Most settlers in the American Mid-Atlantic region and in New England were Calvinists, including the English Puritans, the French Huguenots, the Dutch settlers of New Amsterdam (New York), and the Scottish-Irish Presbyterians of the Appalachian back country. The majority of the newcomers had Calvinist roots, while Lutherans accounted for only five percent of the population.[33] Most successful among the so-called "free churches" were the Baptists and the Methodists, while the proportion of Roman Catholics also steadily increased as the nineteenth century progressed.[34] One significant factor in the development of the church in North America is, undoubtedly, that America was greatly affected by two powerful waves of revivals, one in each of the eighteenth and nineteenth centuries. This had a significant effect on Calvinist thinking in America, in particular with regard to the fundamental doctrine of predestination. This teaching proved to be a very "contentious" doctrine.[35] Arminian influences that

---

32 See the historical introduction by Dennis Fortin to a special 125th anniversary edition of Ellen White's book *Steps to Christ* (Berrien Springs, MI: Andrews University Press, 2017), 22–58. See also the special section, "Adventism's Methodist Roots" in *Spectrum* 25 (September 1996): 26–54.

33 Roger Finke and Rodney Stark, *The Churching of America, 1776–1990: Winners and Losers in Our Religious Economy* (New Brunswick, NJ: Rutgers University Press, 1992), 25.

34 Reinder Bruinsma, *Seventh-day Adventist Attitudes toward Roman Catholicism, 1844–1965* (Berrien Springs, MI: Andrews University Press, 1994), 15–19.

35 As expressed in the title of an important book on the history of the idea of predestination in North America: Peter J. Thuesen, *Predestination:*

had come from Europe had already convinced many that this basic Calvinist tenet was not correct, but the revivalist preaching that emphasized "free will" in an often very popular manner also had a profound influence.[36] The fact that the very idea of predestination did not fit well with the American idea of choosing and working hard to reach one's own destiny should also be remembered.

Many immigrants ("pilgrims") to North America had suffered religious persecution in Europe, but it did not necessarily follow that in their new country they would always favor full religious freedom and total separation of church and state. There were, however, some significant developments in colonial America as the initial supremacy of "established" churches came increasingly under fire.[37] Roger Williams, a Puritan turned Baptist leader "was perhaps the foremost spokesman for religious freedom in seventeenth-century America."[38] We might also mention the relative freedom granted to Roman Catholics in the state of Maryland,[39] as well as the struggle for religious freedom by the Quakers in the state of Massachusetts.[40]

The American Revolution brought political freedom from Great Britain, but it also resulted in many changes in the area of church and religion. The churches faced the challenge to "adjust to the ideology of democratic republicanism that had driven the war."[41] The new republic, of course, needed a constitution. This Constitution

---

The American Career of a Contentious Doctrine (Oxford: Oxford University Press, 2009).

36 The last two paragraphs are mostly dependent on an earlier (and as yet unpublished) lecture entitled 'The Sixteenth Century Reformation and Adventist Ecclesiology", delivered in the spring of 2016 at Friedensau University. See also Reinder Bruinsma, *Geloven in Amerika: Kerken, Geschiedenis en Geloof van Christenen in de Verenigde Staten* (Uitgeverij Zoetermeer: Boekencentrum, 1998), 86–88.

37 Robert T. Handy, *A Christian America: Protestant Hopes and Historical Realities* (New York/ Oxford: Oxford University Press, 1994 ed.), 3–23.

38 Edwin S. Gaustad, *Liberty of Conscience: Roger Williams in America* (Grand Rapids, MI: Eerdmans, 1991), back cover.

39 Sydney E. Ahlstrom, *A Religious History of the American People* (New Haven/London: Yale University Press, 1972), 331–334.

40 Ahlstrom, *Religious History,* 176–181.

41 Mark A. Noll, *A History of Christianity in the United States and Canada* (Grand Rapids, MI: Eerdmans, 1992), 144.

was signed on September 17, 1787. The First Amendment of the US Constitution took effect in 1791. It stipulated that "Congress shall make no law respecting the establishment of religion or prohibiting the exercise thereof." However it may well be asked, "How did the First Amendment come to coexist with what, from a modern vantage point, looks like a thorough intermingling of church and state."[42] Church historian Mark Noll reminds us, however, that " ... the colonial background of the new states was so overwhelmingly Protestant that it was simply assumed that such things as Sunday legislation, laws prohibiting atheism and promoting public morals ... were appropriate." [43]

Adventism, which was a new, Sabbath-keeping religious movement that originated in this nineteenth century Sunday-keeping context, could thus expect to meet with considerable opposition. This explains why, almost from the beginning, Adventists would be strongly interested in the promotion of full religious freedom and of a total separation between church and state. The early Adventists saw some large dangers looming. In 1864, a group of "zealous opponents of the growing secularization in the United States" established the National Reform Association. Their aim was to convince Congress that the state should enforce the general principles of Christianity. To begin with, God should be put into the Constitution. They failed in their plans and from 1874 onwards, shifted gears to emphasize legally enforced Sunday observance.

In some states Sunday laws were enacted, resulting in the persecution of the violators of these laws. In the 1880s some hundred Adventists were either given jail sentences, condemned to enforced labor, or fined. Matters came to a head in 1888 when Senator Henry Blair of New Hampshire tried unsuccessfully, despite a gigantic petition drive, to make Congress adopt a national Sunday law.[44] It was in this climate that Ellen G. White wrote *The Great Controversy*[45] in

---

42 Noll, *History*, 144.

43 Noll, *History*, 145.

44 Richard W. Schwartz and Floyd Greenleaf, *Light Bearers: A History of the Seventh-day Adventist Church,* rev. ed. (Nampa, ID: Pacific Press, 2000), 241–245. For a detailed historical survey of the attempts to enforce Sunday legislation in the United States, see Warren L. Johns, *Dateline Sunday, USA: The Story of Three and a Half Centuries of Sunday-law Battles in America* (Mountain View, CA: Pacific Press, 1967).

45 The original 1888 edition of *Great Controversy* was revised in 1911.

which she developed an end-time scenario that, in many ways, was a reaction to the lack of freedom many Seventh-day Adventists were experiencing in very concrete ways through the opposition of other Christians. At the same time in the entire Protestant world of the United States, anti-Catholicism was being fed by the millions of immigrants from Catholic countries who constituted an economic as well as religious threat. In addition to this general anti-Catholicism, White saw the United States itself as a future persecuting power.

Early on—in 1889—the Adventists decided to establish the Religious Liberty Association. It stated as its key principle that civil governments do not have the right to legislate on religious matters, and it underlined the importance of complete freedom of conscience.[46] Ever since, the promotion of religious liberty, through its department[47] and through independent organizations, has been an important concern for the Adventist Church. The International Religious Liberty Association (IRLA) was established in 1946, at the initiative of the Adventist Church. It is headquartered in the Adventist head office in Silver Spring, but enjoys the participation of many non-Adventists experts.[48] The religious liberty efforts of Adventists have been focused on protecting the religious rights of Adventist believers, but not exclusively so, as it is recognized that all people must enjoy full religious freedom.

Issues and Questions

At the present time, Adventists are entitled to some sense of pride and satisfaction with regard to religious freedom. Their ideas of what religious freedom means have matured and their efforts to promote

---

See Denis Fortin, "The Great Controversy Between Christ and Satan", in *The Ellen G. White Encyclopedia,* ed. Denis Fortin and Jerry Moon (Hagerstown, MD; Review and Herald, 2013), 847–850.

46 Don F. Neufeld, ed., *Seventh-day Adventist Encyclopedia*, 2 Vols. (Hagerstown, MD: Review and Herald, 1996), s.v. "Religious Liberty".

47 The church department that is devoted to religious liberty as one of its main concerns since 1962 has been named Department of Public Affairs and Religious Liberty (PARL). See *SDA Encyclopedia*, s.v. "Public Affairs and Religious Liberty, Department of (PARL)". See also Douglas Morgan, *Adventism and the American Republic: The Public Involvement of a Major Apocalyptic Movement* (Knoxville. TN: University of Tennessee Press, 2001), 108–110.

48 *SDA Encyclopedia*, s.v. "International Religious Liberty Association".

it—both through public events and by silent diplomacy—have often paid off, and Adventist contributions in this domain have been recognized by many.

Adventists have traditionally been very hesitant—to put it euphemistically—to get involved in interfaith or interdenominational projects, but they have been more than willing to cooperate with other faith communities with regard to humanitarian and developmental projects and in the promotion of religious freedom.

When considering the topic of religious freedom in an Adventist context, a few important issues come to mind. It is unfortunate that among Adventists the conviction that liberty of conscience and of religion should be recognized as an essential right of every person is not always matched by a genuine *interest* in what others actually believe. Often Adventists continue to cherish stereotypical views of what other faith communities stand for, or to hold on to facts that are now outdated.[49] The traditional Adventist understanding of the Roman Catholic Church and of the Protestant churches as apostate communities has all too frequently led to disrespectful statements and unbecoming conduct towards those whose beliefs differ from those held by Seventh-day Adventists. It would show a mature Christian attitude if Adventists would not just grant others the right to worship and believe as their conscience dictates, but also show respect and a greater willingness to understand what they stand for, and to give praise where praise is due.

Another major issue arises in regard to the "freedom of a Christian" in its most fundamental sense. In his 1520 booklet, *Freedom of a Christian,* Martin Luther tended to undervalue the role of God's law in the life of the Christian. Seventh-day Adventists have often erred in the other direction and have neither understood sufficiently nor experienced the true Christian freedom that is based on an adequate understanding of justification by faith. In spite of the debate in Minneapolis in 1888 and its aftermath (and other developments since), the problem of legalism[50] has remained an ever-present danger. "Christ

---

49 See Bruinsma, *Adventist Attitudes toward Roman Catholicism,* 299–300.

50 For a succinct but in-depth discussion of legalism, see Edward W.H. Vick, *Let Me Assure You* (Mountain View, CA: Pacific Press, 1968), 117–120. For a broader treatment, see George R. Knight, *The Pharisee's Guide to Perfect Holiness* (Boise, ID: Pacific Press, 1992).

our Righteousness" must remain the basis for a correct understanding of the doctrine of salvation and of the concept of justification by faith.

This is an even more essential point today than in the past, considering the increasing popularity of the so-called "Last Generation Theology", with its dangerous emphasis on perfectionism and its often undue stress on the human role in the salvation process. This alternative theology, which was fiercely presented by Milton L. Andreasen seventy years ago,[51] has in recent years been vigorously promoted by a number of (mainly independent) ministries and is also clearly present in the writings and sermons of some of the church's world leaders. Here, Luther should remind Adventists of the true freedom that comes when we reject any tint of legalism, and live freely on the basis of justification by faith. It is unfortunate that "Last Generation Theology" leads many of its adherents to doubt or deny that their salvation is only and completely based on the merits of Christ.

Freedom of conscience and the freedom to express one's beliefs can be a complicated issue. How much freedom can a denomination tolerate with regard to diversity in religious and doctrinal views (a) on the part of its leaders and ministers and (b) among its lay-members?[52] To put it plainly, in the context of recent developments in Adventism, should Adventist church members have to agree with every detail of Adventist teaching, especially as outlined in the 28 Fundamental Beliefs, in order to qualify as "true" Adventists? If not, at what point may/should the church organization introduce sanctions (church discipline), or refuse to continue to recognize a person's membership?

One cannot be a Christian unless one accepts the basic tenets of the Christian faith. Likewise, it becomes meaningless to claim to be an Adventist Christian while denying the basics of the Adventist teachings. There must be certain parameters within which one must stay. There may not be enough dialogue in many places in the church about what constitutes these "basics". Yet there seems to be a reasonably broad consensus that, for instance, the Sabbath doctrine

---

51 See in particular Milton L. Andreasen, *The Sanctuary Service*, (Washington, DC: Review and Herald, 1947). 299–321. The chapter is entitled "The Last Generation".

52 An enlightening article is: Lydia Veliko, 'Criteria for Unity and the Limits of Diversity: Towards an Ecclesiology of United Churches,' *The Ecumenical Review*, 62 (2010): 30–40.

is more "basic" than the distinction between "clean" and "unclean" food, or that Christ's second coming is a more vital belief than the identity of the "beast from the earth" (Rev 13:1–18).

In actual practice there has always been, and still is, both a considerable degree of consensus and a considerable amount of theological diversity in the Adventist Church. Most Adventist church members consider some degree of diversity to be acceptable. In fact, it might justifiably be argued that a fair degree of diversity is not only inevitable but even desirable in an organization that is alive. But the question is, *how much* of such diversity can be tolerated without losing the necessary degree of unity?[53] Many would suggest that requiring absolute uniformity in assent to all doctrines is unnecessary and undesirable. Moreover, it goes against the genius of Adventism, which from its formative years has shown a considerable degree of diversity in doctrinal matters. Recent attempts at codifying in ever more detail what a "real" Adventist must believe are lamentable. This is a form of coercion that limits the freedom a follower of Jesus must be able to experience.

Related to this point is the gradual growth of the church's corpus of policies. A few decades ago the General Conference Working Policy Book was a 250–300 page book. Over time it has grown into a tome with a multitude of pages. In itself the creation of extra policies and making further refinements is not limiting the freedom of the church's workers or the members. In fact, some policies may protect that freedom. A problem arises when policies receive a status that is almost on a par with church doctrine and when one ecclesial body claims to provide the only correct interpretations of those policies, as is the case with regard to some policies that directly or indirectly impact on the debate over the ordination of female pastors.

Many would agree that Church entities below the General Conference level ought to have considerable freedom to adapt policies to their regional or local circumstances. At the San Antonio General Conference Session that freedom was denied to those Divisions of the

---

53 See e.g. Reinder Bruinsma, "Theological Diversity: A Threat, an Asset or What?" *Ministry*, (December 2010): 17–20; Reinder Bruinsma, "Are all Truths True? Some Thoughts on the Classification of Beliefs," in *Encountering God in Life and Mission: A Festschrift Honoring Jon L. Dybdahl,* ed. Rudi Maier (Berrien Springs, MI: Department of World Mission Andrews University, 2010), 173–188.

world church that wanted to have the possibility of ordaining women pastors. The very reason why the church towards the end of the nineteenth and at the beginning of the twentieth century decentralized church authority by creating a series of other church bodies (unions and later divisions) with considerable authority was to make regional and local adaptations of ecclesial practices possible. There is a feeling on the part of many that this freedom to adapt rules and regulations has in recent years been limited.

Another question that has become quite urgent is the matter of academic freedom. How much space can be given to those who teach theology—or for that matter, other disciplines—in Adventist colleges and universities?

Few will deny that there must be some parameters as to what is acceptable and what is not, however difficult it may be to reach a consensus in this matter. The educational institutions that are operated by the denomination must retain their Adventist identity (whatever that is exactly must continue to be a topic for dialogue!). But it would seem that there are tendencies in the church to go overboard in controlling everything that happens in the theological departments of church-run institutions of higher learning by establishing a process for the systematic screening of all theology teachers with regard to their orthodoxy. This hotly debated screening process for all university and college level theology professors, entails that they should not only agree with all the 28 Fundamental Beliefs of Seventh-day Adventists, but must also, among other things, subscribe to the document, "Methods of Bible Study", that was voted by the Annual Council of the church in Rio de Janeiro in 1986.[54] Many question whether this goes too far and whether this does not, in fact, limit the possibilities for research and may inhibit creative theological thinking. Some also feel that it is a factor in creating a climate of fear in which freely expressing one's ideas and having an open dialogue with colleagues becomes rather risky, as it may easily create the suspicion of a lack of orthodoxy and even cause the loss of one's job. They wonder whether this development does not eventually lead to precisely the kind of system of ecclesial control against which the Reformers protested. Does "religious freedom" not demand a significant degree

---

54 The document is found on the official website of the Adventist World Church: https://www.adventist.org/en/information/official-statements/documents/article/go/-/methods-of-bible-study/

of academic freedom, even when this might entail some risks? No doubt this discussion will continue.

It is fair to ask the question, should a denomination that has been and is so much in the forefront with regard to the promotion of freedom of conscience and religion not be willing to extend a fair amount of that freedom to its own members and to its theology professors?[55] After all, is what President Ronald Reagan once said during a speech at Moscow University not true?— "Freedom is the right to question and change established ways of doing things"[56] And would that not also include established ways of thinking and of formulating things in the domain of theology and of adapting church policy to varying situations?

Conclusion

This year sees the 500th anniversary of Martin Luther's courageous step towards freedom: freedom from an organization that had no place for those who disagreed with its codified beliefs, and from a system that did not allow people the freedom to study the Bible and think for themselves. That the Reformers themselves often did not grant this same freedom to their followers and to those who disagreed with them ought to be a warning, that great care should be taken in any restriction of the freedom of thought of fellow-believers.

The Adventist "pioneers" insisted that we should have no creed but the Bible, having themselves found freedom from the codified creeds and confessions of faith in the denominations from which they had come. Does that not suggest that extreme care should be taken with regard to any measures that restrict freedom to explore truth anew and to formulate findings in perhaps new and more profound ways? This must not be construed as an appeal for playing loose with the basic Adventist tenets of faith, but must rather be seen as a call to protect—within certain parameters—the freedom of conscience and of belief that Adventist tradition has so much emphasized in the past.

In many ways Luther's views—and those of Calvin and other magisterial Reformers—remained defective. Five centuries after that momentous morning in Wittenberg when Luther nailed his 95 theses

---

55 See also my most recent book: *Facing Doubt: A Book for Adventist Believers 'on the Margins'* (London, UK: Flankó, 2016), pp. 151–172.

56 http://www.notablequotes.com/f/freedom_quotes.html#EO7SMl0qRmgotYBo.99.

on the door of the castle church, human rights are high on the agenda in most countries and religious freedom is defended and practiced by many. It is gratifying to see that the Adventist Church has made freedom of conscience and of religion a point of major emphasis. But the time may have come for the Adventist Church to look critically at itself and determine whether or not this freedom of religion and conscience is perhaps being jeopardized by an over-emphasis on uniformity with the unintended result that that true underlying unity is at serious risk.

5. Justice and Equality: Is God Interested?

Ray C. W. Roennfeldt
Avondale College of Higher Education

Introduction

It is obvious that a complete coverage of the topic of God's attitude to justice and equality is beyond the scope of this chapter. Therefore, a more focused approach is taken here, in which several key passages and stories (cases) are examined in order to explicate Scripture's overall perspective. While the area under discussion is much wider than God's attitude towards women, given the contemporary debate regarding the ordination of women in Seventh-day Adventism, this dimension of the topic will often appear in the foreground.

The approach taken is as follows. First, the Genesis account of the creation of humankind is examined to find the divine ideal for human relationships. The fact that God creates all of humankind in his making of Adam and Eve is surely significant for attempts to discover the divine attitude towards humankind and their relationships with each other. Humans, of course, did not remain as God made them, and it needs to be asked whether their "fall" into sin changed God's expectations in terms of his original ideal.

Second, the divine attitude towards justice and equality in general as shown in Scripture is examined. The Old Testament material will be examined chiefly through the lens of two case studies that conveniently combine several characteristics; both of the individuals involved were women and they were not of the "chosen people." The New Testament material will be entered initially via Jesus' own mission statement, then through some of the many outstanding instances of Jesus' interactions with women, and briefly through the *locus classicus* of Galatians 3:28.

Third, as with any biblical teaching or doctrine, there are difficult passages that cannot be easily 'squeezed" into a systematic approach.[1] Not all of these passages are examined in detail. Rather a sampling of texts is examined via a threefold approach: the nature of Scripture itself, the overall perspective of biblical teaching, and the concept of divine accommodation.

Fourth, as the global, multicultural church grapples with the issue of justice and equality a possible path ahead is plotted through the hermeneutical system portrayed as the Wesleyan Quadrilateral and through the Jerusalem Council of Acts 15 viewed as a case study in church politics.

Human Relationships: the Divine Ideal

The climax of the Genesis account of creation is the creation of human beings. Everything that has gone before on the previous five days and earlier on the sixth is a prelude to the creation of humans. However, there is something quite distinctive in this creative act. Humans are the last creatures mentioned in the account and, as pointed out in Genesis 2:7, 22, they are "separately formed by God ... and made from the dust of the ground."[2] The human is not merely called into being as was the rest of creation, but is specifically "shaped" as a potter shapes the clay. Gordon Wenham points out that this "[s]haping' is an artistic, inventive activity that requires skill and planning."[3]

It should be observed that although the Pentateuch provides the Israelite people with an explanation of their existence as a people, in the creation of Adam and Eve is the creation of all of humankind. This is made obvious in the genealogy from Adam to Noah (Gen 5) and in its continuation in the table of nations (Gen 10). To be specific, all of humankind finds its reason for being, its dignity, and its equality in a special divine creation, and it is apparent that God planned and intended it to be so.

---

1 For instance, there are difficult passages that do not appear to "fit" neatly into a doctrine of the perpetuity of the Sabbath and texts that seem to teach a doctrine of the immortality of the soul.

2 Allen Ross and John N. Oswalt, *Cornerstone Biblical Commentary: Genesis and Exodus* (Carol Stream, IL: Tyndale House, 2008) 39. Ross is the author of the section on Genesis and henceforth this work will be referred to as Ross.

3 Gordon J. Wenham, *Genesis 1–15*, Word Biblical Commentary 1 (Waco TX: Word, 1987) 59.

Furthermore, all humans are made in the "image of God." This is stated explicitly in Genesis: "So God created man in his own image, in the image of God he created him; male and female he created them" (Gen 1:27[4]).

What does this mean? Various explanations have been offered, ranging from (1) the natural human qualities in which humans resemble God (e.g. reasoning and personality); (2) the "mental and spiritual faculties that man shares with his creator;" (3) the human "physical resemblance" to God; and (4) to the image as "God's representative[s] on earth."[5] Laurence Turner comments that "While the text of Genesis 1 does not state explicitly what the image is, it does provide hints. If humans are in God's image then there must be some analogy between God and humans."[6] Turner then explains that the projected human dominion over creation is analogous to God's subjugation of and transformation of the earth from its primeval chaos. He concludes that "This suggests that the 'image of God' in humans refers not only to what humans *are* but primarily to what they *do* …"[7]

There may also be a relational aspect to the concept of the image of God. The Creator-human (or Father-man/woman) relationship is clearly inferred in God's declaration, "Let us make man in our image, in our likeness" (Gen 1:26; c.f., 5:1-3). The same passage also refers to the other two foundational human relationships. The relationship between humans and their environment is explicitly mentioned (Gen 1: 26, 28–30) and the creation of humans as male and female (Gen 1:27) points to the relationship between human and human.[8] If this interpretation is correct, at very least it means that there is something about humans of both genders that equally "images" God in the world.

However, some argue that the order of the creation of Adam and Eve portrays a basic inequality between the two.[9] However, there is

---

4 Unless otherwise noted the biblical citations in this chapter are taken from the NIV.

5 Wenham, *Genesis 1–15,* 29–30; cf., Ross, *Genesis,* 39–40.

6 Laurence A. Turner, *Genesis*, (Readings: A New Biblical Commentary), 2nd ed. (Sheffield: Sheffield Phoenix, 2009) 14.

7 Turner, *Genesis* 15. In pointing to their role as "God's representatives," Ross states that "God's image in humans is functional" (Ross, 40).

8 For this insight, I am indebted to a Christian Anthropology (MA Religion) class taught by Gottfried Oosterwal at Avondale College during the 1980s.

9 See for example Danny Burk, "5 Evidences of Complementarian

no hint of that in the creation accounts of Genesis 1 and 2. While Adam is created first, the "order" of the creation narrative would forbid such a conclusion. Within the account there is a distinct progression from what might be construed as simple living things to the more complex (e.g., vegetation on the third day, birds and fish on the fifth day, and, finally, land animals and then humans on the sixth day. In addition, the "structure" of the creation account indicates the same kind of progression: what is formed on day 1 is filled on day 4; what is formed on day 2 is filled on day 5; and what is formed on day 3 is filled on day 6. It is an ironic fact that, given the inherent structure within the narrative, one could actually argue for the superiority of Eve over Adam!

Adam's declaration concerning the woman contains no indication of inequality between the two: "This is now bone of my bones and flesh of my flesh" (Gen 2:23). In commenting on the relationship between Adam and Eve, Allen Ross remarks that "The woman is described as a helper, which means that she supplied what he lacked ... and by implication the reverse would also be true."[10] With the creation of the woman, the situation of Adam's aloneness described by God as "not good" (Gen 2:18), is now "very good" (Gen 1:31). Commenting on the symbolism of the creation of the woman, Ellen White aptly says:

> God himself gave Adam a companion. He provided "an help meet for him"—a helper corresponding to him—one who was fitted to be his companion, and who could be one with him in love and sympathy. Eve was created from a rib taken from the side of Adam, signifying that she was not to control him as the head, nor to be trampled under his feet as an inferior, but to stand by his side as an equal, to be loved and protected by him. A part of man, bone of his bone, and flesh of his flesh, she was his second self ... [11]

In summary, it can be concluded safely that the Genesis accounts of creation indicate the intention of God to create humans as equal beings in terms of family of origin and of gender.[12] All of humankind

---

Gender Roles in Genesis 1–2" https://www.thegospelcoalition.org/article/5-evidences-of-complementarian-gender-roles-in-genesis-1-2

10 Ross, *Genesis*, 48.

11 Ellen G. White, *Patriarchs and Prophets* (Mountain View, CA: Pacific Press, 1890, 1958) 46.

12 Susan E. Elliott maintains that gender equality "is a dynamic and repeated theme from Genesis to Revelation". See Susan E. Elliott, "Biblical Gender Equality in Christian Academia," *Forum on Public Policy: A Journal*

is portrayed as finding their common ancestors in Adam and Eve while God's ideal is obviously that women and men will live together in equality. However, Genesis 3 reveals that the parents of the human race fell away from this ideal. We need to examine whether this "fall" destroyed the divine ideal of human equality and whether God now established a different order in which women were subordinate to men.

Clearly, Genesis 3 indicates that the original perfect relationship between male and female was shattered. The disobedience of humanity's first parents led to blame and fractured relationships between each other and God (Gen 3:10–13). God utters "curses" and declares penalties on the serpent, on the woman, and on the man (Gen 3:14-19).[13] A key passage is the pronouncement on the woman for that is the only one that is indicative of a change in the relationship between herself and the man: "I will greatly increase your pains in childbearing; with pain you will give birth to children. Your desire will be for your husband, and he will rule over you" (Gen 3:16).

Is this pronouncement prescriptive or descriptive? In other words, is God here outlining what *must be* the part of women from henceforth, or is he indicating what *would be* in many cultures and societies? The context seems to indicate that this passage is descriptive rather than prescriptive. While Adam would now struggle with the soil to produce what was necessary to sustain life, there is certainly no edict that he was to "submit" to the fact that the soil would "now produce thorns and thistles for you" (Gen 3:18). By analogy, one might legitimately assume that the woman, also, was not predestined to be dominated by the man.[14]

---

of the Oxford Roundtable Summer 2010. (The online version of Elliott's article cited in this chapter, does not contain page numbers.)

    13 In fact, the "curses" are only on the serpent and the ground (Gen 3:14 and 17), so they are better seen as divine pronouncements. See Wenham, *Genesis 1–15,* 81.

    14 In the past it was sometimes argued that the woman should not receive analgesia during childbirth because God has decreed that she was to have pain. For instance, during the 1800s "many members of the British clergy argued that this human intervention in the miracle of birth [i.e., the use of analgesic drugs] was against the will of God" (Bhavani Shankar Kodali [of Harvard Medical School], "A Brief History of Pain Relief in Labour," available at http://www.papapetros.com.au/HistoryPainRelief.pdf (accessed 4 June 2017).

While the fall into sin "changed the game" in every way for humankind, it did not mean that everything was lost. Humans still reflected God's image, although rather more dimly.[15] Clark Pinnock insightfully observes that

> ... the Fall into sin is the most empirical of all the Christian doctrines. Few things are more obvious about human nature than its deeply flawed character and the misuse of human freedom. It explains much of what we see in and around us. What Adam [and Eve] did in this story is repeated and confirmed practically every day in the lives of all of us (Rom. 7:9–10).[16]

The remainder of the Old Testament witnesses to fractured relationships between God and humankind, between humans and their environment, and between humans and humans. The latter, as illustrated most starkly in the injustice and inequality experienced by women speaks volumes, as does the divine intention to ameliorate the situation not only through the promise of the "offspring" of the woman (Gen 3:15), but also in day-to-day life situations.

Justice and Equality in the Old Testament

The Old Testament provides stories in which God (almost surprisingly) treats women with justice and equality when culture and society would have prescribed otherwise. One clear example, told in Genesis 16, is the case of Hagar. Not only was Hagar a woman, but she was a woman of no account, being an Egyptian slave to Sarai, the wife of Abram. Being unable to bear a child herself at Sarai insists that Abram sleeps with Hagar in order to conceive a child.

There are several interesting dimensions to this story. It is clear that Sarai, while very clearly burdened by her barrenness, is hardly the submissive wife in this instance. She arranges the impregnation of Hagar by her husband as a means to overcome "the curse of her childlessness."[17] However, Hagar then "began to despise her mistress" (Gen 16:4) and Sarai complained to Abram: "You are responsible for the wrong I am suffering. I put my servant in your arms, and now

---

15 See, for instance, Gen 9:6, where God continues to refer to humans as being in his image.

16 Clark H. Pinnock, *Tracking the Maze: Finding Our Way through Modern Theology from an Evangelical Perspective* (New York, NY: Harper and Row, 1990) 195.

17 Turner, *Genesis,* 75.

that she knows she is pregnant, she despises me. May the Lord judge between you and me" (Gen 16:5). Abram's spineless reply is, "Your servant is in your hands. Do with her whatever you think best" (Gen 16:6). The result is that Sarai mistreats Hagar and she flees into the desert (Gen 16:6–7).

The angel of the Lord now comes to Hagar and asks her where she has come from and where she is going, to which she replies that she was running from her mistress Sarai (Gen 16:8). Hagar is instructed to "Go back to your mistress and submit to her" and "I will so increase your descendants that they will be too numerous to count" (Gen 16:10). The angel promises her: "You are now with child and you will have a son. You shall name him Ishmael, for the Lord has heard of your misery" (Gen 16:11).

While modern (or postmodern) sensibilities might wish for a different ending to this story, Hagar's positive response is to name the Lord who spoke to her, "You are the God who sees me," for she said, "I have now seen the One who sees me" (Gen 16:13). In Hagar's view, God had revealed himself as a God of justice, albeit as viewed through the lens of Ancient Near Eastern (ANE) culture.

A second example is provided by the story of Ruth, again a foreign woman—a Moabite. Once again the scenario is not particularly positive. During a severe famine in Israel, Elimelech and his wife Naomi moved from Bethlehem to the land of Moab. There, against a divine prohibition, their two sons had married Moabite women (e.g., Deut 7:3; 23:3). About ten years later, after the death of her husband and her two sons, and hearing that there was now food to be had in Israel, Naomi decided to return home. Ruth, one of Naomi's daughters-in-law, declared her intention to accompany her: "Don't urge me to leave you or to turn back from you. Where you go I will go, and where you stay I will stay. Your people will be my people and your God my God. Where you die I will die, and there I will be buried. May the Lord deal with me, be it ever so severely, if anything but death separates you and me" (Ruth 1:16-17).

In one of Scripture's great love stories, Ruth meets Boaz in Bethlehem, Boaz acts the part of a kinsman-redeemer, and Boaz and Ruth are married. It is very significant that Ruth is received so completely into Israel that she is declared by the women of Bethlehem to be better than seven sons to Naomi (Ruth 4:15), and the narrative concludes with the family line of Boaz and Ruth: Boaz, Obed, Jesse, and David (Ruth 4:17).[18] Against all odds, Ruth is treated with equality and justice, and receives the blessing of the covenant.[19]

These two narratives are probably sufficient to conclude that in the Old Testament God appears to be on the side of the marginalised and he treats them with justice and equality. The prophets—especially the Minor Prophets (see for example, Amos 2:6–7, 4:1; Mic 6:8; Hos 6:6[20]—with their focus on justice, or on the Sabbath commandment which provided Sabbath rest or household slaves and the "alien within your gates" (Ex 20:10), might have also been investigated with profit.

Justice and Equality in the New Testament

Any examination of the New Testament in regard to God's attitude toward justice and equality must begin with Jesus' attitudes. After all, Jesus is the incarnate expression of the person of God (see, for example, John 1:1–5; 10:30; and Heb 1:1–3). Luke records that Jesus began his ministry with the reading of the Isaiah scroll in the synagogue in his hometown of Nazareth. According to Luke, this was not a reading of Scripture chosen at random for when the scroll of the prophet Isaiah was handed to him, Jesus unrolled it and "found the place where it was written":

> The Spirit of the Lord is on me because he has anointed me to preach good news to the poor. He has sent me to proclaim freedom for the prisoners and recovery of sight for the blind, to release the oppressed, to proclaim the year of the Lord's favor (Luke 4:16–21; c.f., Isa 61:1–2).

With the eyes of the congregation fastened on him, Jesus said, "Today, this scripture is fulfilled in your hearing" (Luke 4:21). It seems obvious (at least from Luke's perspective) that Jesus takes this passage from Isaiah as his mission statement since Luke goes on to describe how, on being driven out of Nazareth, Jesus drives out an evil

---

18 Ruth is one of the few women named in Matthew's genealogy of Jesus (Matt 1:5).

19 Significantly, the Book of Ruth is Scripture's clearest illustration of the role of the kinsman-redeemer although there are some hints in the Pentateuch: e.g., Lev 27:9–25; 25:47–55; Num 3:9–34; and 25:47–55.

20 M. Daniel Carroll underscores the significance of justice in the prophetic writings with his observation that "in a sense, the calling of the prophet may be described as that of an advocate or champion, speaking for those who are too weak to plead their own cause." See R. Daniel Carroll, "A Passion for Justice and the Conflicted Self: Lessons from the Book of Micah," *Journal of Psychology and Christianity,* 25 (2006): 172.

spirit possessing a man in Capernaum, heals Simon's mother-in-law and many others, calls his first disciples to give away their fishing in order to henceforth "catch men," heals a man with leprosy, and heals a paralysed man; all of this before he tells one parable or engages in a direct teaching or preaching ministry.[21]

Jesus' revelation of God's interest in justice and equality for the oppressed and marginalised in first-century Jewish society is illustrated in the starkest terms in Jesus' interactions with women. Hans Küng comments that

> In the time of Jesus women counted for little in society. As in some cultures today, they had to avoid the company of men in public. Contemporary Jewish sources are full of animosity toward women, who according to the Jewish historian Josephus are in every respect inferior to men.[22]

Küng notes that the writers of the four Gospels "have no inhibitions about talking about Jesus' relations with women." Rather, they portray Jesus as including women, showing no contempt for them, and being "amazingly open towards them."[23]

A couple of examples of Jesus' contact with women clearly demonstrate the truth of Küng's observations. The obvious prime example is Jesus' interaction with the Samaritan woman as found in the narrative of John 4. It is very significant that John places this incident near the beginning of his Gospel. In John's schema Jesus has just conversed with Nicodemus, the quintessential Jewish man (John 3:1–21); John the Baptist testifies that "He [Jesus] must become greater; I must become less" (John 3:22–36); and then Jesus encounters the Samaritan woman, the quintessential outsider, at Jacob's well in the town of Sychar (John 4:1–38). A number of elements in this narrative are very significant: (1) contrary to Jewish practice at the time, in travelling from Judea to Galilee, Jesus chooses to go through the region of Samaria; (2) Jesus initiates a conversation with a Samaritan woman, something no Jewish man would do;[24] (3) Jesus, for the first

---

21 In Luke Jesus relates his first parable (Luke 5:36–39) after being accused of eating and drinking with the tax-collectors and sinners (Luke 5:30), that is, those who were identified as being on the fringes of Jewish society.

22 Hans Küng, *Women in Christianity*, transl. by John Bowden (London,: Continuum, 2001) 2. Küng cites Josephus, *Contra Apionem* 2, 201.

23 Küng, *Women in Christianity*, 2.

24 Jesus' request for water is met with shock on the part of the Samaritan

time, forthrightly reveals himself as the Messiah to this marginalised woman by saying, "I who speak to you am he" (John 4:26);25 and (4) the woman becomes the first Christian evangelist with many of the Samaritans from the town believing in "him because of the woman's testimony" (John 4:39–42). So, here there is a woman, and a Samaritan at that, a person of doubtful morals, and a believer in an apostate offshoot of Judaism being treated with respect and equality by Jesus. Is God interested in justice and equality? To the disciples' surprise, he was and is (John 4:27).

Another, perhaps even more startling, example is the story of the Syrophoenician woman recorded in Mark 7. Again, Jesus is outside of his own territory, near Tyre. A Greek woman comes to Jesus begging that he drive out a demon possessing her daughter.[26] This time Jesus appears at first to treat the woman's request as any Jewish male might: "it is not right to take the children's bread and toss it to their dogs" (Mark 7:27). The woman's feisty reply is that "even the dogs under the table eat the children's crumbs" (Mark 7:28), and Jesus' response is that the demon has already left her child (Mark 7:29–30).[27] In the accounts of both Mark and Matthew (Mark 7:24–30; Matt 15:21-28) the story of this Canaanite woman's faith follows a discussion of what constitutes cleanness and uncleanness (Mark 7:14–23; Matt 15:10–20). Jesus is surely indicating that this "unclean" woman was truly part of God's kingdom of justice and equality.

Example after example could be cited from the ministry of Jesus in which he demonstrates divine mercy and justice being directed to the marginalised and the oppressed. However, perhaps it is Paul in Galatians 3:28 who sums up best the implications of the revolutionary ministry of Jesus Christ: "There is neither Jew nor Greek, slave nor free, male nor female, for you are all one in Christ Jesus." Clearly, for Paul, God makes no difference between race, social status, or gender in regard to salvation: "You are all sons [and daughters] of God

---

woman: "You are a Jew and I am a Samaritan woman. How can you ask me for a drink? (For Jews do not associate with Samaritans)" (John 4:9).

25 This is in spite of Jesus' recognition that the Samaritan woman was living in an adulterous relationship (John 16–18).

26 Mark seems to go out of his way to indicate that this was a non-Jewish woman: "The woman was Greek born in Syrian Phoenicia" (Mark 7:26).

27 Matthew's version of this narrative has Jesus responding: "Woman, you have great faith. Your request is granted" (Matt 15:28).

through faith in Jesus Christ" (Gal 3:27) and as such all who "belong to Christ ... are Abraham's seed, and heirs according to the promise" (Gal 3:29). In light of this affirmation, one might legitimately ask if all racial, social, and gender differences are now *passé* in the Christian community, yet it is other writings from this same Paul that appear to be the primary seedbed for the church's practice of treating women inequitably.[28] How are such biblical passages to be regarded in light of what has already been seen in terms of God's keen interest in justice and equality?

Two Faces of Scripture?

A persuasive case has been built for a positive answer: Yes, God is vitally interested in justice and equality. But is the case "watertight"? What of the passages of Scripture—in both the Old and New Testaments—that appear to support slavery, and why does the Bible contain no clear prohibition in regard to slavery? What about the texts that appear to justify the dominance of the male in church and society, and why does Scripture contain no clear direction on the ordination of women to the gospel ministry?

Some, like Marcion in the early church era, are tempted to reject the Hebrew Scriptures because they reveal a god different from the God of the New Testament. However, even Marcion himself found that it was also necessary to "edit" the Christian Scriptures in order to maintain their harmony, and in general the Christian church has resisted such a radical approach.[29] There is insufficient space in a single chapter to provide a complete coverage of this issue, but it is possible to illustrate the diversity of Scripture in regard to its attitude to slaves and women.

Slaves who were not part of Israel itself were considered to be the legal property of their masters and were listed as "property", as were cattle, gold, and silver (e.g., Gen 12:16; 20:14; 24:35; 30:43; 32:5;

---

28 Samuel L. Adams sums up his article with the following: "Despite arguments to the contrary, social justice and economic fairness are core themes in Scripture." See Samuel L. Adams, "The Justice Imperative in Scripture," *Interpretation* 69(2015): 399–414.

29 A convenient summary of Marcion's differentiation between the Creator God and the Redeemer God can be found in E. Ferguson, "Marcion," in *Evangelical Dictionary of Theology*, ed. Walter A. Elwell (Grand Rapids, MI: Baker, 1984), 685–86.

Ex 20:17). In this regard the status of slaves in Israel was similar to that in other areas of the Ancient Near East. However, the Old Testament does contain legal instructions that ameliorate the situation of slaves, unlike anything in other ANE codes. For example, slaves were not to be required to work on the Sabbath (Ex 20:10); slaves born in the house of their master were to be circumcised in order for them to share in Israel's religious life (Ex 12:44; Deut; 12:12,18; Lev 22:11); and murder of a slave was considered a crime (Ex 21:20). If a master put out the eye of his slave or knocked out a tooth, the slave was to be granted freedom (Ex 21:26–27). In summary, "Hebrew law was relatively mild toward the slaves and recognized them as human beings subject to defense from intolerable acts, although not to the extent of free persons."[30]

In contrast to the Old Testament, the New Testament does not contain detailed legal material in relation to slavery. Instead there are prominent Pauline passages that provide instruction for Christian slaves and the Letter to Philemon is written as advice to him regarding his escaped Christian slave, Onesimus. It is noteworthy that the advice Paul directs Timothy to pass on to Christian slaves is that they respect their masters "so that God's name and our teaching may not be slandered." And, "Those [slaves] who have believing masters are not to show less respect for them because they are brothers" (1 Tim 6:1–2). Again, Paul sends the escapee Onesimus back to Philemon with the request that he be treated "better than a slave [and] as a dear brother" (Philemon 16), but he resists instructing Philemon to release Onesimus. Eventually though, "The early Christian ideology undermined the institution of slavery, declaring an equality of all people in Christ."[31] However, the journey to that conclusion was far from smooth.

In spite of its largely positive stance toward women,[32] and with many women playing key roles as judges and military leaders, diplomats, and prophetesses in Israel,[33] the Old Testament also

---

30 Muhammad A. Dandamanyev, "Slavery: Old Testament," in *The Anchor Bible Dictionary,* 6 vols., ed. David N. Freedman (New York, NY: Doubleday, 1992) 6:64.

31 Dandamanyev, "Slavery," 65.

32 An outstanding example is to be found in Prov 31:10–31.

33 See Patricia Gundry's excellent chapter, "What Can Women Do?", in her *Woman be Free: The Clear Message of Scripture* (Grand Rapids, MI: Zondervan, 1977), 89–104.

Justice and Equality 97

contains some "hard sayings" in its legal material. For instance, there are regulations pertaining to marriage with "beautiful" captive women (Deut 21:10–14); how to relate in polygamous relationships (e.g., Deut 21:15–17); the necessity of stoning for women who could not prove their virginity (Deut 22:13–21); and the "uncleanness" as a result of childbirth (Lev 12;1–8) and menstruation (Lev 15:19–33), to name just a few. Such passages pose difficulties for the modern mind, especially in regard to the divine attitude toward the equality of women and men. It comes across as small comfort that while a case can definitely be made that women within ancient Israel were treated with greater respect than in the surrounding nations, one is left wondering why God did not promote justice and equality for women more proactively.[34]

One of the prominent Pauline passages regarding the role of women in the church community is to be found in the same letter cited above in regard to slavery—1 Timothy.[35] As part of his instructions about worship, Paul states, "A woman should learn in quietness and full submission. I do not permit a woman to teach or to have authority over a man; she must be silent" (1 Tim 2:11–12). The apostle then provides reasons for his position: (1) "Adam was formed first, then Eve", (2) "Adam was not the one deceived; it was the woman who was deceived and became a sinner", and (3) "women will be saved through childbearing—if they continue in faith, love, and holiness with propriety" (1 Tim 2:13–15). It must be admitted that Paul's reasoning here is quite unusual. The Genesis creation narratives provide no indication that the order of the creation of Eve implied any subordination. Neither does Paul's view that it was Eve who was deceived and sinned comport with Paul's own perspective found in many of his writings that it is "in Adam [that] all die" (1 Cor 15:22). Furthermore, what Paul meant by women being saved through childbearing remains a puzzle to most commentators.

---

34 Perhaps Alden Thompson's *Who's Afraid of the Old Testament God?* (Grand Rapids, MI: Zondervan, 1989) provides some clues for us. See especially his chapter, "Strange People Need Strange Laws" (pp. 71–90).

35 In fact, the majority of this epistle is composed of advice: instructions on worship (chapter 2); instructions to congregational overseers and deacons (chapter 3); personal pastoral instructions to Timothy (chapter 4); and instructions about widows, elders, and slaves (chapter 5:1–6:2).

Perhaps an answer to such diversity is to be found in both the nature of Scripture and the nature of God. Much (perhaps all) of Scripture could be described as "occasional." Certainly, the Pauline epistles are written to particular church communities or to Paul's colleagues to deal with particular situations and issues. Sometimes it is impossible to determine exactly what motivated him to write as he did. For instance, what exactly lies behind Paul's instructions to Timothy regarding women in the church in Ephesus is unknown. Were the women abusing their Christian freedom? Were they speaking out of ignorance and lack of education? Were they "lording it over" the men in the church? Despite this uncertainty, it is clear that Paul wanted to make a statement to correct whatever the abuse was, and that he used arguments that may seem strange to us. Are Christians permitted to argue with Paul in terms of his reasoning while accepting his writings as inspired? Or, to phrase the question even more starkly: Is Paul's logic God's logic? Ellen White describes the Bible as

> ... written by inspired men, but it is not God's mode of thought and expression. It is that of humanity. God, as a writer, is not represented. Men will often say such an expression is not like God. But God has not put Himself in words, in logic, in rhetoric, on trial in the Bible. The writers of the Bible were God's penmen, not His pen. Look at the different writers.[36]

This position readily evokes nervousness. It is all too easy to "slip down the slope" so that the Scriptures which previously were seen as God's authoritative speech become at best good advice from which the reader might pick and choose. Scripture must continue to be seen as God's Word and, operationally, Christians should rightly come to it with an "inerrancy expectation."[37] In order to maintain this attitude of respect for the Bible, the Scriptures must be searched by the believer "as a workman who does not need to be ashamed and who handles correctly the word of truth" (2 Tim 2:15). Understanding the Bible is not something for the faint-hearted or for the slacker. It requires deep study to detect Scripture's overall perspective and a constant listening

---

36 Ellen G. White, *Selected Messages*, vol 1 (Washington, DC: Review and Herald, 1958), 21. This statement comes from Ellen White's Manuscript 24, written in 1886.

37 I am indebted to Clark H. Pinnock for this description of how I personally come to the Scriptures. See Clark H. Pinnock, *The Scripture Principle* (San Francisco, CA: Harper and Row, 1984), 77.

Justice and Equality 99

to the voice of the Spirit of God as he guides the church into all truth (John 16:13).

Again, Scripture portrays God as accommodating himself to the human condition. While this is certainly true in that God has "stooped" to meet us when "he prattles to us in Scripture in a rough and popular style"[38] and in "mean and lowly words"[39], perhaps this is best borne out by reference to the way that God chose to interact with the people of Israel at various times. Regarding divorce, Jesus says, "Moses permitted you to divorce your wives because your hearts were hard. But this was not the way from the beginning." Jesus then goes on to say, "I tell you ... " (c.f., Mat 5:31–32). Paul, in Athens, argues that "in the past God overlooked such ignorance [i.e., that the divine being is an image fashioned by humans], but now he commands all people everywhere to repent" (Acts 17:30).[40] So, while postmodern people might find themselves confronted by some of the diversity in regard to justice and equality in both Testaments, they can, at the same time, detect a distinct thread that clearly affirms God's interest in justice and equality. Georg Braulik has provided an example of this in his comparison of Deuteronomy and the Universal Declaration of Human Rights (1948). He concludes that there are "surprisingly many correspondences or at least common tendencies."[41]

Scripture thus contains a diversity of testimony on the topic of justice and equality. However, it contains clear indications that God is on the side of justice and equality. Furthermore, Scripture also indicates that God works within and even accommodates to the variations of time and place in order to maintain interaction with humanity. In light of these facts, how is the Bible best to be interpreted to aid the church to grow in understanding as a community of faith?

---

38 John Calvin, *Calvin's Commentaries*, edited by John T. McNeill and translated by Ford L. Battles (Edinburgh: Oliver and Boyd, ca. 1960), Commentary on John 3:12.

39 John Calvin, *Institutes of the Christian Religion* (Philadelphia, PA: Westminster, 1960), 1.8.1.

40 Perhaps a similar theme is found in Heb 1:1–3 where God "spoke to our forefathers through the prophets at many times and in various ways, but in these last days he has spoken to us by his Son." Of course, the supreme divine accommodation is to be found in the incarnation of Jesus Christ.

41 Georg Braulik, "Deuteronomy and Human Rights," *Verbum et Ecclesia: Skrif en Kerk* 19 (1998): 207.

Plotting a Path Ahead

It may prove helpful for conservative Christians such as Seventh-day Adventists to consider the "Wesleyan Quadrilateral"—a framework of authority composed of Scripture, tradition, reason, and experience—as at least one of the tools for the interpretation of Scripture; especially when the biblical materials show evidence of diversity. The Methodist theologian and historian, Albert C. Outler is generally credited with this description of John Wesley's approach to theology as critically and faithfully familiar with Scripture, cognizant of Christian history, logically analytical, and growing out of "a vital, inward faith that is upheld by the assurance of grace."[42]

Susan Elliott applies the Wesleyan Quadrilateral to the issue of women's roles in church leadership and the pulpit. She begins her survey by pointing out that John Wesley himself did not begin with a positive view in regard to the role of women, and this was in spite of the contributions of his own mother, Susanna.

While some conservative Christians might be concerned that tradition, reason, and experience could subvert the Protestant principle of *sola Scriptura*, Elliott describes Scripture as "the inerrant Word of God, truth as the foundation of reason, tradition and experience." Obviously, in her view the "Quadrilateral" is not an equilateral parallelogram; Scripture always maintains the dominant position (and certainly this would have been the case for Wesley). So the task of discovering the breadth of the biblical perspectives on the justice of God and the equality of women has to be taken seriously. However, that is not the end of the task. Tradition, reason, and Christian

---

42 Albert C. Outler, "The Wesleyan Quadrilateral in John Wesley," *Wesleyan Theological Journal* 20 (1985): 7–18. It should be observed that in the same place Outler confesses some regret at having coined the term since it has been sometimes misconstrued. However, he concludes that the "conjoint recourse to the fourfold guidelines of Scripture, tradition, reason and experience may hold more promise for an evangelical and ecumenical future than we have realized as yet—by comparison, for example, with Biblicism or traditionalism or, rationalism, or empiricism." Note that a more complete coverage of the "Wesleyan Quadrilateral" can be found in Don C. Thorsen, *The Wesleyan Quadrilateral: Scripture, Tradition, Reason and Experience as a Model of Evangelical Theology* (Grand Rapids, MI: Zondervan, 1999). For a helpful introduction to the pros and cons of using the Wesleyan Quadrilateral as a hermeneutical tool from an evangelical perspective, see Pinnock, *Tracking the Maze*, 71–74.

experience need also to be taken into account, even if only to raise questions to send us back to the Bible for better answers.

Elliott points out that there is a wealth of tradition in the interactions of Jesus with women that should inform us in regard to the equality of women in the church. She cites the fact that Jesus constantly "challenged the traditional social norms about women and modelled equality of women." However Elliott considers that the fact that Jesus called only men as disciples and leaders cannot be ignored. She cites approvingly Kent Brower and Jeanne Serrao: "to our knowledge no ... group insists that all ordained leaders must be circumcised and Jewish. The Twelve are symbolic and representative of the whole, restored, holy people of God."[43] Church communities have a prime responsibility to take account of the new "tradition" inaugurated by Jesus Christ, not just the traditional understandings that have been passed down through Christian history.

What role does human reason play in the interpretation of Scripture? Again, on the equality of women, Elliott maintains that "the core of theological conflict on gender equality is grounded in human interpretation and application."[44] Everyone uses reason when coming to the Scriptures, even when claiming to accept the "plain" or literal meaning of the Bible. For example, Dennis Bratcher maintains that

> a "plain sense" reading actually takes far less notice of the actual story itself, and must read far more things into the text to make it all "work," than do other ways of interpreting the text. The main reason for this is because what the "plain sense" of the text says to us, it says in the context of a 21st century view of the world.[45]

Reason leads us to ask a variety of questions related to the matter of the ordination of women: If no watertight case can be made for ordination as it is practiced in most denominations, on what basis

---

43 Kent Brower and Jeanne Serrao, "Reclaiming the Radical Story," *Holiness Today* 11 (2009): 23, as cited in Elliott, "Biblical Gender Equality".

44 Elliott, "Biblical Gender Equality".

45 Dennis Bratcher, "The Problem of a 'Plain Sense' Reading of Scripture," available at http://www.crivoice.org/plainsense.html (copyright 2016), accessed on 8 June 2017. See also my own discussion in "Our Story as Text," in Ross Cole and Paul Petersen, eds., *Hermeneutics, Intertextuality and the Contemporary Meaning of Scripture*, (Adelaide, South Australia: Australian Theological Forum/Avondale Academic Press, 2014), 81–88.

can it be denied to women? If women are contributing positively to society in leadership roles, why would God deny them such a role in the church? At very least, such questions should send thoughtful Christians back to Scripture to ask whether the Scriptural perspective has not been misunderstood.

Elliott then turns to the role of Christian experience. She points to the fact that Paul repeatedly acknowledged "the importance of women in ministry and in leadership positions."[46] Yet, "([t]wo verses taken from the whole of scripture (proof texting) ... have created centuries of oppression."[47] The contemporary church might point positively to the experience of the many women engaged in pastoral ministry and even in church leadership. Surely the fruitful work of women pastors in the Republic of China and areas like the United States, Europe, and Australia should raise the question, "How is God not in this?", and force a re-examination of Scripture.[48]

The Jerusalem Council reported in Acts 15 provides a case study in how 21st-century Christians might wrestle through an issue that clearly involves biblical hermeneutics and church politics. In fact, this account provides a case study in how to do church and it is instructive that the four dimensions of the "Wesleyan Quadrilateral" were allowed to function creatively together. **Scripture** is certainly to the fore, since James says "The words of the prophets are in agreement with this ..." (Acts 15:15).[49] In this instance, the traditionalist party clearly had what would have appeared to be the "weight" of Scripture behind it.[50] **Tradition** and traditional understandings of Scripture were obviously under discussion. In fact, the Council would not have taken place except that "Some men came from Judea to Antioch and were teaching the brothers: 'Unless you are circumcised, according to the custom taught by Moses, you cannot be saved'" (Acts 15:1).

---

46 Elliott ("Biblical, Gender Equality") cites Rom 16:1–16; Phil 4:2–3; and Acts 18.

47 Elliott ("Biblical Gender Equality") cites 1 Tim 2:11–12; and 1Cor 14:34–35, ironically both passages from Paul.

48 In Matt 12 Jesus points out that to attribute what is obviously of God to Beelzebub is blasphemy against the Holy Spirit which cannot be forgiven (see especially Matt 12:31–32).

49 James cites Amos 9:11–12.

50 Circumcision was undoubtedly the sign of the covenant with Abram, the father of the Jewish race (Gen 17). However, Paul, for instance, picks up the concept of "circumcision of the heart" from such passages as Deut 30:6 and expands on it in Rom 2:25–29.

Reason and logic were also taken into account. James argued, "It is my judgment, therefore, that we should not make it difficult for the Gentiles who are turning to God" (Acts 15:19) and the letter sent to the Gentile believers in Antioch, Syria, and Cilicia stated, "It seemed good to the Holy Spirit and to us not to burden you … " (Acts 15:28). In addition the **experience** of God's Spirit working with Peter, on the one hand, and Barnabas and Paul, on the other, carried great weight (Acts 15:7–14).

From the perspective of the 21st century, it is difficult to grasp the revolutionary impact of this first church council. If a totally conservative position had been taken, it would have stymied the growth of the fledgling Christian church. If it had been too progressive it would have completely severed the church from its Jewish roots.[51] Perhaps even today, the implications of the position taken at this Jerusalem council, which made circumcision nothing, and uncircumcision nothing, are not completely understood. No longer was the mark of the covenant something that only pertained to males, rather "Keeping God's commands is what counts" (1 Cor 7:19; cf., John 14:15, 23).

What enabled the church to move on in regard to this issue? The weight of biblical evidence and tradition were on the side of the circumcision party. But the Spirit had been leading the community in a different direction and that caused the church to look again at the Scriptures, raising to prominence some passages that had been overlooked previously. In addition, the earliest church was blessed with courageous leaders such as Peter, James, Barnabas, and Paul who were willing to stand up—sometimes literally (Acts 15:7)—for a biblical and pragmatic solution to a divisive issue.

Conclusion

It may be concluded with great confidence that God is vitally interested in justice and equality. This is seen clearly in the manner in which God created all of humankind in his own image, irrespective of race or gender. It can also be observed in the way God dealt with the issues of race, slavery, and gender in the Old Testament. But the issues of justice and equality are given even greater clarity through Jesus' mission to provide freedom and healing to the marginalised

---

51 Note the cautiousness implied in Acts 15:21, "For Moses has been preached in every city from the earliest times and is read in the synagogues on every Sabbath."

and oppressed. However, this divine interest is not merely to remain the domain of Deity. Rather God's attitude to justice and equality is to be played out in the way his followers interact with each other: "We are to adopt as our standard his law and precepts. We are to treat others justly and fairly (Amos 5:15; Jas 2:9) because that is what God himself does."[52] The Church's mission is to work with God in "repairing the world."[53]

Today a new paradigm is needed—one that will assist in breaking through the hermeneutical tangle that is dividing Church member from Church member and region from region. It is not enough to say that the Christian community should now ignore issues of justice and equality and focus on the mission and message of the church. For Jesus himself, there was no dichotomy or separation between mission and message; the two were actually one and the same. Preaching righteousness by faith without doing justice and righteousness is heresy(see, for example, James 2:14–26), preaching Sabbath sacredness without living out the freedom and equality it stands for is legalism (e.g., Mark 2:23–28), and preaching the second advent without helping the alienated and marginalised is downright dangerous (e.g., Matt 25:31–46).

Perhaps the "quadrilateral" of Scripture, tradition, reason, and experience will provide an interpretive key and that might assist in breaking the impasse. And, the Jerusalem Council of Acts 15 may provide a model for "doing" church; even for dealing spiritually and pragmatically with issues of church party politics!

---

52 Millard J. Erickson, Christian Theology (Grand Rapids, MI: Baker, 1985), 289.

53 For this idea, I am indebted to Sheryl Sandberg's *Lean In: Women, Work, and the Will to Lead* (London: W. H. Allen, 2015), 54, where she cites a rabbi's sermon on civil rights and *tikkun olam*, a Hebrew phrase which means "repairing the world."

Ellen White's Perspectives

6. Unity in the Writings of Ellen G. White

Wendy A. Jackson
Avondale Seminary

The success of Adventist evangelistic outreach means that the Seventh-day Adventist Church in the twenty-first century "is marked by great diversity in culture, values, traditions, and practices." While "such diversity has the power to enrich the church" it also
> threatens to pull it apart, as its membership reads Scripture through different cultural and experiential lenses. Even within single cultural contexts diversity is growing. With increasing frequency, this diversity contributes to conflicts on theological issues and church practices in the Seventh-day Adventist Church.[1]

While the church seeks to maintain unity in the face of such apparent threats, approaches to unity often overlook the complexity of the issues involved. Too often single statements on unity are considered in isolation without regard to the complexity of the concept. Such practices leave readers to interpret statements in ways consistent with their own ideas rather than understanding what the author originally intended. Furthermore, most of the discussion fails even to define what is meant by unity and simply assumes that everyone is agreed about what it means.[2]

---

1 Jackson, Wendy A., "The Unity of the Church and Church Authority: A Comparative Study of the Views and Practice of Alexander Campbell and Ellen G. White" (PhD diss., Andrews University, 2015), 445. This chapter is based largely on research conducted during my doctoral studies and follows closely some sections of my final dissertation. The dissertation can be downloaded in its entirety from the Andrews University Website at the following URL: http://digitalcommons.andrews.edu/dissertations/1584/.

2 Many recent decisions appear to be based on an understanding of unity as uniformity of practice although is not explicitly stated.

The Christian church has struggled from its inception with the tension between the declaration that unity is intrinsic to the nature of the church, and the reality that the church is far from united. The difficulties and challenges this tension poses have resulted in many attempts to explain the nature of unity in a way that solves the apparent gap between belief and reality. While such theological exercises may seem pointless, they are in fact fundamental to thinking through questions of praxis since any consideration of church unity presupposes an understanding of the nature of unity. We cannot consider how unity can be achieved and manifested by the church without first discussing the actual nature of the unity that we are seeking.

In this chapter the concepts of unity and disunity from the perspective of Seventh-day Adventist prophet and co-founder Ellen White will be examined. In the course of her ministry Ellen White wrote extensively on the topic of church unity. The chapter begins with a statement of several basic assumptions, followed by a note on the importance White placed on the unity of the church. The foundational question of what White understood by the term unity is explored and what she considered to be the major causes of disunity are noted. An outline of White's contribution to the topic of how unity of the church can be attained concludes the chapter.

Presuppositions

Before becoming immersed in the thinking of White, three important presuppositions on the part of the author need to be stated.

The first presupposition is that the views of Ellen White are not those of a theologian who is removed from the everyday life, but rather a hands-on leader whose views were incubated in real-world crises. Her first statements suggesting brethren press together were made in the shadow of the Great Disappointment. These were followed by statements directed to specific crises in the 1850s and 1860s, while her views came to maturity during the last decade of the 19th century as she dealt with the ongoing conflicts that emerged out of the 1888 General Conference and the drama surrounding the controversial figure of John Harvey Kellogg. Her ideas matured and developed over time as she was involved in an increasing number of crises. This means we must take care in considering the context of her statements on unity, and explore her ideas in some chronological fashion. In this chapter an overview of the key ideas will be presented first, and then their chronological development will be considered in order to construct a model of her views.

The second presupposition is that any consideration of the theme of unity in the writings of Ellen White also needs to be cognizant of her main themes, particularly her emphasis on the love of God and the great controversy theme.[3]

The third presupposition arises from the nature of unity itself. Since unity of the church is a characteristic of the church, an exploration of unity of the church cannot be viewed in isolation from Ellen White's wider ecclesiological perspectives, including the function and role of the church's authority structure and the relationship of the organization to biblical authority.

It is beyond the scope of this paper to provide a full ecclesiology of Ellen White. Instead, several foundational concepts that impact the discussion directly will be outlined. The most important of these ideas is that White's ecclesiology was primarily functional. Her writings defined the church in terms of its relationship to God and its divinely appointed mission. White specifically identified the church as God's appointed representatives to testify to the love of God and to "win them to Christ by the efficacy of that love."[4] White's understanding of the Seventh-day Adventist Church as the end-time remnant extended the representative role of the church. With a specific message to call people back to forgotten truths and a final message of warning to the nations, both the remnant's actions and its faithfulness to truth are to be a witness to the character of God and his law.[5] Moreover, given her understanding of the church as a voluntary society, White considered representing God as an obligation on every member who chose to join the church. In consequence she expected that all members of the church would give priority to the interests of God at all times.[6]

---

3 George Knight presents an excellent summary of the main themes evident in the writings of Ellen White. See George Knight, *Meeting Ellen White* (Hagerstown, MD: Review and Herald, 1996), 109–127.

4 Ellen G. White, "The Church and Its Mission - No 1," *East Michigan Banner*, January 18, 1905, 1.

5 Ellen G. White, "The Remnant Church, Not Babylon," *Advent Review and Sabbath Herald*, September 12, 1893, 579; Ellen G. White, "Preparation for the Testing-Time," *Signs of the Times*, April 22, 1889, 242.

6 Ellen G. White, "Scattered Churches," *Advent Review and Sabbath Herald*, September 6, 1881, 161.

A second ecclesiological understanding having an impact on the topic of unity relates to order and the structure of church authority. White noted that order was essential for the church to function in the way God intended; however, she did not dictate any specific form this order should take even in the face of an urgent need for reorganization in 1901.[7] Her calls for restructuring when the existing structure was not serving the needs of the church adequately, coupled with her failure to dictate any one form of organizational structure suggest that organization was to remain flexible enough to serve the mission of the church. Nevertheless, centralization of power, no matter how convenient it seemed, was to be avoided.[8] Furthermore, even a flexible structure which met the needs of the church was dependent upon its leaders. The characters of these leaders were as important as the nature of the church structure itself, not only for the success of mission, but for the maintenance of unity. Leaders were to be humble and accountable Christians who called on God for wisdom.[9]

With these presuppositions in mind, Ellen White comments about unity can now be discussed.

The Mandate of Unity

The biblical basis of Ellen White's discussion on unity is found primarily in John 17, Ephesians 4:3–6, Philippians 2:2, and the various biblical metaphors of the church which imply its oneness.

John 17 provides the impetus and mandate for unity since it is in this passage that Jesus himself explicitly expresses that it is his desire for his followers to be one. Because it is the will of God, the call to unity

---

7 Early calls for order in the church can be found in such places as, Ellen G. White, *Supplement to the Experience and Views of Ellen G. White* (Rochester, NY: James White, 1854), 18–19. White's specific call for reorganization in 1901 can be found in Ellen G. White, "A Call to Reconsecrate, Reorganize, and Advance," MS 43, April 1, 1901) in *Manuscript Releases: From the Files of the Letters and Manuscripts Written by Ellen G. White*. Edited by the Ellen G. White Estate, 21 Vols. Silver Spring, MD: Review and Herald, 1981–1993, 13:192–207.

8 See for instance Ellen G. White to W. W. Prescott and Wife, Letter P-088, September 1, 1896, in *Manuscript Releases*, 13:1616–1620.

9 Ellen G. White, "Judge Not," *Advent Review and Sabbath Herald*, November 14, 1907, 8; Ellen G. White, "Thou Shalt Have No Other Gods before Me," Manuscript 15, 1895, in *Testimonies to Ministers and Gospel Workers* (Boise, ID: Pacific Press, 1923), 360.

is to be taken seriously by all who take the name Christian.[10] Thus in 1894 White asked, "What can I present before my brethren and sisters in Christ, that is more important for their study and practice than the Savior's prayer for His disciples? The entire seventeenth chapter of John is full of marrow and fatness."[11] Similarly in 1904 she declared, "The instruction given me by One of authority is that we are to learn to answer the prayer recorded in the seventeenth chapter of John. We are to make this prayer our first study."[12]

Also in 1906, in relation to the prayer she wrote, "Such oneness as exists between the Father and the Son is to be manifest among all who believe the truth. Those who are thus united in implicit obedience to the word of God will be filled with power."[13]

The prayer in John 17 was also a reminder for White that unity is not an end in itself. Rather, unity is to be understood as a crucial precursor to the successful mission of the church. Writing in 1906 she stated,

> If all would completely consecrate themselves to the Lord and through the sanctification of the truth, live in perfect unity, what a convincing power would attend the proclamation of the truth! How sad that so many churches misrepresent the sanctifying influence of the truth, because they do not manifest the saving grace that would make them one with Christ, even as Christ is one with the Father! If all would reveal the unity and love that should exist among brethren, the power of the Holy Spirit would be manifest in its saving influence. In proportion to our unity with Christ will be our power to save souls.[14]

The connection between unity and mission was critical enough to suggest that there was a direct correlation between unity and the success of mission. Unity was essential for the church to fulfil its mission because it provided witness to the transforming power of

---

10 Ellen G. White, "One, Even as We Are One," *Bible Training School*, February 1, 1906, 129.

11 Ellen G. White, "The Living Testimony," *The Bible Echo*, April 23, 1894, 124.

12 Ellen G. White, "One with Christ in God," *The Southern Watchman*, February 2, 1904, 60. See also Ellen G. White, *Testimonies for the Church*, 9 vols. 1885–1909. Reprint, (Mountain View, CA: Pacific Press, 1948), 8:239.

13 Ellen G. White, "One, Even as We Are One," *Bible Training School*, February 1, 1906, 130.

14 Ellen G. White, "One, Even as We Are One," *Bible Training School*, February 1, 1906, 130.

the gospel.[15] In addition, White also emphasized the difference unity makes to the spiritual health of both individuals and congregations.[16]

The Nature of Unity

There are hundreds of passages in the writings of Ellen White in which she wrote about unity, union, harmony, and working together in peace. The frequency with which they occur leaves no doubt that unity within the church was considered important by Ellen White. What is crucial to understand, however, is what Ellen White meant when she used the term "unity" in relation to the church.

Since Ellen White's writings emerged largely from responses to specific crises, there is no nicely formed stand-alone definition of unity in her writings. Consequently, an attempt must be made to draw out an understanding by looking at the words and phrases she employs when discussing unity, and the implications of her statements about unity.

The strong tie between mission and unity precludes White from understanding unity as something that belongs only to the invisible church as some theologians have concluded, or as something that only occurs in the eschaton. Rather, the unity for which Christ prayed was to be a present and visible reality in the historical church. Only a visible unity could testify to the reality and transforming power of the gospel and fit the purpose outlined in John 17.[17]

Unity is considered by most Christian theologians as an intrinsic or essential characteristic of the church which exists whether or not it is visible in the historic church. Ellen White clearly embraced the biblical models of the church which recognize the unity of the church, and quoted texts that imply an intrinsic unity through one baptism and one Lord. However, her discussions do not focus on a unity which already exists in the church. In keeping with her wider functional ecclesiology, Ellen White focused instead on human responsibility in the maintenance of unity. That is, unity is something that requires personal attention and active choices. This prevents excusing one's behaviour, living in complacency, or a failing to engage personally

---

15 Ellen G. White, "Strength and Power in Unity," *Bible Training School*, April 1, 1903, 161; Ellen G. White, "Words of Counsel," *Australasian Union Conference Record*, November 15, 1903, 1–2.

16 Ellen G. White, "Christ Is out Hope," *Bible Training School*, May 1, 1903, 177.

17 White, *Testimonies for the Church*, 3:446.

in the will of God for his church. In her eyes, all must strive actively to obtain unity.[18] Furthermore, White made it clear that unity requires ongoing daily effort. Thus she wrote to John Harvey Kellogg that unity is something that "must be cultivated day by day."[19]

An examination of the phrases White used in relation to unity reveals that she did not use only one expression to describe the nature of unity. Rather, her writings provide a variety of phrases including unity of purpose, unity of action, unity of spirit, unity of thought, unity of faith and being of one mind. At first glance this would seem to portray an array of concepts about unity. Although unity of purpose, unity of action, and unity of the Spirit would seems to be overlapping, the ideas of unity of thought, unity of faith and being of one mind seem to portray quite a different slant on unity. The great majority of phrases fall into the first of these groups, with the context of statements about unity of action being similar to that of unity of purpose. The idea of uniformity of practice is not envisaged here. Rather, what is seen is the wish that God's people should live harmoniously and work together to achieve a common purpose. For instance, she wrote in 1908:

> In the work of soul saving, the Lord calls together laborers who have different plans and ideas and various methods of labor. But with this diversity of minds, there is to be revealed a unity of purpose. Oftentimes in the past the work the Lord designed should prosper has been hindered because men have tried to place a yoke upon their fellow workers who did not follow the methods which they regarded as the best.[20]

Working in harmony not only made pragmatic sense, it harmonized with White's understanding of the church as a voluntary society. In the nineteenth-century context, a voluntary society existed for a

---

18 White, "Christ is Our Hope," *Bible Training School*, May 1, 1903, 177; White, "Unity of the Church," *Advent Review and Sabbath Herald*, February 19, 1880, 113; Ellen G. White, "Notes of Travel," *Advent Review and Sabbath Herald*, February 12, 1885, 8.

19 Ellen G. White to J. H. Kellogg, Letter K-073, April 17, 1899 in Ellen G. White, *Testimonies for the Church*, 8:172–176. White emphasizes the role of human choice in the attainment of unity, but that unity should not be seen as something manufactured by humans. As will become obvious as in this chapter, unity is only possible in connection with Christ and actively involves the Holy Spirit's transformation in the life.

20 Ellen G. White, "A Missionary Education," *Advent Review and Sabbath Herald*, February 6, 1908, 24.

single purpose, and those who joined did so for the express purpose of furthering its aims. Thus, White assumed that those who choose to join the church voluntarily would be willing to work together to prioritize the mission of the church.[21]

The terms unity of thought, and being of one mind require more careful analysis. The phrase "unity of thought" arises in three contexts: a call for people of different ethnicities and nationalities to work together under a single sovereign rather than letting national pride prevent united action;[22] working together to find the best methods to mission;[23] and a call to peace and harmony instead of criticizing and tearing other leaders down.[24] In none of these contexts is unity of thought intended to convey uniformity of doctrine or understanding all scripture or all church practices in the same way.

Likewise, examination of the context of the idea of being of one mind reveals four main meanings of the term:[25] working together to do God's work; working in harmony without selfish ambition and fault-finding;[26] coming together in humility before God;[27] and teaching the

---

21 Ellen G. White, "Scattered Churches," *Advent Review and Sabbath Herald*, September 6, 1881, 161.

22 Ellen G. White, "The Swiss Conference and the European Council," *The Bible Echo*, February 1, 1886, 27.

23 Ellen G. White, "Who are Partners with Christ," *Advent Review and Sabbath Herald*, July 17, 1894, 449.

24 Ellen G. White, "Unity a Test of Discipleship," in *Manuscript Releases*, 15:165.

25 The idea is found in the phrases "unity of mind" and "being of one mind." While the term "unity of mind" only occurs in one context, the term "one mind" occurs frequently in White's writings. A significant number of these occurrences are simply quotations from Scripture including 1 Peter 3:8; Philippians 2:1–2; Romans 15:5, 6; 2 Corinthians 13:6 and 1 Corinthians 1:10. For the single reference to unity of mind, see Ellen G. White, "The Work Before Us," MS 11, 1912, in *Loma Linda Messages* (Payson, AZ: Leaves of Autumn, 1981), 601.

26 White makes this direct connection when she wrote to S. N. Haskell in 1900 noting, "We are often exhorted, 'Be ye all of one mind,' which means the same as 'Endeavour to keep the unity of the Spirit in the bonds of peace.'" See Ellen G. White to S. N. Haskell, April 5, 1900, in *Manuscript Releases*, 8:68.

27 Ellen G. White, "An Important Letter from Sister E. G. White," *Advent Review and Sabbath Herald*, December 11, 1900, 796; White, *Testimonies for the Church*, 6:469.

same doctrines. With regard to teaching the same doctrine, she wrote to Dr Kellogg in 1886,

> The soldiers of Jesus Christ must move in concert, else it were better that they do nothing. For if one speaks one thing, and another presents ideas and doctrines contrary to his fellow laborers, there is confusion, discord, and strife. Therefore the apostle charges that all who believe on Christ be of one mind, one faith, one judgment, each moving in concert, influencing one another beneficially, because they are both obedient to the precious truth of the Word of God, attached to one Savior, the great Source of light and truth.[28]

Several instances of the use of the phrase "unity of faith" also appear to call for a unity in doctrine. For instance in *Christian Experience and Teachings* she noted that

> "God is leading a people out from the world upon the exalted platform of eternal truth, the commandments of God and the faith of Jesus. He will discipline and fit up His people. They will not be at variance, one believing one thing, and another having faith and views entirely opposite; each moving independently of the body. Through the diversity of the gifts and governments that He has placed in the church, they will all come to the unity of the faith. If one man takes his views of Bible truth without regard to the opinion of his brethren, and justifies his course, alleging that he has a right to his own peculiar views, and then presses them upon others, how can he be fulfilling the prayer of Christ? And if another and still another arises, each asserting his right to believe and talk what he pleases, without reference to the faith of the body, where will be that harmony which existed between Christ and His Father, and which Christ prayed might exist among His brethren?"[29]

Yet while calling for unity of faith in relation to what is believed, other passages remind us that this is not uniformity.[30] The diverse

---

28 Ellen G. White, "Christians, Like Soldiers, May Face Hardships, and Must Work Together in Unity," (Letter to J. H. Kellogg, July 1886) in *Manuscript Releases*, 14:29.

29 Ellen G. White, *Christian Experience and Teachings* (Boise, ID: Pacific Press, 1940), 201.

30 See for instance Ellen G. White, "The Vine and the Branches," MS 66, 1897, published in part in *Manuscript Releases*, 6:104; Ellen G. White to P. T. Magan, Letter M-111, June 16, 1903 published in *Manuscript Releases* 6:106.

backgrounds and experiences that shape individuals may be expected to lead to different methods of working for the Lord. Furthermore, Ellen White's encouragement that everyone needs to read Scripture for themselves leads to the expectation that variation in understanding of Scripture will occur. In order to maintain harmony amongst this diversity, White advised that members dwell "upon those things in which all can agree, rather than upon those things that seem to create a difference."[31]

In summary, the nature of the unity that White envisaged was a visible, lived unity, something that requires personal involvement and choice. It is primarily expressed in harmonious working together to achieve a common purpose; however, some degree of doctrinal unity is also expected.[32]

Disunity and its Causes

While success in mission is bound up with unity, a lack of unity misrepresents the truth and brings reproach to the name of Christ.[33] The church as Christ's representatives who have an end-time mission is to demonstrate the loving character of God. This is negated by a disunited church since a divided church portrays an unloving and divided God who consequently lacks power. Thus Ellen White suggested that the church actively works against its Lord when it is disunited. At the 1900 GC Conference session she asked,

> Why do those who profess to believe in Christ, who profess to keep the commandments, make such feeble efforts to answer the Savior's prayer? Why do they seek to have their own way,

---

31 Ellen G. White, "Diversity and Unity in God's Work," in *Manuscript Releases*, 8: 68. Furthermore, White counselled that a failure to agree on ideas should not be seen as a reason to separate from the church. See also White, "The Importance of Unity; the Holy Spirit a Mystery," in *Manuscript Releases* 14:177. While agreement on fundamentals is highlighted, those in Christ should not waste their time disputing over "matters of little importance."

32 Late in this chapter it will be shown that unity of doctrine appears to relate to specific core beliefs related to salvation or in which the Holy Spirit has specifically led the church.

33 Ellen G. White to G. I. Butler, Letter *B-023, October 1, 1885, published in White, *Manuscript Releases*, 15:362. Ellen G. White to Missionaries in South Africa, Letter B-004, March 9, 1890, published in Ellen G. White, *Testimonies to Southern Africa* (South African Union Conference of Seventh-day Adventists, 1977), 21–27.

instead of choosing the way and will of the Spirit of God? Those who do this will one day see the harm done to the cause of God by pulling apart. Instead of co-operating with Christ, instead of laboring together with God, many who occupy positions of trust are working in opposition to Christ. The Lord has presented this to me in a most decided manner to present to his people.[34]

Her words were equally strong at the 1903 General Conference session where she equated disunity with sin: "There is a great and solemn work to be done for Seventh-day Adventists, if they will only be converted. The great trouble is the lack of unity among them. This is a sin in the sight of God, — sin which, unless God's people repent, will withhold from them his blessing ... "[35] The consequences of disunity included distraction from mission,[36] negative impact on personal spirituality,[37] and a resulting weakness of the church.[38]

What did Ellen White identify as the causes of disunity? She did not focus on doctrinal differences as a cause for disunity. Disagreements about doctrine are only surface matters that portray a much deeper issue. Disunity at its core is a sign of disconnection from Christ. Writing against the unequal treatment of some groups of believers, White declared, "The reason of all division, discord, and difference is found in separation from Christ."[39] She continued: "Christ is the center to which all should be attracted; for the nearer we approach the

---

34 Ellen G. White, "Unity among Believers," *General Conference Bulletin*, July 1, 1900, 156.

35 Ellen G. White, "The Work before Us," *Advent Review and Sabbath Herald*, April 14, 1903, 7.

36 Ellen G. White, "The Opposer's Work," *Advent Review and Sabbath Herald*, October 18, 1892, 642. See also White's response to the arguments over the meaning of the daily sacrifice: Ellen G. White, to My Brethren in the Ministry, August 3, 1910, in White, *Selected Messages*, 1:167–168.

37 Ellen G. White, "Make Straight Paths for your Feet." MS 157, 1897. Published in part under the title, "Christian Unity" in *Manuscript Releases*, 11:50.

38 White, *Testimonies for the Church*, 8:240.

39 Ellen G. White, "No Caste in Christ," *Advent Review and Sabbath Herald*, December 22, 1891, 785; Ellen G. White to W. Ings, Letter I-077, January 9, 1893, in White, *The Ellen G. White 1888 Materials: Letters, Manuscripts, Articles, and Sermons Relating to the 1888 Minneapolis General Conference*. Edited by the Ellen G. White Estate. (Washington, DC: Ellen G. White Estate, 1987), 1125.

center, the closer we shall come together in feeling, in sympathy, in love, growing into the character and image of Jesus. With God there is no respect of persons."[40]

The other causes of disunity that she identified also have a strong relational focus and flow directly from being disconnected from Christ. These include attitudinal problems such as stubbornness, pride, unwillingness to listen to others, and lack of love as causes for disunity.[41] She also posited as causes of disunity unbelief in the foundations of the Christian faith,[42] a failure of Christians to shoulder any responsibility for the mission of the church,[43] and an unwillingness to allow the Holy Spirit to work.[44]

How can Unity be Attained?

These causes of disunity became the basis for White's discussion about how unity can be attained. Consequently, union with Christ takes prime position among the six factors to which she points in her discussion of the attainment of unity.

Writing in 1904, she claimed

> The cause of division and discord in families and in the church is separation from Christ. To come near to Christ is to come near to one another. The secret of true unity in the church and in the family is not diplomacy, not management, not a superhuman effort to overcome difficulties—though there will be much of this to do—but union with Christ.[45]

The nature of the connection between union with Christ and unity of the church was described by White using the metaphor of a sun

---

[40] Ellen G. White, "No Caste in Christ," *Advent Review and Sabbath Herald*, December 22, 1891, 785.

[41] White, "To W. Ings," 1125.

[42] Ellen G. White to J. H. Kellogg, December, 1904 in White, *Manuscript Releases*, 11:319. The message was written to John Harvey Kellogg when he was promoting panentheistic theories and in outright conflict with church leadership.

[43] Ellen G. White, "Scattered Churches," *Advent Review and Sabbath Herald*, September 6, 1881, 161–162.

[44] Ellen G. White, "The Secret of Victory," *Bible Training School*, March 1, 1909, 177.

[45] Ellen G. White to Sr. Harper, Letter 49, January 24, 1904 published in Ellen G. White, *Mind, Character, Personality* (Nashville, TN, Southern Publishing Association, 1977), 2:501.

and its sunbeams.[46] Beams of light are closest together at the centre of the sun, whereas they become more and more widely spaced the further they are from the sun. So, as believers remain close to Christ, they will also demonstrate a love and closeness for other believers. In fact, White stated that "they must of necessity be drawn close to each other, for the sanctifying grace of Christ will bind their hearts together."[47] However, as believers move further from Christ, so they find themselves struggling to remain close to others. Thus White could confidently claim that "True religion unites hearts, not only with Christ, but with one another, in a most tender union."[48]

Using John 15 as the backdrop of her discussion about connection with Christ, White considered individual Christians must be united with Christ just as branches are united to the vine.[49] Such a union provides both a new identity and the means by which spiritual growth can occur.[50] As union with Christ occurs, the Holy Spirit is enabled to transform the life of the individual. Consequently, the life will show evidence of the fruit of the spirit as a more Christlike character is formed.

Of particular importance in the discussion of union with Christ was the need for maintenance of the relationship. For Restorationist Alexander Campbell, union simply occurred at baptism, but for White, union with Christ was more than a profession of faith. It was something dynamic which needed to be maintained and preserved lest disconnection should occur. As in human relationships, both partners in the relationship must bear some responsibility for the maintenance of relationship. While the initiative and work that makes this bond possible comes from God, the relationship cannot work if only one

---

46 White to Uriah Smith, Letter S-024, September 19, 1892, published under the title "The Message of 1888; an Appeal for Unity; the Need for the Indwelling Christ," in *Manuscript Releases*, 15:88.

47 White, Letter S-024, 88.

48 Ellen Gould White, *Gospel Workers* (Review and Herald Publishing Association, 1915), 484.

49 Ellen G. White, "The True Vine," *Advent Review and Sabbath Herald*, September 20, 1881; Ellen G. White, "The Living Vine," *Advent Review and Sabbath Herald*, September 11, 1883.

50 White, "True Vine"; White "Living Vine."

partner is interested in its maintenance.[51] The individual is therefore called to preserve the bond by continual communion[52] and "earnest prayer."[53]

The second factor in the attainment of unity that White listed is having the correct attitudes. White's written responses to individuals involved in conflict, particularly General Conference president G. I Butler and J. H. Kellogg, frequently put the emphasis on right attitudes. Even when they held beliefs which White considered were wrong, she generally devoted more space in her writing to the need for humility and the correct attitudes than she did to the condemnation of the beliefs of the individual.

The most essential attitudes for unity were those of love,[54] humility[55] and teachableness,[56] whereas attitudes of pride, self-centredness, and selfish ambition provide obstacles to unity.[57] Consequently, when looking for unity of the church one of the first steps is to examine your own heart. White wrote,

> Whether superiors, inferiors, or equals, your work is to begin with your own heart. Humble yourself before God. Come into right connection with Him by yielding to the creating power of the Holy Spirit. Then will be seen in the church the unity that is of value in God's sight. There will be sweet harmony, and all the building, fitly framed together, will grow up into an holy temple in the Lord.[58]

---

51 Jackson, Wendy A., "The Unity of the Church and Church Authority: A Comparative Study of the Views and Practice of Alexander Campbell and Ellen G. White," 280.

52 White, *Desire of Ages*, 676. Elsewhere, she suggested communion must occur daily or hourly. See for instance White, *Testimonies for the Church*, 5:47.

53 *Testimonies for the Church*, 5:47, 231.

54 See, for example, White, *Christ's Object Lessons* (Hagerstown, MD: Review and Herald, 1969), 49; White, *Acts of the Apostles* (Boise, ID: Pacific Press, 1911), 551; Ellen G. White to Brethren Who Shall Assemble in General Conference, Letter B-20, August 5, 1888 in *1888 Materials*, 41.

55 White, "The Message of 1888; an Appeal for Unity; the Need for the Indwelling Christ," in *Manuscript Releases*, 15:81.

56 Ellen G. White, "Love among the Brethren." *Advent Review and Sabbath Herald*, June 3, 1884, 353–354.

57 See, for example, Ellen G. White to Brethren Who Assemble in Week of Prayer, Letter B-20a, December 15, 1888, in *1888 Materials*, 196–198.

58 Ellen G. White, "The Danger of Rejecting Light," MS 64, 1898, in *Manuscript Releases*, 20:321.

Indeed, she suggested that if all believers had a teachable heart, there would be no divisions between them.[59] It must be noted however, that right attitudes are only obtained by connection with Christ and by the recognition that all are sinners dependent upon the mercy of God. Humility before fellow-believers grows out of Christians' correct understanding of themselves as sinners who are often wrong. It is demonstrated by a willingness to listen to the ideas of others, and weigh their counsel in the light of scripture and experience rather than just pushing personal opinion.[60]

The third factor White identified as important to attainment of unity is to ensure that Scripture is the rule of faith and practice. The Bible itself was to be the only creed for Christians and the bond of union between members. She declared:

> When God's Word is studied, comprehended, and obeyed, a bright light will be reflected to the world; new truths, received and acted upon, will bind us in strong bonds to Jesus. The Bible, and the Bible alone, is to be our creed, the sole bond of union; all who bow down to this Holy Word will be in harmony. Our own views and ideas must not control our efforts. Man is fallible, but God's Word is infallible. Instead of wrangling with one another, let men exalt the Lord. Let us meet all opposition as did our Master, saying, "It is written." Let us lift up the banner on which is inscribed, The Bible our rule of faith and discipline.[61]

While this quote is from 1885, it is representative of her earliest thoughts about unity after the Great Disappointment. That is, the bond which tied the small discouraged remnant of believers together was their commitment to the authority of the Bible.

In choosing Scripture as the guide and authority for the Christian life, the individual is necessarily drawn towards both Jesus and fellow-believers, while at the same time being brought to a place where truth can be discovered. As the only rule of faith, White considered the Bible was both a sufficient and unerring guide for the believer, and the means to determine truth. To move away from an explicit "thus

---

59 White, "Love among the Brethren", 353–354.

60 Ellen G. White, "Do Not Lord It over Others," (1870) in *Manuscript Releases*, 15:126.

61 Ellen G. White, "A Missionary Appeal," *Review and Herald,* December 15, 1885, 770.

saith the Lord" was to risk not only moving away from truth, but total separation from Christ.[62]

The fourth factor in the attainment of unity was the avoidance of non-essential issues.[63] Instead of focusing on controversial and minor issues, leaders were encouraged to focus on core or vital truths which were clearly understood and with which everyone agreed. In practice the identification of which truths fell into these categories was not straightforward. Ellen White's lists of vital truths (also identified as pillars of the faith, landmarks, or waymarks) are not always consistent. However, the truths seem able to be divided into two main categories: those which are foundational for Christianity as a whole, and those which she considered the Spirit had led the Seventh-day Adventist Church to understand. These truths included but were not limited to inspiration, salvation, incarnation, atonement, the perpetuity of the law, Sabbath, creation, the Three Angel's messages, the non-immortality of the soul, the cleansing of the sanctuary, baptism and the Lord's Supper.[64]

---

62 Ellen G. White, "The Word of God," *Bible Training School*, May 1, 1913, 193.

63 See, for example, Ellen G. White, "Non-essential Subjects to be Avoided," MS 10, September 12, 1904 published in part in *Manuscript Releases*, 17:303–304. Non-essential things were not to occupy the mind or the preaching of the word. "We are not to allow our attention to be diverted from the proclamation of the message given us. For years I have been instructed that we are not to give our attention to non-essential questions." Similar ideas are expressed in Ellen G. White, "Ministers should Cooperate and Preach Practical Truths," September 10, 1899, Letter 233, 1899, in *Manuscript Releases*, 21:398–401.

64 White, "Standing by the Landmarks," MS 13, 1889, in *1888 Materials*, 518; White, *Great Controversy*, 582; White, *Testimonies for the Church*, 4: 211; White, *Christian Experience and Teachings*, 246; Ellen G. White, "Build on a Sure Foundation," *Advent Review and Sabbath Herald*, September 24, 1908, 7; Ellen G. White, "The Relationship of Christ to the Law Is Not Understood," *Advent Review and Sabbath Herald*, February 4, 1890, 66. Doctrines which fall into these categories have been gleaned by looking at passages where White uses the phrases or terms "vital truth," "pillars of the faith," "waymarks," and "landmarks" which are used almost interchangeably in reference to doctrines she considered indispensable. The mixture of core Christian doctrines with those more specific to Seventh-day Adventism highlights White's conviction that the Spirit continues to lead the church in truth.

The fifth key to the attainment of unity was to be found in organization, or gospel order. In 1853 she wrote:

> There is order in heaven. There was order in the church when Christ was upon earth; and after his departure, order was strictly observed among his apostles. And now in these last days, while God is bringing his children into the unity of the faith, there is more real need of order than ever before ... 'The church must flee to God's word, and become established upon gospel order which has been overlooked and neglected.' This is indispensably necessary to bring the church into the unity of the faith.[65]

Ellen White's earliest recommendations regarding order were limited to choosing suitable individuals to teach and preach, along with finding ways of appropriate recognition of these individuals by churches. While ordination of other church-officers would follow later, the fact that other officers of the early church are not discussed at this time suggests that White was not calling for an exact replication of the New Testament system of order as Alexander Campbell and the Restorationists had done, but rather an application of the principles of order demonstrated in the New Testament. Thus the principle of orderliness appears to be more important than a specific system of order.

The sixth and final key to attaining unity had to do with maintaining the right relationship with the church. In this area, White highlighted two means of right relationship. First, White emphasized the need for believers to take personal responsibility for the success of the church in accomplishing its mission.[66] Practically this meant being personally involved in the mission of the church and prioritizing the needs of the church over personal desires.[67] When members work for the prosperity of the church it focuses them on mission rather than the issues which divide them, thus promoting unity. Consequently, in 1881 White wrote, " ... churches whose members feel that they are not responsible for its prosperity will fail to show to the world the

---

65 Ellen G. White, *Supplement to the Experience and Views of Ellen G. White* (Rochester, NY: James White, 1854), 18–19.

66 White, "Scattered Churches," *Advent Review and Sabbath Herald*, September 6, 1881, 161–162.

67 White, "Scattered Churches," 161-162.; Ellen G. White, "We Shall Reap as We Sow," *Advent Review and Sabbath Herald*, August 21, 1894, 529–530.

unity, love, and harmony that exist with the true children of God."[68]

The second way in which church members were to maintain the right relationship with the church was by yielding their opinions to the voice of the church unless the issue was of vital importance.[69] This instruction, as difficult as it seems, reflects several of White's core beliefs: that God reveals truth to multiple individuals in his church,[70] that the church has been delegated authority by God,[71] and that the true Christian will be sensitive to the feelings and opinions of others.[72] Thus we find statements such as "God has bestowed the highest power under heaven upon His church. It is the voice of God in His united people in church capacity which is to be respected."[73]

Since White believed there was more truth to be uncovered, individuals are still called to search for truth. However, any new insights should be subject to investigation by mature Christians who are to consider the matter prayerfully in the light of the rest of Scripture.[74] Consequently, leaders and mature Christians are expected to exercise their authority responsibly and prayerfully.

Chronological Development of the White's Views on Unity

When Ellen White's ideas on unity are considered in a chronological sequence it becomes apparent that White's emphasis moved from a primary understanding of unity in terms of doctrine prior to formal church organization, to a primary understanding of unity of action and purpose in the wake of denominational organization. This did not mean that doctrine was no longer important,[75] simply that it did not

---

68 White, "Scattered Churches," 161.

69 White, "The Unity of the Church," *Bible Echo*, September 1, 1888, 129; White, "Unity in the Home and in the Church." *Manuscript Releases*, 19:68.

70 White, "The Unity of the Church," *Bible Echo* September 1, 1888, 129.

71 White "Unity of the Church," 129; White, *Acts of the Apostles*, 122, 164; White, *Testimonies for the Church*, 5:108.

72 White, *Testimonies for the Church*, 4:17, 19.

73 White, *Testimonies for the Church*, 3:451.

74 White, *Christian Experience and Teachings*, 203.

75 White still mentioned the need for unity of doctrine or belief at later dates. See for instance Ellen G. White, "Christians, Like Soldiers, May Face Hardships, and Must Work Together in Unity," (Letter to J. H. Kellogg, July 1886) in *Manuscript Releases*, 14:29. However, doctrine is not the focus of her unity discussions during these later time periods.

form the center of her mature definition of unity. While the church existed as loosely organized congregational bodies, doctrine was one of the few features each congregation had in common, and therefore naturally would be seen as a uniting factor. However, after the formal creation of the Seventh-day Adventist Church, a degree of unity in doctrine was already implied by membership of the church. White's supposition that the church was a voluntary society led her to believe that anyone who joined the church already agreed with its core beliefs, and that this therefore no longer needed to be emphasized to members who were by choice committed to the same beliefs. Rather, focusing on a unity of action and purpose in this context allowed the church of likeminded individuals to fulfill its missional purpose.

Thus the earliest factor identified as necessary for unity is the use of the Bible as the rule of faith and practice. This was followed closely by the need for order and organization. The context helps us understand why these issues figured prominently. Between 1850 and 1860 there were no safeguards against visiting preachers presenting conflicting ideas and personal opinions. New converts were beginning to be admitted as the church moved away from its understanding of the shut door.[76] These converts had not experienced the specific leading of the Spirit in the same way as those who had been through the Great Disappointment. In addition, 1854 saw the rise of the first formal schism in the breakaway of the Messenger Party.[77] Organization and faithfulness to biblical teaching were thus crucial for the survival of the Advent groups. Thus, in this period, White called on believers to focus on maintaining unity through prayerful study of Scriptures, adherence to key doctrinal truths, obedience to the commandments of God, and the institution of gospel order.

While White also spoke of union with Christ as being essential for unity in her earlier discussion of unity, she made no direct linkage between union with Christ and these elements of visible unity.

---

76 *Seventh-day Adventist Encyclopedia*, rev. ed., Commentary Reference Series Volume 10 (Washington, DC: Review and Herald, 1976), s.v. Open and Shut Door.

77 *Seventh-day Adventist Encyclopedia*, rev. ed., Commentary Reference Series Volume 10 (Washington, DC: Review and Herald, 1976), s.v. Messenger Party; Knight, *Organizing for Mission and Growth: The Development of Adventist Church Structure* (Hagerstown, MD: Review and Herald, 2006), 39.

Furthermore, the earlier writings lack any consideration of the role of interpersonal and relational issues in the attainment of unity. These ideas were only developed in the context of the later conflicts of the 1888 General Conference and those associated with John Harvey Kellogg.

The issues of the 1888 General Conference—the identity of the ten horns of Daniel 7, the meaning of the word "law" in Galatians, and the implications for righteousness by faith— appeared doctrinal.[78] But White did not attribute the discord at the 1888 General Conference to doctrine. Her talks at the conference were focused on a deeper cause for the disunity, disconnection from Christ. The un-Christlike attitudes and actions which marred the conference were evidence in her eyes that many of those present were not united with Christ. Every member of the church had a responsibility for maintaining unity and this would be possible only when all remained connected to Christ who was both the source of truth and the source of unity.[79]

The 1888 General Conference also provided White with an opportunity to readdress the role of truth in maintaining unity. All delegates were called to prayerful personal study of the Word so that they would recognize the truth or error of the views presented in the meetings.[80] Nevertheless, White made it clear that knowing truth by itself was not all that was required of the Christian.[81] Truth needed to be lived.[82] This meant more than keeping the Sabbath and preparing for the second coming of Christ. Lived truth for White meant that every action exhibited the character of Christ, and every word was spoken with the best interests of the individual at their core. If truth

---

78 For a good overview of the 1888 General Conference see George R. Knight, *A User Friendly Guide to the 1888 Message* (Hagerstown, MD: Review and Herald, 1998).

79 Ellen White, "Counsel to Ministers," MS 8a, October 21, 1888, in *1888 Materials*, 132–145.

80 White's call for delegates to study Scripture for themselves begun even before the General Conference began. See Ellen White to Brethren who shall assemble in General Conference, August 5, 1888 in *1888 Materials*, 38–46. During the conference she continued to advocate the need for personal study. See for instance Ellen White, "The Need of Advancement," Morning Talk October 18, 1888 in *1888 Materials*, 117.

81 Ellen White, "The Scriptures a Sufficient Guide," Week of Prayer Reading for Sabbath, December 15, 1888, in *1888 Materials*, 201.

82 White, "Scriptures a Sufficient Guide."

was lived, even those who disagreed about the meaning of the key issues should have been able to work together without jealousy and accusation. But such was not the experience of those at the 1888 General Conference.

The growing issues with centralization and abuse of power around the same time also led White to speak again on the authority structure of the church. While White did not believe that the authority structure was the basis of unity of the church, she recognized that authority structures can either aid or hinder unity. Moreover, unity needed to occur within some form of structure. Four features of authority structure were identified as important for maximizing unity: functionality; flexibility to meet the needs of the church; avoidance of centralization of authority;[83] and avoiding giving too much power to any one individual.[84] Based on her advice to G. I. Butler, E. T. Waggoner and A. T. Jones, it can be concluded that White expected leaders to be examples of Christ-like attitudes and behavior."[85] They were to spend time prayerfully studying Scripture in order to determine for themselves what was true.[86] However, they were not to stand in the way of new expressions of truth, nor should they consider that their position meant they were infallible in their understanding or that they alone could determine truth.[87]

The Big Picture

In attempting to build a model of White's suggestions for attaining a unity of action and purpose, it is logical to begin with the group within which unity is to occur. Although Ellen White suggested that the prayer of Jesus in John 17 applies to anyone who has taken

---

83 See for instance Ellen G. White to W. W. Prescott and Wife, Letter P-088, September 1, 1896, in *Manuscript Releases*, 13:1616–1620; Ellen G. White to the General Conference Committee and the Publishing Boards of the Review and Herald and the Pacific Press, Letter R-071, April 8 1894, in *Manuscript Releases*, 11:272–273.

84 Ellen G. White, "A Call to Reconsecrate, Reorganize and Advance," MS43, April 1, 1901, in *Manuscript Releases*, 13:192–207. See especially, 192–193; White, "No Kingly Authority to Be Exercised," MS 26, 1903 in *Manuscript Releases*, 14: 279.

85 Ellen White to George I. Butler, October 1888, Letter 21a-1888, in *1888 Materials*, 85–106.

86 White, Letter 21a-1888.

87 White, Letter 21a-1888.

the name Christian, she only addresses the unity of those who she identifies either as the remnant or as lovers of truth. This provides a clear identity of the group within which unity is to occur. The next step is to add the Bible as the rule of faith which provides an authority for the church upon which all can agree. Necessity also suggests that unity occurs with a specific structure. Although order was important to Ellen White, it was the principle of organization which took priority over the actual details of structure. Indeed, structure rather than being fixed was to be flexible in the service of the mission of the church.

Together these ideas—the identity of the group in which unity was to occur, the authority of the group, and the structure in which unity was to occur—provided a tangible basis for beginning to write a definition of unity. It would be easy simply to put boundaries on these areas such as by specifying how the biblical authority is to be interpreted, concentrating on a core set of doctrines or emphasizing the importance of the authority structure.[88] However, these elements alone are insufficient to produce an adequate unity because they do not deal with the core and essentially intangible issues which centre on understanding the relationships of the Christian.

The keys to unity that have already been identified in the writings of Ellen White now need to be incorporated in the model. A start can be made by adding the invisible foundation of unity which Ellen White understood as union with Christ. In White's earliest writings on unity it is unclear how union with Christ related to the tangible elements of unity that we have noted. This connection became clearer as she wrestled with the crises from 1885 onward. As White focused more on Jesus connections began to become obvious. She recognized that a living connection with Christ impacts all the believer's relationships in a way that promotes unity. Union with Christ promotes the fruit of the Spirit and the development of a Christ-like character as the Holy Spirit does its work. Amongst this fruit would be a transformation of attitudes so that pride and self-centredness are replaced by love and humility. At the same time union with Christ would impact the relationship between the Christian and the church. As following

---

88 Restorationist Alexander Campbell did this very thing. He believed that if authentic Christians resisted organization beyond the congregational level, interpreted the Bible with a consistent hermeneutics, only used biblical terminology and concentrated on the facts of Scripture rather than opinions, unity would follow.

Christ became a priority, Christians would give precedence to the mission of the church over their own desires. This in turn would impact their relationships with other Christians, exhibiting itself in a willingness to submit to one another for the sake of harmony. Union with Christ is also expected to help the Christian to understand "truth as it is in Jesus." Being right in the interpretation of Scripture is to be accompanied by a humility and love for others where we "practice truth as it in in Jesus."[89]

The foundation that connects union with Christ with its practical results highlights three major understandings required for unity: what it means to be a Christian, what it means to be a church, and the ability to recognize truth as it is in Jesus.

These in turn affect willingness to accept the Bible as the rule of faith, willingness to work within the structure of the church, and to identity formation. The identity of those who are called to unity is thus transformed. It is still the remnant defined in Revelation, but it is the remnant that understands truth in the light of Jesus. It is a remnant whose identity is forged through understanding of one's relationship to Christ, of one's role as a member of the body of Christ, and of faithfulness to truth as it is in Jesus. Thus White's view of unity in the Adventist Church also emphasizes identity in Christ. It can be concluded that unity of purpose can only occur between authentic Christians whose relationships and identity are being transformed in connection with Christ.

Strengths of White's Views on Unity

The mature thinking of Ellen White on the topic of unity is complex, with multiple interactions, but it has a number of important strengths.

1. It demonstrates a clear connection between union with Christ and Christian unity, while at the same time, clearly delineating both divine and human roles in the process of attaining church unity.

---

[89] Ellen White to George I. Butler and Uriah Smith, April 5, 1887, in *1888 Materials*, 32–37; Ellen White, "The Scriptures a Sufficient Guide." Week of Prayer Reading for Sabbath, December 15, 1888, in *1888 Materials*, 198, 201; Ellen White, "The Secret of Unity." Sermon at Chicago, IL on April 4, 1889, in *Review and Herald* July 2, 1889, 147–148.

2. It recognizes the biblical principle that connection with Christ does not leave individuals unchanged.

3. It focuses on authentic Christianity. While White saw unity as occurring between those who loved truth and displayed the characteristics of the remnant, the foundation of her model requires individuals to be authentic Christians first and foremost.

4. It recognizes that relationship is at the heart of unity. Unity of the church is impacted by multiple relationships including the relationship with Christ, the church, truth and other people.

5. It recognizes the impact of sin on relationships; in particular, the human tendency to pride, selfishness, and thirst for power or control. Consequently, it places emphasis on correction of attitudes and relational problems through connection with Christ.

6. By including active involvement in the mission of the church, White enables members to focus on something outside of themselves. When focus is persistently directed internally, differences of opinion become more prominent.[90] But when focus is upon a common goal outside of themselves, members are led to focus on their common identity in Christ rather than on the issues that divide them.

Weaknesses of White's Views on Unity

Three major weaknesses of White's view and their relevance to unity also need to be considered.

1. The intangible and personal nature of union with Christ makes it difficult to discuss or work as an organization. Any judgment in relation to the status of an individual's connection or disconnection from Christ is likely to be met with a defensive response from the individual concerned.

2. The understanding that Christians who come to scripture with a teachable spirit and a willingness to be led by the Holy Spirit would always come to the same conclusions does not seem to be

---

90 Christena Cleveland, *Disunity in Christ: Uncovering the Hidden Forces that Keep Us Apart* (Downers Grove, IL: InterVarsity Press, 2013). Social psychologist Christena Cleveland suggests that our human tendency to categorize is done in order to protect our identity and self-esteem. But this self-protective mechanism creates division rather than helping our pursuit of unity.

borne out in practice. White's solution was to label individuals who do not come to consensus as disconnected from Christ. But how can it be determined which group is disconnected from Christ? There is no clear answer here.

3. While organization aided unity by creating order, and streamlined communication between diverse geographic areas, it also risked creating disunity by the abuse of power and centralization of power.

Application in the Adventist Church in 2017: What are the lessons that can be learned and that are applicable to the situation today?

1. Unity is at its heart personal and therefore cannot be manufactured or constructed by leaders' wielding their authority or attempting a forced consensus.

2. Unity of purpose and action neither requires nor endorses uniformity of practice. Rather it recognizes that various practices and methodologies are needed in different places and contexts to achieve the one purpose.

3. Authentic unity of the church can only occur between authentic Christians who are united in Christ and are being transformed by his power.

4. Unity involves a variety of relationships within the church: the relationship with God, with doctrine, with individuals, and with the church as a whole. Emphasizing one type of relationship without the others is not sufficient to achieve a visible unity. Rather, all forms of relationship must be nurtured and developed.

5. Personal responsibility needs to be taken by individuals for their own attitudes and actions. The importance of personal attitudes of humility and kindness are often overlooked in discussions as each side attempts to establish that their own view is the correct one. White clearly reprimanded those who considered being right was more important than displaying the character of Christ and truth as it is in Jesus.

6. Our focus should be directed at Jesus who is both the foundation and the creator of unity. Unfortunately, the tendency is often to focus directly on the creation of unity, but the reality

is that unity is not created by Christians, or by their plans. While believers should strive to be united, unity can only occur if we are connected to Christ.

7. "Circumstances Change the Relation of Things":

Ellen White's Attitude toward Theological Continuity and Change and its Implication for, and Application to, Issues of Church Authority, Policy and Structure

Rolf J. Pöhler
North German Union Conference

Introduction

How would the pioneers of Seventh-day Adventism deal with the present crisis hurting the church? How would they handle the disagreement between General Conference leadership and a number of Union Conferences on such wide-ranging issues as church structure and authority, unity and diversity, ethics and policy, justice and equality, conscience and coercion? The plain answer is: no one can know for sure. Changing times and circumstances call for and bring forth different responses and do not allow us to predict with certainty what the former leaders of the church would do if they were facing our challenges today. Nonetheless, much can be learned from the past by looking at the principles, values and convictions that had guided the pioneers and by drawing lessons for the present time from their accomplishments and failures.

What would Jesus do? In the 1990s, this question became a popular motto of young Christians who regarded Jesus as a definitive role-model for everyday life. But it is easier to wear a bracelet or wristband with the engraved acronym "WWJD" than to know what Jesus would actually do if he was living among us as a human being. Did he not often surprise, and even shock, his disciples by his words and deeds? Why should his modern followers feel certain that they would not also be stunned or disappointed by him today? Again, the spiritual and ethical principles he taught and lived transcend his times and culture and serve as guide posts for all later generations.

This applies equally to Ellen White whose prophetically inspired guidance helped steer the Adventist movement through rough waters for seven decades. What would Ellen White say and do if she was alive today? How would she position herself with regard to the current stalemate? People trying to answer this question should be aware that by doing so they may reveal more about their own views than about the prophet's position. Often enough, surmising about the past is more like a look in the mirror than an accurate lesson about history. The attempt to settle controversial issues by pointing to the prophet entails the risk of cementing one's own prejudice rather than speaking accurately in her name. Still, the attempt may, and should, be made to gain insights from her life and teaching for overcoming the current impasse between the various duly elected and responsible entities in the Adventist church. By studying Ellen White's life and legacy, we need to recognize that her views are not all timeless truths, that her actions are not all prescriptive, and that quotations from her writings are not all directly applicable today. She was, after all, just as much a child of her time as were prophets and apostles in biblical times. While the literary bequest of other Adventist pioneers quite obviously reflects their limited contemporary understanding, it is tempting to use Ellen White's legacy as if it was unaffected by its historical and cultural context. However, before using her writings and example as authoritative in a one-to-one manner, it must be established that the specific situations and concerns of the past are truly comparable to those of today. In drawing lessons from history, it is therefore mandatory to take into consideration the actual context that prompted a particular response. As the prophet once said, "Circumstances alter conditions. Circumstances change the relations of things."[1]

In this chapter, Ellen White's attitude toward theological and doctrinal continuity and change and its impact on her view on church authority, policy and structure will be examined. By implication, this may also contribute to a better understanding of the options for dealing with the current challenges and tensions in the Adventist church.

---

1 Ellen G. White, Report of an Interview/Counsel on Age of School Entrance (St. Helena, CA, 1904), Manuscript 7, 1904, EGWE; Ellen G. White, *Selected Messages*, vol. 3 (Washington, DC: Review and Herald, 1980), 217; idem, *Manuscript Releases*, 21 vols. (Silver Spring, MD: Ellen G. White Estate, 1981, 1987, 1990, 1993).

PART I—Ellen White on Theological Continuity and Change[2]

Ellen White held a surprisingly dynamic view on "present truth." "In every age there is a new development of truth, a message of God to the people of that generation."[3] In the context of the Minneapolis conference of 1888 she wrote: "What would not have been truth twenty years ago, may well be present truth now."[4] Thus, she could declare that the message of justification by faith as presented by E. J. Waggoner and A. T. Jones was "the third angel's message in verity."[5] Prior to that, "present truth" had been regarded essentially as prophetically announced truth, found in the apocalyptic books and passages of the Bible and presently being fulfilled.

In the 1880s and beyond, Ellen White was repeatedly called upon to resolve doctrinal controversies, which tended to divide the church on specific theological issues. Those holding traditional views—apparently sanctioned by the prophet herself—pleaded with her to confirm the historic faith of the church and to reject the new views that seemed to threaten the doctrinal landmarks of Adventism. Ellen White, however, consistently refused to do so, calling upon the church again to give serious study to the controversial points and to remain open to new interpretations of Bible texts, additional doctrinal insights, and possible revisions of erroneous views.[6]

In order to prevent these new views from being taught at Battle Creek College, where A. T. Jones was slated to teach in 1889, a resolution was proposed which recommended " ... that persons holding views different from those commonly taught by us as a

---

2 The following is based on the chapter "Prophetic Authority and Doctrinal Change: An Analysis" in my dissertation, published in *Continuity and Change in Adventist Teaching: A Case Study in Doctrinal Development* (Frankfurt: Peter Lang, 2000), 225–244.

3 Ellen White, *Christ's Object Lessons* (Washington, DC: Review and Herald, 1900/1941), 127. 4 Manuscript 15, 1888, EGWRC, AU, Berrien Springs, MI.

4 Ellen G. White, Manuscript 15, 1888 EGWRC, AU, Berrien Springs, MI.

5 Ellen White, *Evangelism* (Washington, DC: Review and Herald, 1946/1970), 190.

6 The debate on the law in Galatians and on "the daily" are illustrations of this.

denomination" should first present them to various committees for approval.⁷ Ellen White, however, strongly opposed such a restrictive decree because, in her judgment, it would only serve to hinder the progress and advance of truth.⁸

White's role in the development of Adventist theology may be described as "formative, not normative."⁹ While she contributed significantly to the development, acceptance, preservation and revision of doctrines, she was not regarded or used by the church as the final criterion and arbiter of truth—though, sometimes, this was done by some of her ardent followers. Neither did she ever want to be regarded as such. Support for this comes from an analysis of her personal involvement in doctrinal development.

As Alden Thompson has suggested in 1981, Ellen White experienced "significant changes" during her lifetime in her "theological development" by which "her theological understanding grew" with regard to several basic Christian teachings. The general direction of

---

7 "S. D. Adventist General Conference "*Review and Herald*, 13 November 1888, 714. A similar resolution had been adopted already by the 1886 General Conference saying that "doctrinal views not held by a fair majority" of Adventists should not be taught or published until they had been "examined and approved by the leading brethren of experience." See "General Conference Proceedings," *Review and Herald*, 14 December 1886, 779.

8 "When the resolution was urged upon the conference that nothing should be taught in the college contrary to that which has been taught, I felt deeply, for I knew whoever framed that resolution was not aware of what he was doing." See Ellen White, Manuscript 16, 1889, EGWRC, AU, Berrien Springs, MI. "Instructors in our schools should never be bound about by being told that they are to teach only what has been taught hitherto. Away with these restrictions. There is a God to give the message His people shall speak. Let not any minister feel under bonds or be gauged by men's measurements. The gospel must be fulfilled in accordance with the messages God sends. That which God gives His servants to speak today would not perhaps have been present truth twenty years ago, but it is God's message for this time." See Ellen White, Manuscript 8a, 1888, EGWRC, AU, Berrien Springs, MI. In 1896, White wrote: "The God of heaven sometimes commissions men to teach that which is regarded as contrary to the established doctrines." See Ellen White, *Testimonies to Ministers and Gospel Workers* (Mountain View, CA: Pacific Press, 1923/1962), 69.

9 Richard Hammill, "Spiritual Gifts in the Church Today," *Ministry*, July 1982, 17.

this process seems to have led her from a rather discouraging, law-centered position ("Sinai") to a more encouraging, love-centered attitude ("Golgotha"). In Thompson's view, "the transition from fear to love in her experience resulted in a remarkable shift of emphasis."[10] The reactions to these articles indicated that the church did not readily accept the idea that Ellen White's theological understanding evolved significantly over the years. Still, the underlying assumption that Ellen White's perception of truth developed in time seemed to accord well with her own view. "For sixty years I have been in communication with heavenly messengers, and I have been constantly learning in reference to divine things."[11]

George R. Knight has noted "three distinct types" of change in Ellen White's writings related to matters of doctrine and lifestyle. The first involved the "clarification" of vaguely or, perhaps, implicitly held views; in other words, "a change from ambiguity to clarity." The second type refers to the "progressive development" of new positions or changing emphases on doctrinal and other questions. Such change was progressive, not contradictory, in nature and happened "against the background of the ongoing development of present truth." Some changes even came by "contradiction, or reversal, of her earlier position." This happened, for example, with "Ellen White's changing belief in the shut door" which also involved certain "contradictory aspects," and "her later understanding contradicted that of her earliest years in the post-1844 period." In other words, "Ellen White was capable of both believing error and growing in her understanding" of truth.[12]

More than any other Adventist pioneer, Ellen White directly addressed the issue of doctrinal continuity and change. Her remarks were scattered through the years, but partly collected in the books compiled from her writings.[13] The following brief overview should

---

10 Alden Thompson, From Sinai to Golgotha—Nos. 1–5," *Adventist Review*, 3–31 December 1981, 4–6, 8–10, 7–10, 7–9, 12–13.

11 Ellen G. White, *This Day with God* (Washington, DC: Review and Herald, 1979), 76. Cf. idem, *Testimonies for the Church,* vol. 5 (Mountain View, CA: Pacific Press, 1948), 686.

12 George R. Knight, Adventists and Change," *Ministry*, October 1993, 12–13 (10–15).

13 See esp. *Counsels to Writers and Editors* (Nashville: Southern Publishing, 1946), 28–54; *Early Writings* (Washington, DC: Review and Herald, 1945), 258–261; *Spiritual Gifts,* vol. 1, *The Great Controversy*

be undergirded by a detailed historical analysis that interprets the different, and partly conflicting, statements in their respective historical and literary setting in order to determine their proper meaning and point of reference. Such a study cannot be presented here. Still, the following summarizes what appears to be White's basic approach to the issue of doctrinal development.

1. The Twofold Nature of Truth

In Ellen White's view, divine truth is eternal, changeless and immovable. At the same time, it is infinite and inexhaustible, capable of unlimited expansion, ever developing and unfolding in its meaning. Because of the progressive and advancing nature of truth, the church should see a continual advancement in the knowledge of truth. While the church is to teach the fundamental truths of the Scriptures, it must also proclaim present truth, i.e., doctrines fit for the times and embracing the whole gospel.

2. The Dialectic between Continuity and Change

According to White, Seventh-day Adventists must ever remain open and receptive to new light. Such increasing insight into truth usually will be in addition to previous beliefs, providing a clearer understanding of the word of God. At times, however, new light will be in conflict with our expositions of Scripture, with long-cherished opinions and long-established traditions. In other words, though new light does not contradict old light, it does collide with erroneous doctrines and misinterpretations of the word of God. She declares, for example, that,

> We must not for a moment think that there is no more light, no more truth, to be given us ... While we must hold fast to the truths which we have already received, we must not look with suspicion upon any new light that God may send.[14]

(Battle Creek, MI: James White, 1858), 168–173; *Selected Messages*, vol. 1 (Washington, DC: Review and Herald, 1958), 160–162, 185–191, 201–208, 383–388, 401–405, 406–416; ibid., vol. 2, 387–391; *Testimonies to Ministers and Gospel Workers*, 24–32, 105–111; *Gospel Workers* (Washington, DC: Review and Herald, 1948), 297–310; *Christ's Object Lessons*, 124–134; and *Testimonies*, vol. 5, 698–711. The following summary outline is based mainly on her published writings; all references can be found in Pöhler, *Continuity and Change in Adventist Teaching*, 236ff.

14 White, *Gospel Workers*, 310.

> The God of heaven sometimes commissions men to teach that which is regarded as contrary to the established doctrines ... Seventh-day Adventists are in danger of closing their eyes to truth as it is in Jesus, because it contradicts something which they have taken for granted as truth but which the Holy Spirit teaches is not truth.[15]
>
> If ideas are presented that differ in some points from our former doctrines, we must not condemn them without diligent search of the Bible to see if they are true.[16]
>
> There are errors in the church, and the Lord points them out by His own ordained agencies, not always through the testimonies.[17]
>
> In closely investigating ... established truth ... we may discover errors in our interpretation of Scripture.[18]

Therefore, we need to examine carefully, investigate candidly, test critically and review constantly our doctrines in the light of the Scriptures and discard everything that is not clearly sustained by the Bible. On the other hand, satisfaction with the church's present understanding of truth, opposition to a critical and persevering examination of its teachings, avoidance of controversial doctrinal discussions, prejudice against those who present new doctrinal insights, refusal to accept newly discovered truths, and general resistance to theological change betray a "conservative"[19] mind-set which results from spiritual lethargy. Those would-be guardians of the doctrine who prevent the much-needed re-examination for fear of removing the old landmarks are hampering the cause of truth.

At the same time, the pioneers of Seventh-day Adventism have laid well the doctrinal foundation of the church under the guidance of the Holy Spirit. These fundamental principles were firmly established in the early years through careful and prayerful Bible study; they were

---

15 White, *Testimony to Ministers*, 70–71.

16 Ellen White, "Candid Investigation Necessary to an Understanding of the Truth," *Signs of the Times,* 26 May 1890, 307 (305–307).

17 White, *Selected Messages*, 2:81.

18 Ellen G. White, "Treasure Hidden," *Review and Herald,* 12 July 1898, 438.

19 "Although the words *conservative* and *conservatism* occur in Ellen White's published writings some 30 times, they are always used in a negative sense." See David Thiele, "Is Conservatism a Heresy?" *Spectrum* 23:4 (1994): 12–15.

confirmed by divine revelation; they are based upon unquestionable authority; they have withstood test and trial and are unmovable, indispensable, unchangeable and irreplaceable. No interpretations or applications of the Scriptures must be entertained that would undermine or weaken these distinctive doctrines, contradict the special points of our faith, unsettle faith in the old landmarks, remove the pillars from their foundation, or move a block or stir a pin from the three angels' messages. Instead, Seventh-day Adventists are to preserve the waymarks which have made us what we are, hold firmly to the fundamental principles of our faith, and stand firm on the platform of eternal and immovable truth.

At first glance, Ellen White's statements on doctrinal continuity and change appear somewhat contradictory. The seeming discrepancies are largely due, however, to the different contexts in which she was expressing herself throughout the years. During and after the 1888 General Conference, she called for openness to theological change in order to counter the reluctance of the church to accept the new light which Waggoner and Jones were presenting on the subject of righteousness by faith. But when the church seemed to be threatened by heresy and apostasy, particularly in the 1850s, 1880s and 1900s, White particularly emphasized the doctrinal continuity and identity of the Adventist faith. Thus, her seemingly conflicting statements on doctrinal continuity and change may be seen as actually complementary when interpreted in their respective historical setting.

There is still another, related reason that may help explain the seeming contradiction in White's statements on theological development. To her, the landmark doctrines of Seventh-day Adventism were central to the message, mission and self-understanding of the church. Any change with regard to these foundational truths tended, therefore, to jeopardize the very *raison d'être* of the church. Other teachings, however, that did not directly belong to the unchangeable platform of Adventist truths were of secondary importance. Their revision would not constitute a threat to the identity and mission of the church. Thus, they could be freely reinvestigated and possibly be modified significantly.

It should be kept in mind that when such minor doctrinal matters were debated among Adventists, they were often regarded as being closely tied to the old landmarks, making their readjustment look like an attack on the fundamentals themselves. In order to be true to Ellen

White's intention, it seems therefore important to distinguish the core doctrines of the Adventist faith from other teachings and practices that are related but not foundational to it.

However, any authentic doctrinal development may and will somehow affect either the fundamental or the distinctive truths of Seventh-day Adventism in some, albeit positive, way. Otherwise, the deepening insight into truth would, in the final analysis, be irrelevant and not worth arguing or even talking about. Ellen White, on her part, held no low view of theological growth. To her, doctrinal progress was of crucial significance for the church: "Much has been lost because our ministers and people have concluded that we have had all the truth essential for us as a people; but such a conclusion is erroneous and in harmony with the deceptions of Satan, for truth will be constantly unfolding."[20]

As only those theological insights which, in some real sense, are related to the central beliefs of the church can be regarded as essential, it follows that—for Ellen White—doctrinal development was not a superfluous or even dangerous process but rather an indispensable aspect of the spiritual growth and theological maturation of the church.

3. The Twofold Process of Theological Development

An analysis of Ellen White's view on theological development reveals two major aspects which, to her, were involved in this process. They reflect the balance she sought between the need for substantial doctrinal continuity and the demands for authentic doctrinal change. On the one hand, truth develops through restoration and rediscovery; on the other hand, it involves reinterpretation and recontextualization.

a. Restoration and Rediscovery

For Ellen White, doctrinal development was first and foremost a process in which old truths were rediscovered and restored to the church. "There are old, yet new truths still to be added to the treasures of our knowledge."[21] What appears to be new light is, in reality, "precious [old] light that has for a time been lost sight of by the people."[22] After all, no doctrine must be taught in the church

---

20 Ellen White, "Candid Investigation Necessary to an Understanding of the Truth," *Signs of the Times*, 26 May 1890, 305–306.

21 Ellen G. White, "Need of Earnestness in the Cause of God," *Review and Herald*, 25 February 1890, 113.

22 White, *Selected Messages* 1:384; cf. ibid., 401.

which cannot be shown to be contained in the word of God. But there are many "precious rays of light yet to shine forth from the word of God. Many gems are yet scattered that are to be gathered together to become the property of the remnant people of God."[23] White wrote powerfully about the importance of this reclamation of truth:

> Gems of thought are to be gathered up and redeemed from their companionship with error ... Truths of divine origin, are to be carefully searched out and placed in their proper setting, to shine with heavenly brilliancy amid the moral darkness of the world ... Let the gems of divine light be reset in the framework of the gospel. Let nothing be lost of the precious light that comes from the throne of God. It has been misapplied, and cast aside as worthless; but it is heaven-sent, and each gem is to become the property of God's people and find its true position in the framework of truth. Precious jewels of light are to be collected, and by the aid of the Holy Spirit they are to be fitted into the gospel system.[24]

b. Reinterpretation and Recontextualization

Obviously, then, there is something really new about new light. While truth itself is eternal and unchangeable, the understanding of its meaning and the realization of its full significance may grow constantly in the church. Taking Christ as the model and norm of theological progress and doctrinal advance, White repeatedly pointed out that his work consisted in recontextualizing and reinterpreting divine revelation. New meanings resulted from placing old truths in different and proper settings. The true significance of Bible teachings can, at times, only be seen when they are related to new scriptural contexts or changing situations which make old truths appear in a different, new light. Correcting misinterpretations of the Bible and properly reinterpreting old truths, new doctrinal insights reveal new facets and the true import of divine revelation. Thus White wrote:

> Great truths which have been neglected and unappreciated for ages will be revealed by the Spirit of God and new meaning will flash out of familiar texts. Every page will be illuminated by the Spirit of truth."[25]

---

23 White, *Counsels to Writers and Editors*, 35.

24 Ellen G. White, "Truth to Be Rescued from Error," *Review and Herald*, 23 October 1894, 657. See also idem, "Be Zealous and Repent," *Review and Herald Extra*, 23 December 1890, 1–2.

25 Ellen G. White, *Counsels on Sabbath School Work* (Washington, DC:

"When the mind is kept open and is constantly searching the field of revelation, we shall find rich deposits of truth. Old truths will be revealed in new aspects, and truths will appear which have been overlooked in the search."[26]

Some things must be torn down. Some things must be built up. The old treasures must be reset in the framework of truth ... Jesus will reveal to us precious old truths in a new light, if we are ready to receive them.[27]

Summary

Ellen White exerted a significant influence on the development of Adventist doctrines, being involved in the formation, preservation and revision of the teachings of the church. She actively participated in various types of change, encompassing not only theological maturation and doctrinal growth but, at times, even doctrinal readjustments and revisions. To a considerable degree she shared in, and even fostered, the process of theological growth and doctrinal development which the Seventh-day Adventist Church experienced in her lifetime.

At the same time, Ellen White's concept of doctrinal development appears to have surpassed that of her fellow-believers not only in depth of understanding but also in striking a delicate balance between the need for theological continuity and substantial identity, on the one hand, and the possibility of theological revision and doctrinal change, on the other. Tirelessly she warned her church against both the careless rejection of precious old light and the stubborn resistance to much-needed new light.

This concept may still provide guidance to the church now faced by the twin dangers of theological immobilism and doctrinal revisionism. Seventh-day Adventists may do well to emulate the example of their prophet who served both as a strong factor of doctrinal continuity and a constant catalyst of doctrinal change. Her concept of theological development is perhaps best expressed in the following quotation which is worth pondering for its rich implications.

[Christ] promised that the Holy Spirit should enlighten the disciples, that the word of God should be ever unfolding to

---

Review and Herald, 1938), 35.

26 Ellen G. White, Manuscript 75, 1897, EGWRC, AU, Berrien Springs, MI.

27 Ellen G. White, "Minneapolis Talks," 88–89; see also *Selected Messages*, 1:355, 409.

them ... The truths of redemption are capable of constant development and expansion ... Though old, they are ever new, constantly revealing to the seeker for truth a greater glory and a mightier power.

In every age there is a new development of truth, a message of God to the people of that generation. The old truths are all essential; new truth is not independent of the old, but an unfolding of it. It is only as the old truths are understood that we can comprehend the new ... But it is the light which shines in the fresh unfolding of truth that glorifies the old. He who rejects or neglects the new does not really possess the old. To him it loses its vital power and becomes but a lifeless form ... Truth in Christ and through Christ is measureless. The student of Scripture looks, as it were, into a fountain that deepens and broadens as he gazes into its depths.[28]

PART II—Ellen White on Church Authority, Policy and Structure

What can be learned from Ellen White's view on theological continuity and change for church leadership, authority, organization, structure and policy? What insights can be derived from her position on doctrinal development that are applicable to the issues currently engaging the church? How did she herself apply these principles in different situations? What implications may be drawn from and what applications may be made of both her teaching and her actions? While the answers cannot claim to be comprehensive or exhaustive by any measure, they should be informative, representative and significant. Three main aspects have a direct bearing on the ongoing struggle about "unity in mission" in the Seventh-day Adventist Church.

1. Organizational Readjustment

According to Ellen White, divine truth is eternal and unchanging, but the understanding of truth is subject to development and change. Moreover, there is truth particularly relevant at a certain point in history—"present truth" or truth for today. What pertains to church teachings will—by implication—also hold true for church policies and organizational structures. They, too, may be changed and in need of readjustment. Just as ecclesial traditions are not dependable guides to "present truth", nor are traditional policies or structures.

---

28 White, *Christ's Object Lessons*, 127–128.

They may become outdated and obstructive even when sanctioned by an authority in the past. Therefore, the church should be amenable to changes regarding its policies and structures, just as it should remain open to new doctrinal insights. In many cases, the new is a deepening and unfolding of the old. At times, however, it stands in contrast to previous church teaching, policy or practice. Learning and understanding is progressive, making a conservative stance a possible hindrance to the advance of the church.

This does not mean that everything is subject to change or revision. On the contrary, the foundational truths of faith remain, while secondary teachings are more easily reconsidered. In a similar manner, the basic three-tier (local, regional, global), threefold (pastor, elder, deacon) and representative structure of the church has stood the test of time and proved highly effective in protecting unity and fostering mission. At the same time, structures and policies should be treated dynamically and not be regarded as unchangeable. As there is a kind of hierarchy with regard to truth—with core beliefs being distinguished from, and superior to, peripheral views—so we must also admit to a certain hierarchy of policies and procedures, where the application of foundational principles is dependent on tangible needs and particular circumstances.

This inference from Ellen White's view on theological continuity and change is supported by the following statement: "The place, the circumstances, the interest, the moral sentiment of the people, will have to decide in many cases the course of action to be pursued."[29] This calls for openness and flexibility on the part of the worldwide Adventist church with regard to its rules and regulations, policies and practices, organization and structure. They must not be treated like a "Codex Iuris Canonici" and invested with quasi-divine authority. The following statement bears repeating: "Circumstances alter conditions. Circumstances change the relations of things."[30] In a multicultural world and community, this insight is essential for the unity of purpose and the accomplishment of the mission of the church. Organizational

---

29 Ellen G. White, "To Ministers of the Australian Conference," 11 November 1894; GC Bulletin, 1901, 70.

30 Ellen G. White, Report of an Interview/Counsel on Age of School Entrance (St. Helena, CA, 1904), Manuscript 7, 1904, EGWE; idem, *Selected Messages*, vol. 3, 217; idem, *Manuscript Releases*, 21 vols. (Silver Spring, MD: Ellen G. White Estate, 1981, 1987, 1990, 1993), 6:354.

structures and policies should serve the church, not vice versa, as the following underlines.

2. Situational Re-evaluation

In 1875, Ellen White wrote a testimony to a strong-willed brother who was inclined to act independently of the church: "God has invested His church with special authority and power which no one can be justified in disregarding and despising, for in so doing he despises the voice of God."[31] Later in the same year, she wrote:

> I have been shown that no man's judgment should be surrendered to any one man. But when the judgment of the General Conference, which is the highest authority that God has upon earth, is exercised, private independence and private judgment must not be maintained, but be surrendered."[32]

What may primarily have pertained to the General Conference in session[33] was, in the years following, applied to the General Conference administration. About the latter, President G. I. Butler claimed: "It is the highest authority of an earthly character among Seventh-day Adventists."[34] Likewise, President O. A. Olsen regarded the General Conference as "the highest organized authority under God on the earth."[35] Ellen White, however, became increasingly concerned about the centralization of power in the hands of a few administrators. In the 1890s, she began to criticize the "kingly power" usurped by the leaders in Battle Creek, fearing that it would ultimately lead to "a state of insubordination."[36] She denied that the General Conference was the legitimate voice of God.[37] "We hear that the voice of the [General]

---

31 Ellen G. White, *Testimonies for the Church,* vol. 3 (Mountain View, CA: Pacific Press, 1948), 417.

32 White, *Testimonies for the Church* vol. 3, 492.

33 "It is not clear in the 1875 statement ... whether Ellen White is speaking of the General Conference in session, or whether she is referring to the daily and weekly decisions that were necessary for the advancement of the work." See George E. Rice, "The church: voice of God? *Ministry*, December 1987, 5.

34 *Seventh-day Adventist Year Book* (Battle Creek, MI: Review and Herald, 1888), 50.

35 Minutes of the General Conference Committee, 25 January 1893.

36 Ellen White, *Special Testimonies: Series A* (Payson, AZ: Leaves-of-Autumn, n.d.), 299f.

37 Ellen G White, "Board and Council meetings," n.d., MS 33, 1891; "Relation of the G. C. Committee to Business Interests," n.d., MS 33, 1895;

Conference is the voice of God. Every time I have heard this, I have thought it was almost blasphemy. The voice of the Conference should be the voice of God, but it is not."[38]

After the far-reaching and decentralizing reorganization of 1901 had put a kind of stop to leadership by "dictation," Ellen White again expressed confidence in the General Conference by reiterating, in 1909, the view she had expressed back in 1875. However, she continued to warn leaders about exercising "kingly power":

> I have often been instructed by the Lord that no man's judgment should be surrendered to the judgment of any other one man. Never should the mind of one man or the minds of a few men be regarded as sufficient in wisdom and power to control the work and to say what plans shall be followed. But when in a General Conference the judgment of the brethren assembled from all parts of the field is exercised, private independence and private judgment must not be stubbornly maintained, but surrendered. Never should a laborer regard as a virtue the persistent maintenance of his position of independence contrary to the decision of the general body.[39]

In each case, Ellen White expressed herself clearly and forcefully, though in a seemingly contradictory and antithetic manner. But new situations and developments were calling for a different response. When people acted independently of the church or relied too much on

---

"Concerning the Review and Herald Publishing Association," 12 October, 1895, MS 57, 1895; To Men Who Occupy Responsible Positions, 1 July 1896; To Brother and Sister Waggoner, 26 August 1898, Letter 77, 1898; comments in the 1901 GC Session, in "General Conference Proceedings," General Conference Bulletin 4, extra, no. 1 (3 April 1901): 25; "Consumers, but not Producers," 25 April 1901, MS 35 and "Talk by Mrs. E. G. White in College Library, 1 April 1901," MS 43, 1901.

38 Manuscript 37, April 1901; cf. Manuscript 35, 1901, Manuscript Releases, vol. 17, 250.

39 White, *Testimonies for the Church*, vol. 9 (Mountain View, CA: Pacific Press, 1948), 260. This thought is continued in the next paragraph: "God has ordained that the representatives of His church from all parts of the earth, when assembled in a General Conference, shall have authority. The error that some are in danger of committing is in giving to the mind and judgment of one man, or of a small group of men, the full measure of authority and influence that God has vested in His church in the judgment and voice of the General Conference assembled to plan for the prosperity and advancement of His work."

individual leaders, she emphasized the importance of the collective will of the church as expressed by the General Conference in session. But when the leadership of the church abused their authority by acting in a dominant manner, White stood up against them, calling them to refrain from exercising dictatorial power. Her statements, made in a particular setting, would become misleading or even wrong when applied indiscriminately to other situations.[40]

It may be argued that the apparent tension between Ellen White's various statements on the role of the "General Conference" is due, not to a change of mind on her part, but rather to two different meanings of the term "General Conference". In 1875 and 1909 she referred to the General Conference in session, while the negative statements about "kingly power" etc. made in the 1890s were directed towards the General Conference administration, which consisted of only a few men. Granted that there is truth in this observation, it still remains quite difficult to separate the two and treat them as independent entities. After all, what happens at a General Conference in session is strongly influenced by the top leadership of the General Conference. Decisions made by the assembled delegates usually are in concurrence with the will of the administration. Thus, Ellen White's critical remarks about "kingly power" exerted by some top leaders may still apply, even when decisions are reached in a General Conference Session. Which of the contrasting statements of the prophet are, then, applicable today? That depends on which of them corresponds more closely to the current situation in the SDA church. What would Ellen White possibly write to those Union Conferences who resist what they see as a misuse of power by General Conference leadership? What, on the other hand, would she most likely tell those leaders who reject the appeal to conscience and the fundamental beliefs of the church? No one can know for sure, for all are tempted to use, if not abuse, the prophet as a spokesperson for their own views. The church will be

---

40 While written with regard to health reform, James White's description of the difficulty his wife was facing in leading the church to a balanced position may apply here: "She makes strong appeals to the people, which a few feel deeply, and take strong positions, and go to extremes . . . . What she may say to urge the tardy, is taken by the prompt to urge them over the mark. And what she may say to caution the prompt, zealous, incautious ones, is taken by the tardy as an excuse to remain too far behind" ("To a Brother at Monroe, Wisc.," *Review and Herald*, 17 March 1868, 220).

wise not to quote Ellen White one-sidedly or out of context in order to bolster up a particular view against other legitimate perspectives. Insights drawn from a particular setting need to be balanced by those gained under different circumstances. Together they form a treasure trove of experience that can be a continual blessing to the church.

3. Conscientious Nonconformity

Shortly after the General Conference was founded in 1863, Ellen White wrote to a discontented church member: "You should have submitted to the judgment of the church. If they decided wrong, God could take hold of this matter in His own time and vindicate the right."[41] There are two important insights contained in this statement. First, decisions made by a majority should be accepted even when one personally disagrees with them. Never should a minority impose its will on the church at large. Second, majority decisions may be wrong and may, therefore, need to be corrected. While even God himself bears with unwise and erroneous decisions, he may also work toward correcting them when he sees fit. Such revisions do not come by heavenly fiat but in the same manner as the initial vote, namely, by proposal, debate and voting.

This calls for a mature attitude that respects the result of a vote and, at the same time, remains open to the possibility of correction at a later time. While the "losers" need to submit to the majority opinion—at times a humbling experience—the "winners" must not regard the outcome as sacrosanct. They too need to show humility by recognizing that they may have been wrong after all and need to surrender their personal conviction when the Spirit leads the church into new directions. "Submit to one another out of reverence for Christ" (Eph 5:21 NIV), Paul wrote. What pertained to husbands and wives, parents and children, masters and slaves in Ephesus equally applies to superiors and inferiors or to "higher" and "lower" entities in the church today. The summons to submission and Christ-like humility is not a one-way road of communication.

But what about a situation in which more is at stake than personal opinions and preferences, divergent views on church policies, or disagreements about the filling of leadership posts? What if contentious points become a matter of conscience and of faithfulness to biblical principles and the fundamental beliefs of the church? Are there times

---

41 Ellen White to Brother and Sister Scott, 6 July 1863, Letter 5, 1863.

when it becomes a right or even a duty to voice dissent against church councils and decisions? This question is not new to Adventists.

In 1877, the General Conference in session voted that its "decisions should be submitted [to] by all without exception unless they can be shown to conflict with the word of God and the rights of individual conscience."[42]

Ellen White concurred that no doctrine must be taught in the church which cannot be shown to be contained in the word of God. She also believed that God sometimes commissions people to go against what seems to be the established position of the church.[43] To her, following one's conscience was the epitome of faithfulness toward God. She wrote:

> The greatest want of the world is the want of men—men who will not be bought or sold, men who in their inmost souls are true and honest, men who do not fear to call sin by its right name, men whose conscience is as true to duty as the needle to the pole, men who will stand for the right though the heavens fall.[44]

Describing Martin Luther's appearance before the Diet of Worms, Ellen White spoke in high terms about his "unwavering firmness and fidelity" in view of state and church authorities that expected him to submit his conscience to church traditions, councils and decrees.[45]

But it was not only in theory and in view of an apostate church that Ellen White allowed for dissent in matters of conscience involving established church rules and practices. While she fully supported the idea that the tithe should be given to the church and not be spent according to one's own liking, at times, she withheld tithe and used it for causes she felt were unduly neglected by the church. Her counsel was unequivocal: "Let none feel at liberty to retain their tithe, to use according to their own judgment. They are not to use it ... as they see fit, even in what they may regard as the Lord's work ... The minister should, by precept and example, teach the people to regard the tithe as sacred."[46] Elsewhere she offers this exhortation: "Cannot you see

---

42 "Sixteenth Annual Session of the General Conference of S. D. Adventists," *Review and Herald*, 4 October 1877, 106.

43 See above, fn 8 and 15.

44 Ellen White, *Education* (Oakland, CA: Pacific Press, 1903/1942), 57.

45 Ellen White, *The Great Controversy between Christ and Satan* (Mountain View, CA: Pacific Press, 1950), 166.

46 White, *Testimonies for the Church,* vol. 9, 247.

Circumstances Change the Relation of Things 151

that it is not best under any circumstances to withhold your tithes and offerings because you are not in harmony with everything your brethren do? ... I pay my tithe gladly and freely..."[47]

Although Ellen White

> ... normally 'paid her tithes in the regular way into the conference treasury' ... at a time when there was inadequate funding for ordained ministers working among African-Americans she paid some of her own tithe directly to their employer, the Southern Missionary Society ... And apparently Ellen White agreed to pay a partial salary for some literature-evangelists in different territories ... These exceptions were not, however, her regular practice.[48]

Neither did she justify her behavior by referring to her prophetic authority. Rather, it was the suffering of the workers and the injustice being done to them that caused her to deviate from the principle she herself had laid down.

This example serves to illustrate what may be called "conscientious nonconformity." While accepting and following the rules, there may be exceptions that are due to special circumstances and needs that justify variant actions grounded in a moral necessity that overrules the normal practice. This does not imply a lack of loyalty or a rebellious spirit refusing to act in harmony with church policy and practice. To the contrary, it is exactly out of loyalty to biblically grounded beliefs and values that such dissent, at times, is legitimate and even called for. Exceptions do not question the rules but confirm their basic validity. However, when policy and authority are used in ways that conflict with the mandates of a conscience grounded in the word of God, submission to the latter takes priority over compliance with the former.

Ellen White's course of action with regard to tithing marks off the legitimate parameters of nonconformist behavior in the church. It is not an act of defiance, but one of loyalty; it is not an expression of individualism, but one of solidarity; it is not a matter of self-exaltation, but of conscience. Such behavior is justified only when conformity to

---

47 Ellen White, *Special Testimonies,* Series A, No. 1: "An Appeal to Our Ministers and Conference Committees," 27 (10 August 1890).

48 Johannes Kovar, "Tithe," in *The Ellen G. White Encyclopedia*, ed. Denis Fortin and Jerry Moon (Hagerstown, MD: Review and Herald, 2013), 1226. See also Arthur L. White, *Ellen G. White: The Early Elmshaven Years, 1900–1905* (Washington, DC: Review and Herald, 1981), 389–397.

the rules conflict with the core teachings and principles of the word of God. "The Lord has shown you what is good. He has told you what he requires of you. You must treat people fairly. You must love others faithfully. And you must be very careful to live the way your God wants you to" (Micah 6:8 NIRV).

Conclusion

When being criticized by some for having changed her mind on certain issues, Ellen White referred to the many lessons she had learned in the years and decades of her life-long ministry. "For sixty years," she wrote, "I have been constantly learning in reference to divine things."[49] To change one's mind may therefore not be a sign of weakening faith, but rather an evidence of personal and spiritual growth. What applies to divine messengers also holds true for dedicated leaders. The longer they serve, the more teachable they become under the guidance of the Holy Spirit. "To live is to change, and to be perfect is to have changed often" (J. H. Newman). The following quote pertains, therefore, not only to matters of doctrine and theology, structure and policy, but equally to each of us personally: "Some things must be torn down. Some things must be built up."[50]

---

49 Ellen G. White, *This Day with God* (Washington, DC: Review and Herald, 1979), 76. Cf. idem, *Testimonies for the Church*, vol. 5 (Mountain View, CA: Pacific Press, 1948), 686.

50 Ellen G. White, "Minneapolis Talks," 88–89; see also *Selected Messages*, 1:355, 409.

ORGANIZATIONAL ISSUES

8. Reorganization of Church Structure, 1901–03: Some Observations[1]

Barry Oliver
South Pacific Division (1997–2015)

Introduction

The author's objectives in this chapter are:

1. To describe briefly aspects of the denominational context and the organizational design of the Seventh-day Adventist Church in 1863;

2. To identify and to discuss briefly a number of factors which led to the reorganization of the Church in the period from 1901 to 1903;

3. To list the changes that reorganization brought to the organizational structures of the Church;

4. To locate mission as the primary impetus for reorganization;

5. To discuss the principles which, in 1901, undergirded the introduction of the Union as an added layer of organizational structure;

6. To distil from the historical data lessons that may be instructive for the contemporary Seventh-day Adventist Church.

Perspective of the Author

With respect to the author's perspective, this chapter should be read while keeping in mind that:

1. The chapter reflects the author's abiding sense of loyalty to and love for the Seventh-day Adventist Church. Now retired, he has served as an ordained pastor, evangelist, associate professor, administrator, and finally as president of the South Pacific Division and vice-president of the General Conference of Seventh-day Adventists.

---

[1] Much of the content of this paper is drawn directly from research conducted by the author when preparing and writing a Ph.D. dissertation at Andrews University in 1989, and from the published version of the dissertation. See Barry David Oliver, *SDA Organizational Structure: Past, Present, and Future*, (Berrien Springs, MI: Andrews University Press, 1989).

2. Care has been taken to ensure that all quotations reflect the context from which they are taken.

3. The chapter has been written in a spirit of open enquiry and discussion.

4. It is acknowledged that history is always contextual, as is the application of principle and practice in diverse contemporary contexts.

Limitations

The chapter assumes a working knowledge of Seventh-day Adventist organisational structure. Thus no attempt is made to describe contemporary structure. There is limited discussion of the theological interplay between Alonzo T. Jones and those aligned with him in 1901, and Arthur G. Daniells and those aligned with him. The polemic between these two groups strongly influenced the outcome of the restructuring process.[2] Furthermore, in this chapter there is only passing reference to the impact of the Kellogg debacle on individuals and on decisions made in the early 20th century.

Aspects of the Denominational Context and the Organizational Design of the Seventh-day Adventist Church in 1863

The Seventh-day Adventist Church was formally organized at a meeting of believers at Battle Creek, Michigan, in 1863. At that time the membership was approximately 3500. It was decided that there would be three administrative levels of Church structure: the local church, the conference, and the General Conference with headquarters in Battle Creek. The officers of the General Conference would be president, secretary and treasurer. Three persons were to be appointed as the members of a General Conference executive committee and General Conference sessions were to be held annually.[3]

There were those who had argued that by being organized the Church would become Babylon, but those who saw the necessity for

---

2 For a discussion of the polemic see Barry D. Oliver, "The Development of Organizational and Leadership Paradigms in the Seventh-day Adventist Church," *Journal of Adventist Mission Studies* 3/1 Spring 2007: 4–28.

3 For a detailed discussion of the factors which precipitated denominational organization in 1863 see Andrew G. Mustard, *James White and SDA Organization: Historical Development, 1844–1881* (Berrien Springs, MI: Andrews University Press, 1987).

an efficient system of organization prevailed. Indeed it was James White who was the most vocal proponent of the need for organization throughout the controversies that surrounded the proposed organization in the late 1850s and early 1860s.[4] White, as editor of the Advent *Review and Sabbath Herald* and the unofficial leader of the Sabbatarian Adventists, continually wrote and spoke in support of organization. His wife also supported the need for sound organization. It appears, however, that when it came to denominational structures, the Church understood her role to be more exhortative and advisory than definitive.

For example, in August 1861, Ellen White reproved those who did not have the courage of their convictions:

> The agitation on the subject of organization has revealed a great lack of moral courage on the part of ministers proclaiming present truth. Some who were convinced that organization was right failed to stand up boldly and advocate it ... They feared blame and opposition. They watched the brethren generally to see how their pulse beat before standing manfully for what they believed to be right ... They were afraid of losing their influence ...Those who shun responsibility will meet with loss in the end. The time for ministers to stand together is when the battle goes hard.[5]

The arguments that were used to persuade the believers to organize themselves into a denomination were not based strongly on biblical or theological reasoning.[6] Rather, pragmatism won the day. In 1907 A. G. Daniells, reflecting on the events of the 1860s, listed some of the problems of non-organization, implying that organization would solve these and other issues facing the Church. His list included: failure to keep proper church membership records; paucity of church officers; inability to determine the accredited representatives of the people; no regular support for the ministry; and no legal provision for holding property.[7]

The list of reasons that Ellen White compiled in 1892 was also largely pragmatic, although she did leave room for more latitude. Her

---

4 See Mustard, *James White and SDA Organization*.

5 Ellen G. White, "Communication from Mrs White," *Advent Review and Sabbath Herald*, Aug. 27, 1861, 101–2.

6 See Oliver, *SDA Organizational Structure,* 46–48.

7 A. G. Daniells, "Organization: A Brief Account of Its History in the Development of the Cause of the Third Angel's Message," *Advent Review and Sabbath Herald*, February 14, 1907, 5.

reasons for organizing the church in 1863 were: (1) to provide for the support of the ministry; (2) to carry the work in new fields; (3) to protect both the churches and the ministry from unworthy members; (4) to enable the church to hold property; and (5) to enable publication of truth through the press. Additional objectives were offered.[8]

Factors which led to the reorganization of the Church between 1901 and 1903

Despite the simplicity and uniqueness of the structures set up in 1863, the need for major modification of those structures became evident as the Church expanded during the last quarter of the nineteenth century. A number of contextual factors led to the need for change.

1. Numerical Growth and the Beginnings of Diversity

Although Seventh-day Adventists still understood themselves to be simply "a body of believers associating together, taking the name of Seventh-day Adventists, and attaching their names to a covenant simply to keep the commandments of God and the faith of Jesus," with the Bible as "their only creed and discipline," by 1888 there were already thirty organized conferences containing 889 organized churches. There were 227 ordained and 182 licensed ministers. The constituency was supporting six publishing houses, three senior educational institutions, and two medical establishments. By the turn of the century the church had 75,000 members spread not only across the United States, but also in Europe, Australia and New Zealand and, increasingly, in the "mission fields."[9]

As the church continued to grow and diversify, it was evident that the meager organization that was set in place in 1863 could not cope with this numerical and geographical growth.

2. Institutional Growth

The organizational structures of 1863 did not anticipate the increase in the number of organizations to care for the publishing, educational, health, and missionary interests of the Church. These entities were not

---

8 Ellen G. White to the Brethren at the General Conference, Letter 127, December 19, 1892, Ellen G. White Research Centre.

9 *A Brief Sketch of the Origin, Progress and Principles of the Seventh-day Adventists* (Battle Creek, MI: Review and Herald, 1888), 9, 11–12.

a part of the conference administrative structure of the Church, but stood as independent units apart from it. Although they had a separate infrastructure, most shared personnel with the administrative structure of the denomination. Most were located in Battle Creek.

The major auxiliary organizations that were in existence at the beginning of 1888 were the General Tract and Missionary Society, established in 1874, the General Sabbath School Association, established in 1878, the Health and Temperance Association, established in 1879, and the General Conference Association, established in 1887. The National Religious Liberty Association was established in 1889, an autonomous Foreign Mission Board in the same year, and the Seventh-day Adventist Medical Missionary and Benevolent Association in 1893.[10]

3. Loss of Coordination and Integration

The organizations established by 1888 were legally incorporated as independent bodies that had their own officers and executive boards or committees. Although they were all part of the Seventh-day Adventist Church—officers being appointed by and reporting to the General Conference session—they were not administered directly by the General Conference. Because of their independent status, coordination and integration were perennial problems during the 1890s. Not until the 1901 General Conference session and its reorganization of the administrative structures of the church were the auxiliary organizations incorporated into the conference structure as departments of the General Conference.

4. Administrative Centralization

The growing global missionary consciousness of the church during the 1870s and 1880s was accompanied by increased centralization of administrative control. In 1885, George Butler, president of the General Conference from 1871 to 1874 and, again from 1880 to 1888, spoke of the principles upon which the organization of the church was established. He declared:

> Supervision embraces all its [the General Conference] interests in every part of the world. There is not an institution among us, not a periodical issued, not a Conference or society, not a

---

10 For a summary overview of the Seventh-day Adventist Church at the beginning of 1888, see *Brief Sketch*, 9–40.

mission field connected with our work, that it has not a right to advise and counsel and investigate. It is the highest authority of an earthly character among Seventh-day Adventists.[11]

Butler's concept of administration grew out of his concept of leadership. After the General Conference of 1888, Ellen White wrote of Butler:

> A sick man's mind has had a controlling power over the General Conference committee and the ministers have been the shadow and echo of Elder Butler about as long as it is healthy and for the good of the cause. Envy, evil surmisings, jealousies have been working like leaven until the whole lump seemed to be leavened ... He thinks his position gives him such power that his voice is infallible.[12]

In response to some tensions that existed between James White and other church leaders, Butler had written an essay in 1873 in which he encapsulated his attitude toward leadership. His position was clear from the opening sentence: "There never was any great movement in this world without a leader; and in the nature of things it is impossible that there should be."[13]

Butler described a leader as a benevolent monarch. He supported his assertion by references to numerous biblical examples of authoritarian leaders. While he was willing to concede that Christ was indeed head of the church, he insisted that some men were "placed higher in authority in the church than others."[14]

Two years later, in 1875, the General Conference session passed a resolution that called for a revision of Butler's essay.[15] The 1877 session rescinded all parts of the essay that referred to the leadership of the church as residing in one man. This was supported by a resolution which stated that:

> The highest authority under God among Seventh-day Adventists is found in the will of the body of that people, as expressed in the decisions of the General Conference when

---

11 *Seventh-day Adventist Year Book: 1888* (Battle Creek, MI: Review and Herald, 1889), 50.

12 Ellen G. White to Mary White, Letter 82, November 4, 1888, Ellen G. White Estate Office.

13 George I. Butler, "Leadership," *Advent Review and Sabbath Herald*, November 18, 1873, 180.

14 Ibid., 180–81.

15 "General Conference Report," *Advent Review and Sabbath Herald*, August 26, 1875, 59.

acting within its proper jurisdiction; and that such decisions should be submitted to by all without exception, unless they can be shown to conflict with the word of God and the rights of individual conscience.[16]

Although James White made it clear that he did not agree with Butler's position, and despite Ellen White's continuous appeals, Butler did not modify his leadership style very much until well after he was voted out of the presidency at the 1888 General Conference session.[17]

In the early 1880s, Ellen White began to rebuke General Conference administrators for taking too much of the responsibility for decision-making on themselves and failing to give others opportunity to have input. In a letter to W. C. and Mary White in 1883, Ellen White pointed out that "every one of our leading men" considered that "he was the very one who must bear all the responsibilities" and "failed to educate others to think" and "to act." In fact, she charged, the leading men gave the others "no chance."[18]

Implicit in her condemnation of those who followed that practice was reproof for those who permitted them to do it without seeking to correct the situation. Conference leaders, for instance, were told that they were to make their own decisions. The president of the General Conference could not possibly "understand the situation as well as you who are on the ground."[19]

As a corrective for centralization of control, Ellen White advocated proper use of the committee system that had been established when the General Conference had been organized in 1863. She made it clear that even in the operation of institutions one man's mind was not to control the decision-making process. She emphasized that "God

---

16 "General Conference Report," *Advent Review and Sabbath Herald*, October 4, 1877, 106.

17 For a discussion of the conflict between James White and George Butler over the concept of leadership, see Mustard, *James White and SDA Organization*, 175–78; and Bert Haloviak, "SDAs and Organization, 1844–1907" (paper presented at the Central California Camp meeting, August 1987), 39–41.

18 Ellen G. White to W. C. White and Mary White, Letter 23, August 23, 1883, Ellen G. White Estate Office.

19 These words were spoken to the delegates assembled at the General Conference session in 1883. Ellen G. White, "Genuine Faith and Holiness," Manuscript 3, 1883, Ellen G. White Estate Office.

would not have many minds the shadow of one man's mind," but that "in a multitude of counselors there is safety."[20]

5. Financial Crisis

Another precipitating factor which led to restructuring was the state of the finances of the church. When G. A. Irwin assumed the presidency of the General Conference in 1897, he had to face a woeful financial predicament. Within a few weeks of his appointment, the situation was so desperate that he wrote to N. W. Allee that the General Conference was "living from hand to mouth, so to speak." He told Allee that "some days we get in two or three hundred dollars, and other days we have nothing." On the particular day that he was writing, he lamented that the treasury was "practically empty," even though there were at that time "a number of calls for means."[21]

Despite concerted effort by General Conference leaders, the situation did not improve substantially. While there were some periods when the predicament was not as desperate as it was at other times, at all times the situation was out of control. The financial statement for 1899 showed that at the beginning of that year the General Conference had only $55.33 cash in hand. The same report showed that by October 1 of the same year there was an operating deficit of $9,529.74.[22] At the beginning of 1901 the deficit was $41,589.11. In August the deficit was still $39,600.[23]

Because of the chronic shortage of operating capital, nothing was being done to repay debts that had been incurred in order to establish various institutions. Percy Magan, who realized that part of the problem lay in the ease with which institutions borrowed money and the ease with which church members lent it to them, charged that "all our institutions" had been in "the borrowing business." He

---

20 Ellen G. White to John Harvey Kellogg, Letter 7, April 26, 1886, Ellen G. White Estate Office.

21 G. A. Irwin to N. W. Allee, May 5, 1897, Record Group 11, Letter Book 18, General Conference Archives, Silver Spring, Maryland.

22 General Conference Committee Minutes, Oct. 10, 1899, Record Group 1, General Conference Archives, Silver Spring, Maryland.

23 A. G. Daniells to Members of the General Conference Committee, August 2, 1901, Record Group 11, Letter Book 24, General Conference Archives, Silver Spring, Maryland. See also A. G. Daniells to J. E. Jayne, August 3, 1901, Record Group 11, Letter Book 24, General Conference Archives, Silver Spring, Maryland.

advocated that it was time for them "to quit" borrowing. But not only were institutions to cease borrowing, church members were to cease dabbling in "the lending business." Had the members not been "in the lending business," then it was certain that the institutions "would never have been in the borrowing business."[24] Desperate times called for desperate measures.

6. Decreasing Ability to Support Missionary Expansion

The inability of the denomination to support its growth financially was having an effect on its missionary expansion. In the last five years of the nineteenth century there was a slackening of missionary activity by the denomination. At the 1899 General Conference session, Allen Moon, president of the Foreign Mission Board, reported that

> During the last two years we have opened up no new work in any part of the world. It has been an impossibility. There have been demands for opening the work in China. That work ought to have been opened a year ago, yet we have been utterly unable to do anything toward opening it.[25]

The failure to commence any new work between 1897 and 1899 and the decrease in the number of missionaries being sent abroad between 1895 and 1900 does not appear to have been the result of any marked decrease in the church's eschatological or missiological vision. A more likely explanation for the problems is that the centralized organization as it existed was just not able to cope financially and administratively with its missionary enterprise.[26]

---

24 Percy T. Magan, "Denominational Debts," *Advent Review and Sabbath Herald*, April 11, 1899, 235–36.

25 *General Conference Bulletin* [hereafter *GC Bulletin*], 1899, 73.

26 The missionary program was being stifled because decisions which should have been made by "those on the ground" had to be referred to Battle Creek. See W. A. Spicer to A. G. Daniells, October 5, 1893, Record Group 9, A. G. Daniells Folder 2, General Conference Archives, Silver Spring, Maryland; A. G. Daniells to E. H. Gates, May 23, 1901, Record Group 11, Letter Book 23, General Conference Archives, Silver Spring, Maryland. In his letter to D. A. Robinson, White focused on the dilemma caused by centralization. In reference to a "pioneer to a new mission field," he said: "If he consults with the Board in everything he will be forced sometimes to vary from instruction. If he does not consult them he will get the credit of moving independently. Whichever way he does, he will wish he had done the other." In a letter to Percy Magan, W. C. White said that "mother has been cautioned not to give sanction to any arrangement in connection with

Arthur Daniells realized that such a situation confronted the church as he visited Africa and Europe on his way from Australia to the 1901 General Conference session. In August 1900, while in Europe, he wrote to W. C. White that

> "My heart is filled with interest that I cannot express in behalf of these foreign fields, and I sincerely hope that the next session of the General Conference will rise to the high and important position it should take in behalf of these countries ... I see much to encourage us, and some things that need careful management in the way of reorganization ... In all these places I have secured all the details I can regarding the work, the same as I did in Africa, and shall arrange these data for future use if needed."[27]

Change was needed not only to accommodate the growth of the past but also to facilitate growth in the future.

The Changes that Reorganization Brought to the Organizational Structures of the Church

For all of these and perhaps other additional reasons, the 1901 General Conference session saw a major reorganization of the administrative structures of the Church. The impetus for change continued at the 1903 General Conference session. The changes that were made at those sessions were based on the principles of organization that were established at the denomination's founding from 1861 to 1863. By 1901 it was recognized that those principles needed to be updated and applied in the contemporary context. Ellen White was particularly pointed in her endorsement of change. On the day before the official opening of the 1901 General Conference session she declared, "God wants a change ... right here ... right now."[28] The following day, when reiterating the concerns which she

---

this [missionary] enterprise by which one class of men or of institutions shall lay binding restrictions upon another class of men or institutions; that His servants in one part of the world should not dictate to or lay restrictions upon His servants in another part of the great harvest field" (W. C. White to Percy T. Magan, March 8, 1900, Letter Book 15, Ellen G. White Estate Office.

27 A. G. Daniells to W. C. White, August 23, 1900, Incoming Files, Ellen G. White Estate Office.

28 "Talk of Mrs E. G. White, before Representative Brethren, In the College Library, April 1, 1901, 2:30 P.M.," MS 43a, 1901 (emphasis supplied). This manuscript together with MS 43, an edited edition of Ellen White's speech is available in the Ellen G. White Estate Office. The author

had communicated on the previous day, she added: "according to the light that has been given me—*and just how it is to be accomplished I cannot say*—greater strength must be brought into the managing force of the Conference."[29] She called for change and flexibility. She left it to the assembled delegates to determine just how that change would be accomplished and what organizational structures would be put in place.

The principal changes that were made in from 1901 to 1903 were:

1. The formation of union conferences as the constituent bodies of the General Conference;

2. The decentralization of much decision-making from the General Conference administration to union conference executive committees;

3. The consolidation of departments of the General Conference and the dissolution of independent incorporated entities that had been operating departments and some institutions;

4. The title of the chief officer of the General Conference was to be "Chairman of the Board" rather than "President. At the 1903 General Conference session the title "President" was reinstated.

The Development of Mission as the Major Impetus for Reorganization

At the time of organization in 1863, mission was a relatively insignificant reason among many given for forming an organized church. But by the time of reorganization in 1901, mission was the preeminent reason for organization. It is abundantly clear that when it came to the need for organization, A. G. Daniells and his associates began with the certainty and imminence of the return of Jesus Christ. The imminence of the second coming of Christ determined the urgency of the mission.

For those allied with Daniells, ecclesiology was more a function of their eschatological and missiological perceptions. The church existed because it had been commissioned to perform a specific task. That task was missionary in nature. The missionary nature of the church was the

---

commends a thorough and careful reading of these manuscripts.

29 *General Conference Bulletin*, 1901, 25 (emphasis supplied). Bulletins which report on General Conference sessions are available at the Ellen G. White Research Centre at Avondale College.

theological perspective that informed the need for and shape of the structures of the church. Writing to W. C. White in 1903, Daniells stated that "the vital object for which Seventh-day Adventists have been raised up is to prepare the world for the Coming Christ; the chief means for doing this work is the preaching of the present truth, or the third angel's message of Rev. 14:6–12."[30]

Because the need for organization arose from a perception of eschatological and missiological necessity, there was no doubt among those who held this view that the structure which they erected was biblically based. They understood that the New Testament affirmed that Christ was returning and that the transmission of the gospel to the world was the primary precondition for his return. With a consciousness of divine providence, they understood that Seventh-day Adventists had been specifically chosen within a precise time reference in order to herald the "everlasting gospel" to all the world. It was a conviction born of commitment to the necessity of a biblical foundation for their faith and practice, including their organizational practice. Daniells reflected the conviction of the denomination when, in 1906, he confidently declared that

> The doctrines we hold not only created our denomination, but our denominational aim, purpose, or *policy*, as well. *This denominational purpose or policy is formed by our view of what the Bible teaches*. It is peculiar to our denomination. It differs from the policies of other denominations and organizations as widely as our doctrinal views differ from theirs.[31]

Some years later, W. A. Spicer was even more emphatic than Daniells. Challenging the church to take up the "world-wide proclamation of the everlasting gospel and the finishing of the work," he contended that "every principle in the organization of our work ... is found in the Word of God." Clarence Crisler who was the private secretary of Ellen White from 1901 until 1915, began the foreword to a pamphlet that he wrote the year before her death by categorically stating that "the underlying principles of the organization of the Seventh-day Adventist denomination ... may be traced in the records of the New Testament." Both Spicer and Crisler were careful to say

---

30 A. G. Daniells to W. C. White, May 17, 1903, Incoming Files, Ellen G. White Estate Office.

31 A. G. Daniells, "A Statement Concerning Our Present Situation—No. 3," *Advent Review and Sabbath Herald*, February 22, 1906, 6 (emphasis supplied).

that it was "principles" and not "forms" that were to be found in the New Testament.[32]

Reorganization was undertaken in the first place not because the end was coming, but because there was a "work" to do before the end could come. Reorganization, or for that matter organization, could not be substantiated on the basis of the return of Christ alone. Those who insisted that organizational form be determined only by the imminence of the return of Christ had, in the history of Adventism, often denied the necessity of any form of organization at all. It was the mission policy of the church that in 1905 was described as "the most important feature of our denominational policy," and it was the urgency associated with that mission that was more the precipitating factor in reorganization than the imminence of the Christ's return.[33]

The Principles Undergirding the Formation of Union Conferences

At the 1901 General Conference session there were two opposing viewpoints with respect to the reasons for and the shape of reorganization. Alonzo T. Jones and his associates derived their principles of organization more from their individualistic understanding of soteriology and their ecclesiological emphasis. Arthur G. Daniells and his associates derived their principles of organization more from their evaluation of the pragmatic situation of the church with respect to the fulfilment of its missionary task. Having just returned from extended periods of foreign missionary service, Daniells, W. A. Spicer, Ellen G. White, and William. C. White were keenly aware of the inadequacy of the existing administrative structure to cope with the needs of the church's global missionary enterprise. Their focus was on the reorganization of the administrative

---

32 W. A. Spicer, "Divine Warnings against Disorganization," *Advent Review and Sabbath Herald*, September 14, 1916, 4; C. C. Crisler, *The Value of Organization: An Historical Study*, (n.p.), 3. See also S. N. Haskell, "Organization—No. 18," *Advent Review and Sabbath Herald*, May 16, 1907, 4; A. G. Daniells, "Organization as Developed by Our Pioneers," *Advent Review and Sabbath Herald*, February 21, 1918, 5; and J. L. McElhany, "Principles of Conference Administration," *Ministry*, March 1938, 5.

33 A. G. Daniells, "The President's Address: A Review and an Outlook—Suggestions for Conference Action," *Advent Review and Sabbath Herald*, May 11, 1905, 8.

structures of the church so that they could be an instrument rather than an inhibitor of mission.

The development of the missionary focus of the church in the years since 1863 certainly did not diminish the need for structures. Daniells contended that the principles which governed the choice of organizational structures should be those which supported the maintenance of the structures, not those which tended to destroy them. In retrospect, he pointed out that the principles which guided the church in its reorganization could not be permitted to lead the church towards disorganization or the abandonment of those "general principles" which in the 1860s had transformed a scattered group of "believers" into a viable denomination.[34]

Daniells would later list the advantages of reorganization and attempts would be made to systematize the theological rationale for reorganization.[35] However, despite repeated reference to "principles," again, no systematic treatment that could be used as a basis for decision-making was forthcoming. Without a systematic ecclesiology, there was really no substantial basis upon which the church could build its principles of organization.

Those principles which can be derived from extant records and which appear to have most strongly influenced reorganization and the formation of unions were as follows:

1. *Decentralization*

For Daniells and his associates decentralization as a principle of reorganization was paramount. In 1902, reflecting with the General Conference committee on what had been accomplished in 1901, Daniells affirmed that "the guiding principle [of reorganization] had been the decentralization of authority by the distribution of responsibility." He added that the application of that principle had led "to the organization of union conferences," and representation "on all operating committees" of the "four features of our work—the

---

34 A. G. Daniells, "A Statement of Facts Concerning Our Present Situation—No. 9," *Advent Review and Sabbath Herald*, April 5. 1906, 6.

35 At the 1903 General Conference session Daniells made reference to some of the "features" of the "work" which were the result of reorganization. See A. G. Daniells, "Some Beneficial Features of Our Organization," *Advent Review and Sabbath Herald,* March 14, 1918, 6.

evangelical, medical, educational, and publishing interests."[36]

At the 1903 General Conference session, while explaining his understanding of the sentence from Ellen White's 1896 letter that had been used by Jones, Waggoner, and Prescott in an attempt to do away with the presidency of the General Conference, Daniells stated that in his view, Ellen White was saying that the leaders of the church needed to "decentralize responsibilities and details and place them in the hands of a larger number of men."[37] In this sentence he was using the term "decentralize" in the sense of the verb "to delegate." He understood Ellen White to be discussing the need for responsibility to be delegated to several persons rather than being concentrated in just one person—the president of the General Conference.

One of Daniells' favorite expressions (one that he had taken from Ellen White), was that those "on the ground" should bear the burden of administration and have the prerogative of decision-making.[38]

---

36 General Conference of Seventh-day Adventists, Minutes of Meetings of the General Conference Committee, 13 November 1902, 2:30 P.M., Record Group 1, General Conference Archives, Silver Spring, Maryland.

37 "Original Reports and Stenographically Reported Discussions Thereof Had at the Thirty-Fourth Biennial Session of the Seventh-day Adventist General Conference, April 19, 1901," Record Group 0, General Conference Archives, Silver Spring, Maryland, 75.

38 Ellen G. White to A. O. Tait, August 27, 1896, Letter 100, 1896, Ellen White Estate; A. G. Daniells to W. T. Knox, May 21, 1901, Record Group 11, Letter Book 23, General Conference Archives, Silver Spring, Maryland; A. G. Daniells to E. H. Gates, May 23, 1901, Record Group 11, Letter Book 23, General Conference Archives, Silver Spring, Maryland; A. G. Daniells to Edith R. Graham, May 24, 1901, Record Group 11, Letter Book 23, General Conference Archives, Silver Spring, Maryland; A. G. Daniells to W. C. White, June 19, 1901, Record Group 11, Letter Book 23, General Conference Archives, Silver Spring, Maryland; A. G. Daniells to Members of the General Conference Committee, August 2, 1901, Record Group 11, Letter Book 24, General Conference Archives, Silver Spring, Maryland. In 1895 Ellen White had used the phrase in a testimony to ministers. She said: "Be sure that God has not laid upon those who remain away from these foreign fields of labor, the burden of criticizing the ones on the ground where the work is being done. Those who are not on the ground know nothing about the necessities of the situation, and if they cannot say anything to help those who are on the ground, let them not hinder but show their wisdom by the eloquence of silence, and attend to the work that is close at hand ... Let the Lord work with the men who are on the ground, and let those who are not on

He saw the implementation of the union structure as the manner in which administrative responsibility was being delegated to those "on the ground." The union administrators were, for Daniells, those "on the ground."³⁹

Under Daniells' leadership the commitment to the principle of decentralization was never revoked. Decentralization continued to be considered as a vital principle which governed the reorganization of the church. However, the confrontation and polemics over organizational issues that began in mid-1902 and continued for the next seven years (until Jones was removed from church membership in 1909), caused a renewal of emphasis on the need for unity in the church. That desire for unity on the part of the administration of the church meant that the structures of the church became more an instrument of the centralization of authority than an instrument of delegation and decentralization of authority. Jones claimed that just such a tendency was built into the very structures themselves. Such was not necessarily the case, but circumstances and the disposition of the leaders themselves did indeed influence just what emphasis was evident in practice.

2. Unity and Diversity

When Daniells discussed the principles which were to govern the reorganization of the church at the 1901 General Conference session and described the benefits which would accrue from the implementation of the union conference plan, he did not particularly mention unity. Certainly Ellen White had done so in the College Library Address and certainly the principle of unity had always been a top priority for Seventh-day Adventists and would continue to be so, but for both Ellen White and A. G. Daniells the immediate priorities were elsewhere. In his single, most significant explanation of the operation of the Australasian Union Conference and its application to the world church, Daniells discussed the simplification of machinery for transacting business, the need to place laborers [administrators] in the field in personal contact with the people, the advantage of having general boards in the field, the necessity of having a general

---

the ground walk humbly with God lest they get out of their place and lose their bearings" (Ellen G. White, *Special Instruction to Ministers and Workers* [Battle Creek, MI: Review and Herald, 1895], 33.

39 A. G. Daniells to H. W. Cottrell, June 17, 1901, Record Group 11, Letter Book 23, General Conference Archives, Silver Spring, Maryland.

organization which did not concern itself primarily with affairs in the United States, the General Conference as a "*world's* General Conference," and the necessity for the boards of institutions and the committees of union conferences to be composed of persons familiar with their geographical areas of administration.[40] But he did not even mention the need for unity.

At the second meeting of the General Conference session in 1903, however, Daniells did include unity among the list of advantages and benefits that were realized by reorganization. Having pointed out that reorganization had resulted in a distribution of responsibility and that "work in all parts of the world" was to be dealt with by those who were "on the ground," and that the "details" were to be "worked out" by them; he summarized: "in short, the plan recognizes one message, one body of people, and one general organization."[41]

By 1903, even though decentralization was still vital, it was now a form of a decentralization which was carried out only along "prescribed lines." In some respects, particularly in the organization of departments of the General Conference, there was more centralization than decentralization. Apparently some were concerned that things were going back to what had occurred during the years leading up to reorganization.[42]

Ellen White sensed the danger of slipping backwards and placing inordinate stress on the oneness of the organization. Her concern was that such a position would result in the need to centralize authority, resulting in organizational uniformity. Specifically with reference to the publishing concerns of the church, she said: "No man's intelligence is to become such a controlling power that one man will have kingly authority in Battle Creek or in any other place. In no line of work is any one man to have power to turn the wheel. God forbids."[43]

She was particularly outspoken regarding failure to implement principles that had been introduced in 1901. Writing to Judge Arthur in January 1903, she maintained that as the delegates who had been

---

40 *GC Bulletin*, 1901, 228–29.

41 *GC Bulletin*, 1903, 17–21.

42 See "Original Reports and Stenographically Reported Discussions Thereof Had at the Thirty-Fourth Biennial Session of the Seventh-day Adventist General Conference, 9 April 1903, Record Group 0, General Conference Archives, Silver Spring, Maryland, 20-20a.

43 Ellen G. White, "Principles for the Guidance of Men in Positions of Responsibility," Manuscript 140, 1902, Ellen G. White Estate Office.

in attendance at the session returned to their homes, they carried with them into "their work the wrong principles that had been prevailing in the work at Battle Creek."[44]

The context does not indicate exactly what "principles" were being discussed. Although structural changes of which she approved had been made in 1901, apparently the new structures could be abused with the same result as the former structures. Thus Ellen White once again found it necessary to reprove the leaders of the church and its departments because of the tendency to gather power about themselves. Whenever the need to promote unity was prioritized to the extent that it disrupted the maintenance of equilibrium between the principles of unity and diversity, and diversity was not taken into consideration as it should have been, centralization was the result.

During the 1890s both unity and diversity had negative and positive aspects as far as the mission of the church was concerned. Diversity was positive when it enhanced the potential of the church to reach diverse "nations, tongues, and peoples," and led to decentralization of decision-making. It was negative when it caused chaos and confusion, such as was the case with the multiplication of auxiliary organizations. Unity was positive when it bound the church into oneness in Christ. It was negative when it was interpreted to require uniformity and unnecessary centralization of authority.

Unity was necessary in order to encompass the dimensions of the mission of the church. There was no way for the Seventh-day Adventist Church with its emphasis on world-wide evangelization to succeed in that task unless there was unity of purpose, belief, and action. Unity of action required administrative co-ordination that could best facilitate strategic initiatives on a global scale. Further, the functional ecclesiological self-image that was characteristic of the church permitted a centralized administration that could co-ordinate and facilitate the mission of the church. It cannot be denied that, given the church's theological and pragmatic priorities, some centralization was necessary and legitimate. But in 1901 the principle of diversity was more determinative than the principle of unity in the establishment of an additional level of administration, and by delegating some functions which had previously been performed by the General Conference to union conferences. The emphasis was

---

44 Ellen G. White to Judge Jesse Arthur, January 14, 1903, Letter 17, 1903, Ellen G. White Estate Office.

on the need to recognize diversity by decentralization. Past growth had made the recognition of diversity necessary, but projected future growth made provision for diversity imperative.

3. Participation/Representation

a. Local Conference Participation

Daniells made a concerted effort to carry his emphasis on diversity and decentralization not only into union conferences but also into the local-conference setting. Soon after the 1901 General Conference session, he began to promote broad-based participation in the decision-making process by encouraging the state conferences to permit all state church-members to participate at their respective state sessions as delegates. Daniells' innovation in this respect was a departure from the system of permitting only duly appointed delegates to vote at the session.

Daniells' idea of representation was that any and every person who was in attendance at a local conference session and a member in that conference should be a delegate to the session. He strongly advocated a participatory election process for local conferences at most of the local conference sessions that he attended in 1901, at the Lake Union Conference session (of which he was president), and at the European Union Conference in 1902. In Europe he stated his concept as a principle. He said:

> As to representation, nobody can represent anybody except himself. All should be the Lord's representatives; but nobody can represent some other person, or a church. A church is "fully represented" in a Conference when all its members are present; but nobody can delegate his mind or his conscience to another. If a person is present at any meeting, he does not want somebody else to speak for him.[45]

It was also reported that while he did not presume "to dictate to any how they should do, he gave it as his conviction that just as in any church meeting all the members present are entitled to speak, so in any Conference all the members present are properly delegates." He added that his plan had "been adopted in quite a number of Conferences in America."[46]

---

45 *Bulletin of the European Union Conference Held in London, May 15-25, 1902,* [Hereafter *European Conference Bulletin*], 2.

46 *European Conference Bulletin,* 2.

Daniells was questioned at length concerning his proposal. Apparently quite a few of the delegates had either read Loughborough's article or were familiar with the early history of the development of the organizational structure of the church and saw pragmatic difficulties with the plan. They were concerned that such a plan could give one district an undue proportional influence and control. Daniells rebuffed such a suggestion on the basis that all were Christians; the implication being that no one member or group of members would exercise arbitrary or political power over others. Daniells countered even further. Given his commitment to mission, he assured the delegates that the principle of numerical representation could not be a satisfactory principle because if it were strictly followed from the local conferences right through to the General Conference, it "would leave the heathen lands wholly unprovided for, and was thus opposed to missionary effort." Each member was to "consider himself as representative of the world, and not merely of his particular locality."[47] He was somewhat inconsistent in his reasoning, however. He was not promoting participatory representation as a principle to be adopted at all levels of church administration. He was only concerned for its adaptation to local conference governance, and, to some extent, to union conferences. At General Conference level, Daniells' ideas of representation, especially with reference to overseas fields, were not at all participatory, nor were they even particularly representative.

b. Union Conference Representation

At the union level of administration, the concept of representation changed from broad-based participation by the people to unilateral representation of the departments and the institutions in the union. The same situation applied at the General Conference. In 1901 Daniells allowed the proposal that the executive committee elect its own chairman because he, along with W. C. White, considered the committee to be a "thoroughly representative one."[48] But the committee selected in 1901 comprised representatives of departments and institutions, with only the union presidents as representatives of "the people" who were supposed to be the authority base in the church. The union presidents were outnumbered seventeen to eight and could very easily be outvoted. Further, as chairmen or executive

---

47 *European Conference Bulletin*, 2.
48 *GC Bulletin*, 1901, 206.

board members of the institutions within their own unions, union presidents were more often focused on institutional concerns than on the concerns of the local churches and the church members. They were, therefore, more likely to be sympathetic to institutional problems and needs than to the needs and concerns of the church at large. The composition of the committee inevitably led to a focus on institutional concerns. In this respect Seventh-day Adventist mission methodology was in accord with that of most mission agencies which depended to a large degree on the establishment of institutions.

c. *International Representation*

The situation with regard to representation of the world-wide constituency of the church was even more troublesome. As the composition of the General Conference executive committee was being discussed in 1901, G. G. Rupert asked if there was any provision for the "different nationalities among us" being represented on the committee. Prescott answered him by quoting Gal 3:28 and assuring the delegates that such was not necessary because "ye are all one in Christ Jesus." The outcome was that the safest course was chosen—only North Americans were elected to the executive committee. But that is not to say that there was no commitment to the principle of representation. Representation was understood as being compatible with the higher principle of decentralization. The church and its members were very much in the mind of Daniells both at the General Conference session in 1901 and in the year that followed. Though he was conscious "more and more" of the "influence and power" that the General Conference had, he was anxious to use that power "rightly" and get into "sympathetic touch" with the "rank and file" of the church constituency. He censured conference officers for failing to consult their constituencies when decisions of importance were to be made. In 1901 he had wanted administration and government in the Seventh-day Adventist Church to be "of the people, by the people, and for the people."[49]

---

49 A. G. Daniells to E. A. Sutherland, December 20, 1901, Record Group 11, Letter Book 25, General Conference Archives, Silver Spring, Maryland; A. G. Daniells to W. C. White, June 18, 1901, Incoming Files, Ellen G. White Estate Office; A. G. Daniells to N. P. Nelson, July 17, 1901, Record Group 11, Letter Book 24, General Conference Archives, Silver Spring, Maryland.

4. Decision by Consensus

Along with his regard for the prerogatives of the members of the church and his desire to implement a participatory decision making process at local conference level, Daniells advocated decision-making by consensus rather than by majority vote in 1901 and 1902. In contrast to his concept of participation which was promoted only on the state conference level, he advocated consensual decision-making at every level of administration. Daniells told E. R. Palmer, his associate and confidant in Australia, that at the 1901 General Conference session no measure "received unkind treatment." Some of the proposals advanced were "amended" and a few "dropped out," but it had all been done by "common consent," not by "majority vote." Daniells declared that he had never seen "anything like it."[50]

One may wonder just what Daniells had in mind when he advocated the concept of consensual decision-making.[51] Whatever was the case, his attitude changed rapidly, again as a consequence of the confrontation with Kellogg, so that by the General Conference Session of 1903, vital decisions were being made on the strength of majority vote.[52]

---

50 A. G. Daniells to E. R. Palmer, May 3, 1901, Record Group 9, A. G. Daniells Folder 6, General Conference Archives, Silver Spring, Maryland.

51 Just before his death in 1932, R. A. Underwood made some terse observations with regard to James White's concept of consensual decision-making. He said: "Elder James White was what men would call a shrewd leader—He understood the effect of being united—and one of his diplomatic moves was this in all the questions that secured a majority vote in the General Conference or district or otherwise whatever carried by a majority of even a few votes—he got the delegates to agree that it should be reported unanimous—and no opposition was referred to in the report" (R. A. Underwood to L. E. Froom, December 8, 1930, Record Group 58, 1920s–1930s Interpretation Development of Folder, General Conference Archives, Silver Spring, Maryland). Underwood's punctuation was not precise and his memory was not acute—districts were not introduced into the administrative structure until eight years after the death of James White. However, one wonders how much correlation there was between the practice of White (as recalled by Underwood) to seek unanimity for the sake of the report, and that of Daniells who was not in the "habit of calling for the opposition vote to any measure" (*European Conference Bulletin*, 3).

52 In the reply to Jones in 1906, it was pointed out that the decision to adopt the new constitution at the 1903 General Conference session was made

The church had some adjustments to make in the years immediately after 1901. Some of the plans that were made and the methods that were followed were not wise. Daniells himself admitted that himself. However, the shift from emphasis on participatory representation and decision-making by consensus to emphasis on more-structured representation and majority-vote decision-making after the clash with Kellogg and the extended polemical arguments with those opposed to the church structure was indicative of a shift from emphasis on the need for diversity (or decentralization) to emphasis on preservation of unity.

5. *Constituent Authority*

In 1901 Daniells intended that the General Conference executive committee should be advisory, not executive. In regard to the plan of organizing unions, he hoped that the General Conference and the Mission Board (which had been integrated into the General Conference executive committee), would "ultimately ... [be] quite free from perplexing details." He was convinced that the new plan of organization would enable the committees "to take the position of general advisory boards."[53] Two weeks later he wrote to the members of the General Conference Committee:

> We are glad that the details in the various Union Conferences are being so fully taken over by those who are on the ground ... Our hope is that we shall be left almost entirely free to study the large questions of policy affecting the entire field, and to devote our energies to fostering the work in the weak parts of the field, and also the great mission fields in the regions beyond. Thus the general machinery is being reduced to a few simple parts.[54]

---

by majority vote. In fact, all the decisions made at the General Conference session in 1903 were adopted by majority vote. By that time majority vote was the method being consistently followed, despite Daniells' stated desire to the contrary less than one year earlier. See *A Statement Refuting Charges Made by A. T. Jones Against the Spirit of Prophecy and the Plan of Organization of the Seventh-day Adventist Denomination,*" (Washington D.C.: General Conference Committee, 1906), 28. The statement can be found at http://ellenwhite.org/content/file/statement-refuting-charges-made-t-jones-against-spirit-prophecy-and-plan-organization#document

53 A. G. Daniells to J. J. Wessells, July 15 1901, Record Group 11, Letter Book 24, General Conference Archives, Silver Spring, Maryland.

54 A. G. Daniells to Members of the General Conference Committee,

Even so, some were concerned that too much power was being centralized in the hands of one board. They may have been beginning to question the wisdom of forming departments in the General Conference to replace the auxiliary organizations. Apparently in response, Daniells wrote to Edith Graham, the treasurer of the Australasian Union, that the General Conference executive committee could not possibly be guilty of centralizing because the facts of the matter were that the authority to act was being placed in the hands of "those on the ground." Daniells continued:

> The General Conference Committee does not propose to deal directly with the affairs in any Union Conference. We propose to interest ourselves in the welfare of every Union Conference, in every line of work ... So instead of centralizing our work, we have been distributing it.[55]

Daniells' answer to the centralization of power in the General Conference committee was that the committee was not going to make executive decisions. It was going to be a fostering, advisory, board whose interest was coordination, not supervision. With Ellen White's advice in mind, no doubt, Daniells was concerned that the General Conference committee should not exercise executive control, but that it should do everything in its power to coordinate the administrative functions of the church so as to respect that authority resident in the church membership. With the reforms that were suggested and implemented and with the movement away from centralization of authority, Daniells hailed the events of 1901 as the "beginning of a new era," the beginning of "our last grand march."[56]

By 1903 Daniells was speaking as though he still held the "advisory" concept of the role of the General Conference executive committee. But he was not speaking with the same certainty. At the General Conference session he stated: "As the work is now shaping, the province of the General Conference Committee is of an advisory character to a large extent—not altogether, by any means—and it is

---

August 2, 1901, Record Group 11, Letter Book 24, General Conference Archives, Silver Spring, Maryland.

55 A. G. Daniells to Edith R. Graham, May 24, 1901, Record Group 11, Letter Book 23, General Conference Archives, Silver Spring, Maryland.

56 A. G. Daniells to E. H. Gates, May 23, 1901, Record Group 11, Letter Book 23, General Conference Archives, Silver Spring, Maryland; A. G. Daniells to M. H. Brown, June 17, 1901, Record Group 11, Letter Book 23, General Conference Archives, Silver Spring, Maryland.

of a missionary character or phase."⁵⁷ No longer was the role of the General Conference executive committee merely advisory. A change of attitude had taken place. Notice, however, that no change had taken place with regard to the priority of mission. Any changes in the role of the General Conference executive committee with respect to coordination as set over against control were being made with reference to the missionary focus of the committee and the church.⁵⁸

6. Simplicity

In view of the complication and confusion that had characterized denominational administration in the 1890s, reorganization was perceived as a simplification of the organizational system. In the 1890s Ellen White had advocated simplicity in organization and insisted that the machinery was not to be "a galling yoke."⁵⁹ Therefore, when reorganization was being considered in 1901, simplicity was understood to be an essential principle. The principles of representation and distribution of authority were related to the principle of decentralization. So also was the principle of simplicity.⁶⁰

---

57 *GC Bulletin*, 1903, 100.

58   Francis Wernick has somewhat astutely made reference to Daniells' 1901–1902 concept of the role of the General Conference as an impartial, advisory, fostering board. He observes, however, that since that time, the General Conference has enlarged its role from a coordinating, counselling body to "more of a supervisory role." Wernick advises that "we need to rethink the role of the General Conference." He adds: "We do need a central office to preserve unity, to give coordination, and to give counsel ... Supervision versus coordination needs further study and definition" (Francis W. Wernick, "Philosophy of the Role of the General Conference" [paper prepared for the committee on the role and function of denominational organizations, 1984], Record Group 500, Monographs Series, General Conference Archives, Silver Spring, Maryland). Wernick's agenda is noteworthy: the preservation of unity heads the list of concerns. It has been that way ever since the mid-1902 crisis.

59   *GC Bulletin*, 1893, 22–24; Ellen G. White, "Overbearing Control Reproved," Manuscript 43, 1895, Ellen G. White Estate Office.

60   In early 1902 Daniells said: "I believe that we have thrown away a great amount of money and energy in trying to keep useless machinery running. I find that the less complex we make our work, and the more we center our efforts on the simple straight lines of missionary evangelization, the heartier is the response of the people, and the greater is the manifestation of life in the enterprise" (A. G. Daniells to C. H. Jones, April 21, 1902,

Daniells expressed himself most succinctly on the need for simplicity at the European Union Conference session in 1902. He said: "Organization should be as simple as possible. The nearer we get to the end, the simpler will be the organization. I have no idea that we have got to the limit of simplicity."[61]

In 1903 simplicity was still described as a desirable principle of reorganization. In his "Chairman's Address" Daniells used the integration of the auxiliary organizations into General Conference departments as an example of the application of the principle of simplification.[62] However, it was admitted that in some regards, the machinery was still too complicated. Simplicity was proving to be an elusive quality in organization and it was to remain so. That would continue to be the case especially in those parts of the world where the administrative machinery that may have been necessary in North America or Europe was just "too complicated."[63]

7. Adaptability

The principle of adaptability was, in 1901, almost too obvious to need extended treatment. The very fact that the church was willing to enter into a process of radical reorganization is sufficient to indicate that priority was given to adaptability in organizational structures. Additional adaptations in 1903 indicate that the commitment to adaptability remained. In 1902, in addition to his remarks at the European Union conference regarding simplicity, Daniells insisted,

"We see many things differently from what we did ten years ago, and I expect that we shall see still more. As new light

---

Incoming Files, Ellen G. White Estate Office).

61 *European Conference Bulletin*, 2.

62 *GC Bulletin*, 1903, 18.

63 At the 1903 General Conference session, Daniells quoted Ellen White with reference to the simplification of machinery. He noted that she had declared that in "some parts of the work it is true, the machinery has been made too complicated" ("Original Reports and Stenographically Reported Discussions Thereof Had at the Thirty-Fourth Biennial Session of the Seventh-day Adventist General Conference, 9 April 1903," Record Group 0, General Conference Archives, Silver Spring, Maryland, 75b). Even in 1909 Ellen White found it necessary to stress that "simple organization and church order" were set forth in the New Testament and that the Lord had ordained such for "the unity and perfection of the church" (Ellen G. White to the Leading Ministers in California, December 6, 1909, Letter 178, 1909, Ellen G. White Estate Office).

comes, we ought to advance with it, and not hold rigidly to old forms and old methods. Because a thing is done a certain way in one place is not reason why it should be done in the same way in another place, or even in the same place at the same time."[64]

More attention could be given to Ellen White's attitude to adaptability and the possibility of subsequent structural change.[65] Apart from Ellen White, W. A. Spicer was probably the most vocal advocate of the importance of allowing adaptability in the form that organization took in the Seventh-day Adventist Church. It was Spicer, an experienced missionary, who was responsible as much as anyone for the success of the missionary enterprise of the church in the early years of the twentieth century. With his wide exposure to different cultures and situations, he said repeatedly, *"The details of organization may vary according to conditions and work,* but ever as God has called his church together there has appeared in it the spiritual gift of order and government, the spirit that rules in heaven."[66]

---

64 *European Conference Bulletin*, 2.

65 For example, soon after the General Conference session of 1901, Ellen White wrote to A. G. Daniells, regarding the work among the "colored people" in the South. She admonished Daniells to be flexible in his administration because of the unique needs of the South. The church was not to become "narrow" and confined by "regular lines." Different methods of organization and approach were necessary in culturally diverse situations. For administration to be tied to an inflexible predetermined policy which could not adapt to diverse cultural and sociological needs was, for Ellen White, an abuse of administrative prerogative. See Ellen G. White to A. G. Daniells, Letter 65, June 30, 1901, Ellen G. White Estate Office. The very same day, Ellen White wrote to her son Edson, who was working in the southern part of the United States. Edson was inclined to be too adventurous in his innovations. Whereas Daniells, the administrator, had to be counseled to allow change and innovation in a different socio-cultural milieu, Edson had to be cautioned not to be too hasty. Ellen White wrote: "You need now to be able to think and judge with clear discrimination. Great care must be exercised in making changes which differ from the old-established routine. Changes are to be made, but they are not to be made in such an abrupt manner that you will not carry the people with you. You who are working in the South must labor as if in a foreign country. You must work as pioneers, seeking to save expense in every way possible. And above all, you must study to show yourselves approved unto God" (Ellen G. White to J. Edson White, Letter 62 June 30, 1901, Ellen G. White Estate Office).

66 W. A. Spicer, "The Divine Principle of Organization," *Advent Review*

Insights which may be Instructional for the Contemporary Seventh-day Adventist Church

1. When major discussion is needed and a decision is to be made, it is necessary for people of influence to speak up and participate in the discussion rather than keeping silent.

2. It is possible for leaders to take too much responsibility for decision-making on their own shoulders and not listen to others or give them opportunity to participate in the process.

3. When utilized properly the committee system can be a corrective for centralization. Ellen White declared that "God would not have many minds the shadow of one man's mind," but that "in a multitude of counselors there is safety."[67] Group-think is not to be in evidence in the decisions of the church.

4. The holding of a position of responsibility by any individual does not in itself guarantee the best opinions or the best decisions by that individual.

5. Position does not grant irrevocable power.

6. Financial crisis can be a powerful catalyst for change.

7. A commitment to a global mission which arises from belief in the imminence of Christ's return is the major catalyst for efficient and effective organization. Organization must serve mission, not vice versa.

8. The determining principles of organization are derived more from an evaluation of the pragmatic situation of the church with respect to the fulfilment of its missionary task than from systematic theological considerations. A pragmatism that takes into account biblical teaching and contextual imperative has been the *modus operandi* of the church.

9. Decentralization was the most pervasive principle of reorganization. As a corrective to centralization, as much as possible and practical, decisions are to be made by those "on the ground."

---

and Sabbath Herald, March 25, 1909, 5 (emphasis supplied).
67 Ellen G. White to John Harvey Kellogg, Letter 7, April 26, 1886, Ellen G. White Estate Office.

10. Confrontation and polemics in the church result in emphasis by leaders on the need for unity. In this context the structures of the church become more an instrument of the centralization of authority than an instrument of delegation and decentralization of authority. Circumstances and the disposition of the leaders themselves have considerable bearing on which is evident in practice.

11. No one person is to become such a controlling power that he/she has too much influence on the direction that the church takes on any issue.

12. Both unity and diversity can have negative and positive impacts on the mission of the church. Diversity is positive when its acceptance enhances the potential of the church to reach diverse "nations, tongues, and peoples," and decentralized decision-making is practiced. It is negative when it is taken too far, appropriate organizational boundaries are not respected, and it results in syncretism. Unity is positive when it binds the church into oneness in Christ. It is negative when it is interpreted to require uniformity and unnecessary centralization of authority.

13. Given the church's theological and pragmatic priorities, some centralization is necessary and legitimate. But in 1901 the principle of diversity was more determinative than the principle of unity in the establishment of unions, and by delegating some functions which had previously been performed by the General Conference to union conferences. The emphasis was on the need to recognize diversity by decentralization.

14. In the reforms of 1901, Daniells affirmed that it was not the intention of the General Conference committee to deal directly with the affairs of any Union Conference. Daniells' answer to the centralization of power in the General Conference committee was that the committee was not going to make executive decisions. It was going to be a fostering, advisory, board whose interest was co-ordination, not supervision. By 1903 Daniells was speaking as though he still held the "advisory" concept of the role of the General Conference executive committee. But in practice, no longer was its role merely advisory. A change of attitude had taken place.

Adaptability and flexibility are vital for the fulfilment of the mission of the Seventh-day Adventist Church. Not everything is to be done the same way everywhere. When there is no direct "Thus saith the Lord," the church must be flexible if it is to be true to its reason for existence.

9. General Conference Working Policy: The Challenge of Enforcement and the Opportunity for Development

Lowell C. Cooper
General Conference - Retired

"... policy never matters until it matters, and then it matters a lot."[1]

Introduction

Policy is not often viewed as a glamorous topic for discussion. News, politics, weather, stock markets, and people rank much higher in conversational preference. Policy questions surface when there is tension—and then only out of necessity. The Seventh-day Adventist Church is currently in one of those moments in its collective life as a worldwide community. The Unity 2017 Conference was convened to consider the cross-currents impacting people and denominational units with respect to ministry and leadership positions requiring ministerial ordination. That this should be called a "Unity Conference' was no accident. Throughout the worldwide church the subject of ministerial ordination, and who is eligible for it, awakens sharply differing views and convictions.

The question has been under consideration for more than a century.[2] In recent decades several commissions have studied the

---

1 Marco Rubio, http://www.thedailybeast.com/articles/2013/11/21/marco-rubio-says-he-ll-do-hillary-clinton-s-foreign-policy-but-better.

2 Bert Haloviak, "The Long Road to Mohaven," *The Adventist Woman*, Sept.-Oct. 1993, 1. The first recorded discussion on the matter of women's ordination took place at the 1881 General Conference Session. In more recent times the Northern European Division, in 1968, forwarded a request from the Finland Union to ordain women to the gospel ministry, but there was no follow-up on that request.

matter of ministerial ordination. Reports have been submitted and recommendations have been made to General Conference Sessions. Those sessions have not embraced the idea of ministerial ordination being available to females, even if they have qualifications equivalent to those required of males. These decisions have not settled the matter. Instead they may have amplified it. A rather strong polarity of views persists. Some unions have already implemented inclusive ministerial ordinations (inclusive here meaning male and female). Such actions have added a new dimension, ecclesiastical authority, and considerable emotion to the whole discussion.

The official studies thus far have focused largely on the theology of ordination in the hope that the Bible would provide clarity in the matter. The biblical text has been examined from virtually all angles and viewpoints. Rather esoteric nuances have been advanced in support of one view or the other. Yet, the result of these studies yields at least two strongly-held opinions. Each side feels that there is sufficient evidence to warrant its conclusions. Both sides concede that neither the Bible nor the writings of Ellen White provide explicit instruction regarding the ordination of women as pastors. However, there is rather broad agreement on the theology of ordination.

Relatively less emphasis has been given to ordination policy and practice. If a conclusive answer is elusive in theology, would there be value in considering ecclesiology and its body of policies and practices? In this chapter it is assumed that a review of policy can provide important insights that may help in creating a path to the preservation, even enhancement, of unity in the worldwide church.

This topic will not be addressed in a coldly detached and purely objective manner. The survey and analysis comes from one who is a member of the church, enthusiastic about its mission, protective of its global structure and keenly devoted to its polity and organizational ethos. The author also holds firm convictions about ministerial ordination.

Underlying Premises

Several assumptions underlie this presentation. The first of these is that further theological study on the question of ordination will not result in consensus regarding ordination. The church will have to live with widely divergent views. This does not need to threaten unity since the church already recognizes diverse practices in other matters and has agreed to varying practices regarding the election and ordination of women as local church elders.

A second assumption is that the Gospel message is meant for the whole world and every culture. In its mission to reach every culture with the Gospel, the church will need to engage increasingly with questions of unity and diversity. The process by which such questions are addressed will be as important as any decision that is reached.

Third, it is assumed that unity and diversity are not necessarily conflicting concepts, and they can co-exist in meaningful partnership. Diversity of sound in a choir or orchestra does not ruin the music. Any organization with the size and global presence of the Seventh-day Adventist Church must make room for differing practices even while rigorously protecting its unity.

The fourth undergirding assumption is that policy development is as important as policy enforcement, perhaps more so, in maintaining a sense of organizational unity and relevance in a rapidly changing world with its very diverse social environments.

The Need for Policy

Every organization requires structure and a system of authority to survive and function effectively. History underscores the importance of organizational structure. Though the church is different from other organizations (government, army, business) there is no debate about its need for policy, systems and a pattern of authority. Among the questions that do arise are what role should policy have and how should authority operate in a faith-based community that considers Jesus as its head?

The Bible provides ample evidence of organizational dynamics connected with the work of God in this world. The Old Testament books of Leviticus and Deuteronomy might be thought of as a policy manual for the covenant people of God. There were rules and guidelines for the community's worship as well as for its internal and external relations.

Several passages in the New Testament offer insights on how Church organization, processes and authority should function. Jesus spoke about the authority of his church. He commissioned the church to regard the whole world as its mission field (Matt 28:18–20; see also Acts 1:7–8, Acts 10–11). It was given the keys of the kingdom of heaven and promised that whatever it bound on earth would be recognized in heaven (Matt 16:19; see also Matt 18:18, John 20:23). Jesus also gave direct admonition about how to deal with an erring brother (Matt 18:15–19) which underscores the idea of group decisions rather than a single individual's making decisions concerning the fate of another individual. Jesus also prayed that His followers might demonstrate unity (John 17: 6–26; see also John15:1–17). Nor is such interest in organization and structure limited to the Gospels. The book of Acts reports a council in Jerusalem dealing with the divisive issue of the acceptance of Gentiles into the Church (Acts 15:1–21. In the aftermath of that Council, leaders "delivered decisions reached by the apostles and elders in Jerusalem for the people to obey" (Acts 16:4). Paul's letters also attest to his concern with structure and organization. Undergirding such concerns is the sociological and gender unity achieved "in Christ" (Gal 3:28, 29) with all its ethical implications. Paul urges the Ephesian church to walk in unity (Eph 4:1–16). However, he also advises the church in Corinth to deal decisively with a person whose immoral behavior harmed the whole congregation: " ... hand this man over to Satan" (1 Cor 5:5). Similarly, Titus is urged to deal with divisive persons (Tit 3:10). Clearly, the New Testament Church experienced differences and developed processes for their resolution (Acts 6:1–7; 15:1–21, Galatians 3:26–29, Phil 2:14–18)

It may be safely concluded, then, that policy, system, structure and authority are appropriate elements in the life of an organization committed to living and proclaiming the Gospel. How then should one think about the purpose of policy?

The Purpose of Policy

Policy outlines or describes, and sometimes prescribes, a course of action designed to perpetuate the organization and facilitate accomplishment of its objectives. If the first purpose of policy is to preserve stability of the organization the second purpose is to translate an organization's vision and mission into effective action. This overarching purpose of policy contains several nuances particularly relevant for large organizations. First, policy protects the organization from autocratic and erratic leadership. From time to time leaders forget the servant nature of leadership and are caught up in a mindset that resorts to the use of power for personal purposes. An abundance of anecdotes illustrates the damage inflicted on organizations by leaders who use the organization for self-serving purposes. Eugene Peterson's observation is pertinent: "Because leadership is necessarily an exercise of authority, it easily shifts into an exercise of power. But the minute it does that, it begins to inflict damage on both the leader and the led."[3]

Second, policy protects an organization from merely reactive decision-making. It facilitates systematic planning and the shaping of structure around collective purposes. Policy expresses the collective wisdom of the church for the continued conduct of essential functions through successive changes in leadership.

Third, policy assists an organization in establishing similar patterns of action across a widespread geographic territory. It links separate parts together into a whole that is more than the sum of its parts. Policy thus contributes to an organization's brand and reputation. It enables leaders to address organizational mission and administrative issues in a context larger than their immediate and local setting.

Policy, then, serves to maintain stability, collective focus and integrity—the same ethos and organizational culture throughout all parts of the whole. Because organizational life is dynamic, policy must also be dynamic and responsive to new realities and environments. Policy must always be the servant of organizational identity and mission, otherwise there is a risk of policy becoming irrelevant and an impediment to the organization and its accomplishment of mission.

The Dynamic Relationship between Policy and Organizational Mission

Policy is an instrument to enable and sustain collective energies applied to mission. This does not mean that policy is the basis for mission. Rather, the consideration of mission needs and opportunities gives rise to policy. The articulation of policy generally follows the thoughtful assessment of new opportunities, new developments (internal or external), and new perspectives in mission. The relationship between policy and mission is dynamic and complementary. Very often the circumstances of mission informed the development of policy while in other instances policy facilitated mission. Numerous examples of this can be provided from denominational structure. For example, the development of unions preceded the policy for unions.

---

3 Eugene H Peterson, "Introduction to 2 Corinthians," in *The Message*, (Colorado Springs, CO: NavPress, 1993).

When church leaders began to recognize the added value that union structures brought to organizational supervision and administration they crafted policy to standardize this feature of denominational structure.

In a similar way, the structural re-organization decisions of General Conference sessions in 1901 and 1903 came as a response to developments taking place in various parts of the world as well as the realization that a revised structure would serve the purpose of worldwide mission better. In this re-organization certain aspects of authority were dispersed while other aspects were concentrated.

More recently, the 1973 Annual Council received a report from the Council on the Role of Women in the Seventh-day Adventist Church (also known as the Camp Mohaven report). One of the main questions under consideration was whether women should function in local church offices that required ordination. No policy existed explicitly permitting or prohibiting the ordination of women as elders. As part of its response to the Camp Mohaven Report the Annual Council voted, "That continued study be given to the theological soundness of the election of women to local church offices which require ordination and that division committees exercise discretion in any special cases that may arise until a definitive position is adopted ..." and "That in areas receptive to such action, there be continued recognition of the appropriateness of appointing women to pastoral-evangelistic work, and that the appropriate missionary credentials/licenses be granted them."[4]

Again, the Annual Council of 1987 voted "To record that if world divisions choose to select a term which applies to individuals who carry major responsibilities or who are placed in leadership roles which do not ordinarily lead to ordination as a gospel minister, the division may request the General Conference to approve the establishment of the Commissioned Minister category for denominational workers in its territory."[5]

Another example comes from the 2001 Annual Council which adopted a policy, "Variations in Administrative Relationships." It begins, "For the purpose of fulfilling the mission of the Church,

---

4 1973 Annual Council of the General Conference Committee, October 18, Role of Women in the Church (emphasis supplied).

5 1987 Annual Council of the General Conference Committee, action 326-87G.

division administrations are authorized to recommend modified organizational structures and or administrative relationships..."[6] The policy was adopted after several organizations had already adopted some variations in administrative relationships.

Similarly, a new policy describing Structural Flexibility was approved in 2007.[7] This policy outlined alternative organizational patterns available under special circumstances. The alternative patterns now approved in policy, though few, were already in existence. The realization that such organizational patterns could improve mission outcomes lead to the development of new policy.

At the 2009 General Conference Annual Council a "Roadmap for Mission" was adopted. This document recognized that "in some situations, Seventh-day Adventist mission may include the formation of transitional groups (usually termed Special Affinity Groups) that lead the people from a non-Christian religion into the Seventh-day Adventist Church ..."[8] Though this document is inserted prior to the Working Policy of General Conference Working Policy it functions as if it were policy. The provision for Special Affinity Groups came into being only after years of frontline experience and experimentation regarding mission among the followers of religions other than Christianity.

More broadly, for many decades, the General Conference Annual Council approved a General Conference Wage Scale that was designed to be used worldwide. This is no longer the case. The General Conference Working Policy contains a philosophy of remuneration and a set of guidelines which divisions are expected to follow in establishing their own wage scale, remuneration and benefit structure.

It would be misleading to conclude from the above illustrations that practice always precedes policy or that policy only responds to, rather than facilitates, mission. The resource-sharing policies of the Church (tithes, offerings and international service employees—often described as 'missionaries') were created to advance mission.

---

6 General Conference Working Policy (2016-2017) p. 70, B 10 30 Variations in Administrative Relationships. First appeared in GCWP in 2001 as B 05 35.

7 General Conference Working Policy (2016-2017) p. 51, B 10 27 and B 10 28. First appeared in GCWP in 2007.

8 General Conference Working Policy (2016-2017) p. 59, A 20 15 Fulfilling the Mission, 5.

Perhaps it is best to see 'policy' and 'mission' as having a symbiotic relationship. The relationship is essential and beneficial, although without continued monitoring to adjust policy in response to circumstances encountered in mission the relationship can become less than beneficial. Policy can function as facilitator and controller—but both functions need to be exercised in the interest of mission.

Policy Expressed in Governance and Authority Documents of the Church

Despite the anti-organizational bias of the church's pioneers, the church has developed a broad framework of policy or governance documents. These include the Seventh-day Adventist Fundamental Beliefs, the Church Manual, the General Conference Working Policy (and the corresponding Division Working Policies, and the Constitutions and Bylaws for Conferences and Institutions. These must be examined briefly in turn.

Seventh-day Adventist Fundamental Beliefs: These statements, and their periodic revisions, expressing Seventh-day Adventist beliefs have been approved by the General Conference Session—the highest organizational authority in the Seventh-day Adventist Church. Proposals for additions or amendments to the Fundamental Beliefs must go through a lengthy and rigorous period of study involving the worldwide church before maturing as a recommendation to a General Conference Session.

The Church Manual: The development of the Church Manual represents the first effort of Seventh-day Adventists to codify *policy* for the organization. In the early years of the church, General Conference Sessions met annually and adopted various decisions affecting church order and church life. But these were not necessarily compiled and circulated as policy. The General Conference Session of 1882 reflected a growing realization that effective and harmonious functioning of a growing organization required a common understanding of procedures. Thus it was voted at the Session to have prepared "instructions to church officers, to be printed in the Review and Herald or in tract form."[9] However, the 1883 General Conference Session rejected the idea of creating a permanent form for these articles and instructions.

---

9 "General Conference: Twenty-First Annual Session," *Advent Review and Sabbath Herald*, December 26, 1882, 787.

Although the church resisted the idea of adopting a formal document of instructions (policies), various leaders took the initiative from time to time to assemble in booklet form the generally accepted rules for church life and operation. A notable case is the 184-page book published in 1907 by J N Loughborough entitled *The Church, Its Organization, Order and Discipline*.[10]

The growth of the church worldwide increased the sense of need for a manual to guide pastors and lay-members. In 1931, the General Conference Committee voted to establish a church manual and this was published in 1932. The preface of the first edition stated, "... it has become increasingly evident that a manual on church government is needed to set forth and preserve our denominational practices and polity."[11]

The Church Manual "describes the operation and functions of local churches and their relationship to denominational structures in which they hold membership. The Church Manual also expresses the Church's understanding of Christian life and church governance and discipline based on biblical principles and the authority of duly assembled General Conference Sessions."[12]

As time passed the Church Manual has experienced numerous changes reflecting the need for order in the worldwide work of the church. The 1946 General Conference Session voted that "all changes or revisions of policy that are to be made in the Manual shall be authorized by the General Conference Session."[13] Consequently, a new edition of the Church Manual is published following each General Conference Session. It is essential that the most recent edition of the Church Manual be used when one desires to know current policies and procedures that apply to the local church.

General Conference Working Policy (and corresponding Division Working Policy): While the focus of the Church Manual is on the local church, the General Conference Working Policy applies to the higher administrative structures, their entities and their employees. Working Policy is the compilation of policy decisions adopted by the General

---

10 See *Seventh-day Adventist Church Manual*, 19th Edition, Revised 2015 (Silver Springs, MD: General Conference of Seventh-day Adventists, 2015), 15.
11 *Church Manual*, 16.
12 *Church Manual*, 16.
13 General Conference Report, No. 8, p. 197 (June 14, 1946).

Conference Executive Committee. The first compilation of General Conference working policies was published in 1926 and contained a digest of decisions by the General Conference Executive Committee and General Conference Sessions.

In connection with the ongoing debate about ministerial ordination there have been some voices claiming that the General Conference Session has no role or right in making policy decisions. These voices assert that the General Conference Session has delegated policy-making authority to the General Conference Executive Committee and thus the Session must refrain from determining any matters of policy. While the assertion concerning delegation of responsibility is true,[14] this does not mean that the General Conference Session is thereby deprived of any right to make or influence policy decisions. The General Conference Session is regarded as the highest authority in the Church. It is therefore contrary to reason to claim that the authority of the General Conference Executive Committee supersedes or can thwart the authority of a General Conference Session.

Accordingly, the first publication of General Conference Working Policy included decisions made by the General Conference Session. Subsequent iterations of the publication have reflected directly or indirectly the decisions of a General Conference Session as well as those of the General Conference Executive Committee.[15]

In practical terms, General Conference Working Policy represents a collective decision-making process. It is the "family code of conduct." Policy is the result of the collective pursuit for unity, not the cause of it.

Policy-making must be a continuing exercise in a growing organization and in the rapidly changing/diversifying environments in which the Church carries on its work. When tension exists on the interpretation or application of policy the family must come together to forge new understandings of mission-sensitive policies.

---

14 See General Conference Bylaws, Article XIII, General Conference Executive Committee.

15 See for example General Conference Working Policy (2016-2017), D 05 "The 54th General Conference Session, in its consideration of the Role and Function of Denominational Organizations, pointed out that the constitutions, bylaws and operating policies of all denominational organizations should be consistent with the Seventh-day Adventist concept of the church, its organization, and governance.

Constitution and Bylaws (for conferences and institutions) and Operating Policy (for units with 'mission' status): These are documents adopted by organizational units that are based upon model documents in General Conference Working Policy and which define an entity's purpose and its relationship to other parts of denominational structure. In addition, the operational procedures outlined are designed to ensure that leadership is accountable to a constituency session.

These four internally-developed types of policy documents address the ethos, polity, and administrative or supervisory functions of denominational structure. However, there is yet another governance authority that has not been established by the church and that is the law of the land. It is easy to overlook the authority of government and its relation to church life. Freedom of religion is highly valued by the church and sometimes this idea translates into the perception that government can have no role whatsoever that affects the church.

General Conference Working Policy clearly acknowledges the domain of earthly government:

> In the event laws/changes in the laws governing a country seem to render compliance with denominational policies a violation of the law, the organization shall act in harmony with the law, provided the following:
> a. Counsel has been sought from the General Conference officers (president, secretary, and treasurer/chief financial officer) and it is established that denominational policies do indeed violate the law.
> b. Compliance with the law does not constitute a violation of scriptural principles.[16]

Unfortunately, the church has experienced some painful moments in its relation to local laws. In some instances where compliance with law was not voluntarily met, court decisions have obligated the church to change policies and practices and to repair past errors. It may be helpful to review a situation that developed out of the United States Civil Rights Act of 1964. Title VII of that Act speaks about equal pay for equal work.

It had been a long-standing practice for the church and its institutions to provide different remuneration to men and women. Men, generally classed as 'head of household', would receive a higher salary/wage than women doing the same work. This situation

---

16 Excerpt from General Conference Working Policy (2014-2015) B 15 10 "Adherence to Policy Required".

was challenged by two female employees of Pacific Press Publishing Association in the 1970s.[17] When rebuffed by administration on the request for equal pay the matter escalated to court. The United States Equal Employment Opportunity Commission became involved as a plaintiff against Pacific Press.

Church leaders presented arguments to the court that all employees were, in a sense, ministers; therefore, the matter of remuneration should be an ecclesiastical decision—and thus beyond the reach of government legislation. The court disagreed. One of four cases settled out of court. The plaintiff (Equal Employment Opportunity Commission) prevailed against Pacific Press in the other three. The ripple effects led to substantial changes in remuneration policy.

The Administration of Policy: Compliance, Enforcement, and Development

What is the use of having a policy if there is no way to enforce it? The question sounds very pertinent. Sanctions and penalties for lack of compliance are a normal part of any regulatory environment. The church has a rather comprehensive policy structure as evidenced in the Fundament Beliefs, the Church Manual, General Conference Working Policy, and Constitutions and Bylaws. What about sanctions and penalties? What are the disincentives to non-compliance? The concept of enforcement, though present, is not a prominent part of denominational life. The process of policy creation is designed to involve broad consensus and thus minimize the need for enforcement measures. However, policy is not silent about compliance and enforcement.

A local church has two disciplinary or enforcement options available: placing an individual under censure (intended for remedial purposes), and removing a person from membership. Either one requires a decision of the church family in a formal church business meeting.

With respect to employees, including leaders, employing units must follow the employment laws of the jurisdiction in which they

---

17 The plaintiffs against PPPA were two female employees, Merikay Silver and Lorna Tobler, and the Equal Employment Opportunity Commission. This ten-year long and sad chapter in institutional history offers many lessons about how a religious institution relates to employees, to fairness in policy and to legislation.

operate. Some areas of the world function within an 'employment-at-will' doctrine. This refers to the presumption that employment is for an indefinite period and may be terminated either by the employer or the employee. In other parts of the world the discharge of an employee can be a very difficult and complex matter.

Employees who hold elective office can be removed from office under disciplinary proceedings documented in the employment policies of their unit. Further, the governance model in the Seventh-day Adventist Church stipulates that election to office is not indefinite. Persons may hold office from the time of their election up to the time of the next constituency meeting. Leaders are accountable to a constituency and the prospect of not being re-elected to a subsequent term can be a powerful incentive to appropriate behavior.

The ethos of Seventh-day Adventist members, their relation to the Church, and the relations among denominational entities is so heavily mission-centered and weighted towards collaboration rather that non-compliance that discipline, sanctions and penalties are often viewed as peripheral matters. Policy expects compliance because policy decisions come out of a collective process of deliberation.

There are recognized disciplinary provisions for church members, employees and elected officials. What about organizational units? Policy is rather sparse in this regard. It provides for one disciplinary measure—dissolution or dismissal of an organization from the Seventh-day Adventist family of organizations. There are no intermediate sanctions. Compliance is assumed by virtue of belonging to the family.[18]

---

18 General Conference Working Policy B 10 25 Structural Stability—Local churches, local conferences/ missions/regions/field stations, union conferences/missions, unions of churches, and institutions are, by vote of the appropriate constituency, and by actions of properly authorized executive committees, a part of the worldwide organization of the Seventh-day Adventist Church. Whereas each has accepted the privilege and responsibility of representing the Church in its part of the world, each is therefore required to operate and minister in harmony with the teachings and policies of the Church, and the actions of the world Church in the General Conference Executive Committee or in General Conference Session. While individual units of the Church are given freedom to function in ways appropriate to their role and culture, no part of the worldwide organization of the Church has a unilateral right to secede.

The negative connotations of enforcement measures in an organization based on voluntary participation can be catastrophic. There are other reasons that make policy enforcement a very difficult challenge. One of those reasons is that authority in the Seventh-day Adventist Church is widely dispersed throughout denominational structure. One cannot find a location in denominational structure that has final authority in everything. Final authority, of one type or another, exists at every level of church structure: local church; the executive committees and constituencies of local conference, union, division, the General Conference; and the General Conference in Session. These differing types of final authority are all interdependent. No one unit can exist by itself because it depends for its very existence on the proper functioning of all other units.

Furthermore, when a member unit is accepted into the family it is assumed that the relationship is permanent. There is no periodic review or reaffirmation of membership. Perhaps there is great wisdom in the church's never adopting a schedule of intermediate sanctions for denominational units. The shared authority structure of the church renders policy enforcement decisions against a member unit a double-edged sword. It is not surprising then that the Annual Council 2016 should have such conflicted views about a proposal to exercise enforcement authority. This is uncharted territory and threatens to awaken many unintended consequences.

Policy enforcement is a legitimate tool in organizational structure. How and when it should be employed are very perplexing questions bound to raise sharply differing views. Certainly it would be expected that all other means of resolution/reconciliation would be exhausted first.

Finding a Pathway Forward

The author of this chapter takes the view that policy documents of an organization must always be dynamic. An organization's mission, vision and values may remain unchanged and anchor an entity in turbulent times. Policies are the instruments that enable an organization to pursue its mission in a stated environment. When that environment changes, fixed and immovable policies become redundant and possibly obstructive. It is for this reason that *policy enforcement needs to be balanced with policy development.*

In the remainder of this chapter the question of ministerial ordination from the perspective of policy and practice will be investigated. The Theology of Ordination Study Committee (TOSC) addressed theological considerations about ordination and produced a very helpful Consensus Statement on the Seventh-day Adventist Theology of Ordination.[19] However, TOSC did not address denominational policy and practices in light of the theology of ordination statement.

Several aspects of policy in relation to ordination practice need to be explored:

1. Policy safeguards unity while allowing for diversity.

2. Policy permits ordination of men and women.

3. Policy functions reserved to an ordained minister are not inherently gender-specific.

4. Policy protects against the abuse of privilege granted by ordination.

Policy Safeguards Unity while Allowing for Diversity

From its earliest days, the idea of unity has been a high priority for the Seventh-day Adventist Church. It was a desire for unity that prompted the development of the Church Manual, the General Conference Working Policy and the statement of Fundamental Beliefs. Unity, however, did not require uniformity, as was acknowledged by W. A. Spicer: "The details of organization may vary according to conditions and work, but ever as God has called his church together there has appeared in it the spiritual gift of order and of government, the spirit that rules in heaven."[20]

Policy decisions of the Church have addressed both issues of unity and diversity. The following illustrations reveal the importance of preserving unity as well as recognizing the need for flexibility.

In the interest of ensuring unity the General Conference Executive Committee, April 4, 1995, voted "To approve the proposal that those sections of the Model Constitutions and Operating Policies *that are essential to the unity of the Church worldwide* be printed in bold print, and to request unions, conferences and missions to include

---

19   https://www.adventistarchives.org/consensus-statement-on-a-seventh-day-adventist-theology-of-ordination.pdf

20   W. A. Spicer, "The Divine Principle of Organization," *Review and Herald*, 25 March 1909, 5.

these sections in Constitutions and Bylaws, and Operating Policies as adopted by their organizations."[21]

However, as outlined above, the General Conference Executive Committee has also adopted policies that permit diversity in structure—Special Affinity Groups in A 20 Roadmap for Mission, Structural Flexibility in B 10 27, and Alternatives in Organizational Structure in B 10 28.

Another instance of recognizing the need for diversity comes from an action of the 1984 Annual Council that said, in part, *"To advise each division that it is free to make provision as it may deem necessary for the election and ordination of women as local church elders."*[22]

Also in 1984, the General Conference Committee received and approved a report from the Commission on the Role and Function of Denominational Organizations. The report has a section on Preserving the Unity of Church and Message. Eleven points are listed on how the Church preserves unity. Point 8 provides an important nuance concerning unity:

> Proper decentralization on various levels and within each level, thus making unity and belonging to the whole more desirable and functional by relating working leadership as closely as possible to local circumstances and to a responsible constituency. Remote control easily becomes a source of frustration and division.[23]

Continued theological study on the question of ministerial ordination only confirms the earlier view, expressed in 1990, that there is no "consensus as to whether or not the Scriptures and the writings of Ellen G. White explicitly advocate or deny the ordination of women to pastoral ministry ..."[24] The Session went on to express the reason for its decision:

> "Further, in view of the widespread lack of support for the ordination of women to the gospel ministry in the world church and in view of the possible risk of disunity, dissension, and

---

21 General Conference Executive Committee, Spring Meeting, April 4, 1995, item 189-95Ga (emphasis supplied).

22 1984 Autumn Council of the General Conference Committee, action 274-84GN (emphasis supplied).

23 1984 Autumn Council, action 208-84GN.

24 Fifty-Fifth General Conference Session, 1990, Session Bulletin #7, p. 15.

diversion from the mission of the church, we do not approve ordination of women to the gospel ministry."[25]

The 1990 General Conference Session decision has been rightfully described as a decision against ministerial ordination for women. What is often left out, intentionally or otherwise, is that *the basis of the decision was "the lack of widespread support" and "the possible risk of disunity, dissension, and diversion from the mission of the church ..."* The reason that prompted the decision should indicate that any further discussion of the matter must consider the issues of support and unity/disunity. The church has spent its energies on looking for a theological answer that might ensure unity. That answer has proved elusive. The church must now determine how it will address unity in the presence of continuing theological differences.

This is where policy development comes to the fore. Numerous illustrations have been given above to demonstrate that, while seeking to preserve unity, policy has made room for diversity in structure, in administration, in licensing/credentialing of employees, and in local church leadership (the ordination of women elders). The development of these policies has not been hostile to unity. Instead, unity has been maintained in the presence of growing diversity.

Policy Permits Ordination of Men and Women

The Seventh-day Adventist Church practices ordination for two offices in the local church structure, deacons/deaconesses and elders, and for selected ministers/pastors. Ordination confirms the faith community's recognition of gifts appropriate for spiritual leadership and the faith community's desire for the person to serve in a leadership role requiring ordination. *There is a hierarchy of service roles but not a hierarchy of ordination.* Ordination does not confer new mystical or spiritual power and authority.[26] Both men and women are already being ordained as deacons/deaconesses/elders. So, the question is not one of female eligibility for ordination. It is a question of female eligibility for certain roles. Denominational policy, by General Conference

---

25 Fifty-Fifth General Conference Session (emphasis supplied).

26 Theology of Ordination Study Committee, Consensus Statement on a Seventh-day Adventist Theology of Ordination. The document includes the following statement: "While ordination contributes to Church order, it neither conveys special qualities to the persons ordained nor introduces a kingly hierarchy within the faith community."

Session actions, has already resolved the question of female eligibility for ordination even though the ordination of deaconesses and female elders is not practiced worldwide.

Attention must now be given to female eligibility for office—particularly any office requiring ministerial ordination as currently practiced. The responsibilities of a church elder, male or female, include many of the responsibilities borne by a local church pastor. The *Church Manual* declares:

> "In the absence of a pastor, elders are the spiritual leaders of the church and by precept and example must seek to lead the church into a deeper and fuller Christian experience. Elders should be able to conduct the services of the church and minister in both word and doctrine when the assigned pastor is unavailable."[27]

However, an elder functions only in the local church where he/she has been elected as an elder for the current term. Policy recognizes that a man or woman, ordained as an elder, can perform these local church functions that are also the responsibilities of an ordained pastor.

Kevin Burton, in an unpublished paper, cites relevant information provided by the General Conference in 1906, 1916 and 1926 to the United States Bureau of the Census. The following statement appeared under the information about Seventh-day Adventists: "Membership in the conferences or the ministry is open to both sexes although there are very few female ministers."[28] In the context of the document, "membership" does not refer to church membership but to leadership roles both in administration and in the ministry. It would appear from this that there were no leadership or ministry roles for which women were ineligible.

Functions Reserved to an Ordained Minister are not Inherently Gender-Specific

Certain local-church functions, however, can only be performed by an ordained minister or by a licensed minister who is also elected as an elder and authorized by the employing conference or mission to perform certain roles ordinarily reserved to an ordained minister.[29]

---

27 *Church Manual*, 73.

28 United States Bureau of the Census, Religious Bodies: 1906, vol. 2, 23.

29 Religious Bodies: 2: 33.

The roles reserved for an ordained minister are:

1. Organizing a church,

2. Uniting churches,

3. Presiding over a church business meeting in which the business of the meeting involves a matter of church-member discipline,

4. Ordaining elders and deacons.[30]

In addition, the president of a local mission/conference, union mission/conference, or the General Conference must be an ordained minister.[31] The General Conference Working Policy explicitly states: "Inasmuch as the conference/mission/filed president stands at the head of the gospel ministry in the conference/mission/field and is the chief elder or overseer of all the churches, a conference/mission/field president shall be an ordained minister."[32]

The roles restricted to an ordained minister include none that inherently require male gender. Neither are these activities such that a woman is incapable of performing them. Nor can these restricted actions be performed solely under the ordained minister's individual capacity. Organizing and uniting churches require Local Mission/Conference Executive Committee authorization. Disciplining members requires the participation of the local church membership. Ordaining deacons/deaconesses and elders requires first that they be elected to the respective positions by their local church. All these actions involve a group process rather than independent decision-making.

The only reason for limiting roles 1, 2 and 4 to an ordained pastor is that only an ordained pastor is authorized to conduct the ordination

---

30 Religious Bodies 2: 36, 39, 64, 73.

31 See the respective Model Constitution and Bylaws or Model Operating Policies in General Conference Working Policy. The *Church Manual* indicates only that the conference president should be an ordained pastor of experience (p. 31). No mention is made of this requirement for a Division President since divisions do not operate under a Constitution and Bylaws. Division presidents are elected at a General Conference Session, or by the General Conference Executive Committee between Sessions, and it will be the case that the qualifications for a president at other levels of organization will also be applied to the selection of a division president.

32 General Conference Working Policy (201602017), E 60.

of deacons/deaconesses and elders. Such ordinations may be required in organizing churches or in uniting churches. The restriction on the leadership functions in these matters is not a question of male or female gender. The restriction is that ministerial ordination is required. Since the church now does not approve of ministerial ordination for women it is not permissible for a woman to perform these tasks. It is not a matter of a woman being incapable of such group leadership tasks. The reason is that the Church has not consented to women being eligible for ministerial ordination even though they are eligible for ordination to other offices.

The third activity reserved for an ordained minister ensures that a person of considerable experience, and one who is not elected/appointed by the congregation, leads the meeting. The pastor is thus at least some distance removed from the internal political processes that may be present in a business meeting at which discipline matters will be decided.

The situation is compounded when one brings credentials and licenses into the picture. As early as 1975 the General Conference Executive Committee considered implementing a Commissioned Minister Credential.[33] By 1981 the General Conference Executive Committee was issuing Commissioned Minister Credentials to senior leaders who were not ordained to ministry.[34] However the Commissioned Minister Credential does not appear in General Conference Working Policy until 1992. The North American Division,[35] as early as 1980, adopted a policy for Commissioned Minister Credentials—intended for persons serving in spiritual leadership positions (administrative, departmental, and institutional).

In 1987, the Annual Council voted that "if world divisions choose to select a term which applies to individuals who carry major responsibilities or who are placed in leadership roles which do not ordinarily lead to ordination as a gospel minister, the division may

---

33 General Conference Executive Committee Spring Meeting, April 2, 1975 "VOTED, To refer to the available members of the General Conference Committee, the item concerning Commissioned Ministerial Credentials."

34 General Conference Executive Committee Minutes, January 29, 1981 p. 81-25.

35 The North American Division did not begin functioning as an entity entirely distinct from the General Conference until 1985. Therefore in 1980 its policies reflected the involvement of many General Conference officers.

request the General Conference to approve the establishment of the Commissioned Minister category for denominational workers in its territory."[36]

The 1989 Annual Council approved that *"commissioned ministers or licensed ministers may perform essentially the ministerial functions of an ordained minister of the gospel in the churches to which they are assigned ... "*[37]

The Commissioned Minister License and Credential was made available

> "... to associates in pastoral care; Bible instructors; General Conference, division, union and local conference treasurers and department directors including associate and assistant directors; institutional chaplains; presidents and vice-presidents of major institutions; auditors (General Conference director, associates, area and district directors); and field directors of the Christian Record Services, Inc."[38]

Not all divisions use this policy. However, several divisions have adopted this policy and grant Commissioned Ministerial Credentials to women who serve as pastors/associate pastors in local churches as well as in officer/departmental roles. The anomaly is that women with Commissioned Minister Credentials may perform essentially the ministerial functions of an ordained minister of the gospel in the churches to which they are assigned. The only functions they cannot perform are those identified above. It has been shown that there is no reason, other than the ineligibility for ministerial ordination, for the denial of these roles to women. Except for the ordination of deacons/deaconesses and elders, the roles reserved to an ordained minister are not primary functions in pastoral ministry.

Policy Protects Against the Abuse of Privileges Granted by Ordination

This section is important because some who object to the ordination of women as pastors are under the impression that doing this in one area of the world imposes the practice elsewhere. It must be admitted

---

36   Annual Council Minutes 1987, 326-87G COMMISSIONED MINISTERS—WORLD DIVISIONS.

37   Annual Council Minutes 1989, pages 35 and 36. See also GCWP L 25 on the functions of licensed ministers (emphasis supplied).

38   *General Conference Working Policy* (1993–1994) D 05 10. The listing is essentially the same in GCWP 2016-2017 E 05 10.

that any variation from normal/standard practice may be cited as precedent-setting and used to pressure widespread adoption of similar practices. Such issues are not unique to the subject of ordination policy and must be addressed through normal decision-making processes of the church. The essential message in what follows is that ordination to any office does not constitute license to function independently. The church has instituted safeguards for the privilege of ordination.

Ordination for local church office (deacon/deaconess, elder) authorizes a person to function as such in the local church in which he/she holds membership and has been elected for the current term of service. The fact of being ordained as a deacon/deaconess or church elder does not give a person the authority to function in this office outside of the local church in which membership is held. However, if an ordained deacon/deaconess, or elder transfers membership to another local church he/she may function in the role if elected to do so by that local church. A new ordination is not necessary. "Once ordained, elders need not be ordained again if reelected, or upon election as elders of other churches, provided they have maintained regular membership status. They are also qualified to serve as deacons."[39] In other words, *their ordination is valid worldwide while their functioning in such a role is dependent upon their being members in the local church that elected them to serve the current term.*

Under the heading "Ordained to the World Church", denominational policy describes ministerial ordination in slightly different and possibly confusing terms. "Workers who are ordained to the gospel ministry are set apart to serve the world Church, primarily as pastors and preachers of the Word, and are subject to the direction of the Church in regard to the type of ministry and their place of service."[40]

What does it mean to be ordained to the world church? There have been some ordained ministers who took this to mean that they could go anywhere in the world, present themselves as ordained ministers and perform any ministerial function without any other permission from anyone. Several of these situations have resulted in serious damage to the church in the areas where these ministers traveled. Ordination to the world church does not mean license to go anywhere and do anything one chooses. But it does mean that, like ordination

---

39 *Church Manual*, 73.
40 General Conference Working Policy (2016–2017), L 40 Ordained to the World Church.

for deacons/deaconesses and elders, a minister's ordination is valid worldwide.

The functioning of deacons/deaconesses and elders is controlled by the requirement of election to office in a local church. The functioning of an ordained minister is controlled by the issuance of appropriate credentials by an employing organization. The possession of ministerial credentials indicates that one is employed and therefore accountable to some unit of organization. Ministerial credentials issued by one organization are accepted elsewhere by denominational entities around the world.

Ministerial ordination does not authorize one to travel the world and conduct ministerial functions independently. Credentials are required. The church has apportioned the world territory to the supervision of divisions, unions and local conferences/missions. Christian courtesy demands that someone knocking on another's door should await their invitation before entering their home. A similar mindset needs to prevail in the activities of persons who have been ordained.

A minister who has been ordained but does not have current credentials is not eligible to function as a minister. "Possession of an expired credential or license gives the person no authority whatsoever."[41]

How can Policy Development Resolve the Present Tension over Ordination?

What follows is *an illustration of how policy can be developed* with respect to ministerial ordination. This is only an example. There may be other paths of policy development on this subject that lead the church towards resolution and away from conflict. The objective is to illustrate that policy development can be an effective conflict resolution methodology in the present circumstances.

    1. Discontinue the practice of ordination altogether. Replace the current ordination service practices with a commissioning service for ministers, elders, deacons and deaconesses. Doing this would be fully consistent with the theology of ordination while avoiding the unbiblical connotations that have become attached to the term 'ordination'.

    2. Suspend the issuance of ministerial licenses and credentials. In their place use the Commissioned Minister License and

---

41 *Church Manual*, 35.

Commissioned Minister Credential. Revise policy language concerning the role and authority of individuals holding Commissioned Minister Credentials.

3. Amend gender-specific language in General Conference Working Policy, section L, The Ministry and Ministerial Training

4. Clarify the territorial authorization associated with Commissioned Minister Credentials. Approve the world-wide validity of the commissioning service for deacons, deaconesses, elders and those holding Commissioned Minister Licenses/ Credentials while re-emphasizing the safeguards that protect the world church from individual abuse of privilege.

5. Revise *Church Manual* and *General Conference Working Policy* credential requirements for a local mission/local conference president. In a similar manner, revise the General Conference Constitution and Bylaws, Model Constitutions and Bylaws, and Model Operating Policies to indicate that the president shall be a 'Commissioned minister of experience'.

6. Amend other policies having language that limits ministerial duties to males.

7. Recognize that permission for women to serve without restriction in ministerial roles does not constitute obligation to do so. The normal selection processes for any employee give discretion to the employing unit. The permissive stance for the ordination of women as local church elders can serve as a pattern for the commissioning of women as pastors.

Some Conclusions

This study of policy and its development through time has led to the conclusion that mission-sensitive practice has generally preceded the development of policy. The church should not be surprised if this situation continues. The opportunities of mission in diverse settings will require creativity which may not yet be embraced in policy. Therefore, policy development must be an on-going priority for the church.

Permissive rather than prescriptive policies have enabled the church to address complex situations in the past where differing circumstances required differing practices. Church policy must allow some room for diversity of practice if the church is to function effectively in all the cultures of the world. Diversity that is mission-sensitive need not be a threat to unity.

The gradual development of decisions respecting the role of women in church leadership has been complicated by uncertainty about the meaning of ordination and the culturally accepted roles of women in society. The theology of ordination, though unchanged, has been more effectively communicated. It is apparent that there is no hierarchy of ordination. The ordination of a deacon/deaconess/elder is not qualitatively different in nature from the ordination of a pastor. There is however, a hierarchy of office and the church's decision to include women as elders, to consent to their ordination, to issue to women Commissioned Minister Credentials with authority to perform virtually all functions of an ordained minister has not threatened unity in the church.

Historically, the Seventh-day Adventist Church has demonstrated a preference for policy development rather than policy enforcement. Emergent circumstances have been addressed by allowing for creative initiatives even in advance of policy creation. Continuing this kind of approach offers the best opportunity for the church to maintain its unity and to resolve the tensions that exist over the matter of ministerial ordination.

10. Catholic or Adventist? The Ongoing Struggle Over Authority (and 9.5 Theses)

George R. Knight
Andrews University

On October 31, 1517, Martin Luther nailed his *Ninety-five Theses* to the door of the Castle Church in Wittenberg, Germany. This year the Protestant world is celebrating the 500th anniversary of that event. On May 8 General Conference president Ted Wilson, addressing the faculty of Middle East University, cited Ellen White who predicted that Seventh-day Adventists would carry that Reformation on until the end of time. Beyond that, he quoted 1 Timothy 1:7: "For God has not given us a spirit of fear, but of power and of love and of a sound mind."[1] It is with that good advice in mind that this study of the history of authority in Adventism begins with Luther and his struggle with the Roman Church.

Given the topic of this chapter, many people might expect it to deal with the theme of the development of ecclesiastical authority in Adventism. But the authority of the church in the denomination is put in the context of Adventism's understanding of the authority of the Bible and of Ellen White. Thus the chapter is divided into three parts: Adventism's approach to biblical authority; Ellen White's thoughts on authority; and the development of authoritative structures in the Seventh-day Adventist Church.

Adventism's Historical Approach to Biblical Authority

Seventh-day Adventists have historically viewed their church as a child of the Protestant Reformation. It is therefore crucial to recognize

---
1 "Lebanese University Encouraged to Reach Middle East through Medicine," *Adventist News Network*, May 9, 2017.

that the Reformation was not primarily about indulgences or even justification by faith. At its heart the Reformation was about the issue of authority. "What is new in Luther," Heiko Oberman writes, "is the notion of absolute obedience to the Scriptures against any authorities; be they popes or councils."[2] That thought is evident in Luther's testimony before the Diet of Worms:

> Unless I am convinced by the testimony of the Holy Scriptures or by evident reason—for I can believe neither pope nor councils alone ... I consider myself convicted by the testimony of Holy Scripture, which is my basis; my conscience is captive to the Word of God. Thus I cannot and will not recant, because acting against one's conscience is neither safe nor sound. God help me. Amen.[3]

Ellen White's comments on Luther in *The Great Controversy* are helpful. Luther "... firmly declared that Christians should receive no other doctrines than those which rest on the authority of the Sacred Scriptures. These words struck at the very foundation of papal supremacy. They contained the vital principle of the Reformation."[4] She declared that the Romanists "sought to maintain their power, not by appealing to the Scriptures, but by a resort to threats."[5] She added:

> ... in our time there is a wide departure from their [the Scriptures'] doctrines and precepts, and there is need of a return to the great Protestant principle—the Bible, and the Bible only, as the rule of faith and duty. The same unswerving adherence to the word of God manifested at that crisis of the Reformation is the only hope of reform today.[6]

At this point it is important to remember that Adventism's primary Reformation heritage is not Lutheranism or Calvinism but Anabaptism or the Radical Reformation, which in essence held that the magisterial reformers had not been consistent in their Bible-only approach. For the Anabaptists it was wrong theologically to stop where Luther, Calvin, or Zwingli did. As a result, they moved beyond such teachings as infant baptism and state support of the church and toward the ideals of the New Testament church.

---

2 Heiko A. Oberman, *Luther: Man Between God and the Devil.* (New York: Image Books, 1992), 204.

3 Oberman, *Luther,* 39.

4 Ellen G. White, *The Great Controversy.* (Mountain View, CA: Pacific Press, 1911), 126.

5 White, *Great Controversy,* 161.

6 White, *Great Controversy,* 204, 205.

Perhaps the best representative religious body in the spirit of Anabaptism in nineteenth- century America was the Restorationist movement, for which there was no creed but the Bible itself. Their drive to get back to the Bible set the stage for Adventism. Both Joseph Bates and James White came to Adventism from the Christian Connexion, a branch of Restorationism. For White, "every Christian is ... in duty bound to take the Bible as a perfect rule of faith and duty."[7]

In summary, Adventism at its best in 2017 stands on a firm platform of the Bible only as the rule of faith and practice. One of the unfortunate features of Roman Catholicism and many other Christian movements in history is that when they could not establish their claims from the Bible they were tempted to use threats and force backed up by ecclesiastical authority.

At this point in the discussion of biblical authority two Biblical passages must be examined: the first deals with the Jerusalem Council (Acts 15) and the second with the binding and loosening function of the church (Matt18:18). These passages have become important to this discussion because of the way they have been used in recent documents produced by the General Conference. In those documents a favorite passage is Acts 15. In a document published in September, 2016, it is noted that "what is often called the 'Jerusalem Council' is significant almost as much for its process as for the theological decision that resulted." The decision of the Council "was regarded as binding on churches everywhere." Furthermore, it is declared that "... in sum, the lesson of the Jerusalem Council is that, in the Church, *diversity of practice can be allowed, but only after a representative body has agreed to allow some variation.*"[8] That is an astounding conclusion, since *the lesson from the Jerusalem Council is exactly the opposite.* In Acts 15 the diversity had already been taking place. The Council met and validated that existing diversity, which previously had been blessed by the Holy Spirit.

That reversal of fact is only one problematic aspect of the September 2016 documents' use of Acts 15 when viewed from the

---

7 James White, "The Gifts of the Gospel Church," *Review and Herald,* April 21, 1851, 70.

8 Secretariat, General Conference of SDA, "Summary of *A Study of Church Governance and Unity,*" Sept. 2016, 5; Secretariat, General Conference of SDA, "A Study of Church Governance and Unity," Sept 2016, 13.

perspective of what has actually taken place in recent Adventist history. But before treating that history it will be helpful to examine Ellen White's remarks on the Council. In *Acts of the Apostles* she notes that "it was the voice of the highest authority upon the earth," a descriptor she would later apply to General Conference sessions. Those words are also found in *The Story of Redemption*, where the section on the Council has the editorial title of "The First General Conference." In this section it is noted that the Council was called because the Jews did not believe that God would authorize a change from traditional practices. But she concludes that "God Himself had decided this question by favoring the Gentiles with the Holy Ghost" to demonstrate the need for change. In short, God had given the Spirit to the Gentiles in the same manner that He had to the Jews.[9] Thus unity in diversity was approved.

The point about the Spirit's settling the matter is an interesting one since at the 2015 General Conference session there was no testimony from female pastors regarding how the Holy Spirit had blessed their ministries in the same way as those of males. This was the very type of testimony that had led to breaking the deadlock over accepting Gentiles in Acts 15 (see vv. 8, 9) and had led the Theology of Ordination Study Committee appointed by the General Conference to approve by a strong majority a proposal to allow those divisions that desired to ordain females to do so. In that sense the decision-making process of Acts 15 was not followed.

Another point to note is that at the Jerusalem Council all of the decisions made had a clear biblical base. The same cannot be said of the 2015 General Conference session vote, as will be shown below in the discussion of Adventism's ecclesiological authority.

Several other points should be made in relation to Acts 15. First, Paul later opted not to follow the Council's decision of Acts 15:20, 29 in regard to abstaining from food sacrificed to idols. That is evident from 1 Corinthians 10:23–30.[10] In verses 25 and 27 he claims that it is permissible to eat meat offered to idols if it does not offend anyone, a ruling that goes directly against Acts 15 with its categorical

---

9 Ellen G. White, *The Acts of the Apostles* (Mountain View, CA: Pacific Press, 1911), 196; Ellen G. White, *The Story of Redemption* (Washington, DC: Review and Herald, 1947), 308.

10 Paul also raises the issue in 1 Cor. 8 and most likely in Rom. 14, but 1 Cor. 10 is the most explicit passage on the topic.

prohibition. Paul adds conditions and makes exceptions based on cultural context. What Paul could have done was to announce that the first General Conference in session had passed a universal rule and that he had a copy of the letter to prove it. That would have solved the problem and saved Paul a lot of ink and explanation. In actuality, Paul does not refer to the Acts 15 Council in any of his letters, even though it could have been helpful to him.

A second point that should be noted is that the Seventh-day Adventist Church does not follow the "universal" rulings of Acts 15:29, 20 in that it does not prohibit the eating of blood by requiring flesh-eaters in its midst to eat only kosher meat that has been killed in the proper way so that the blood is drained completely from it. So, like Paul, Adventists have interpreted and discarded aspects of the Council's ruling largely on the basis of cultural considerations.

With those facts in mind, it can be argued that the real lesson to be gained from Acts 15 is one of unity in diversity, with Jewish and Gentile Christians having freedom to follow differing paths because the Holy Spirit fell in the same way on both groups.

Regarding Matthew 18, in the documents produced by the General Conference Secretariat in September 2016 it is claimed that "Seventh-day Adventists believe the authority granted to the Church by Jesus enables Church leaders to make decisions that bind all members." Such leadership decisions, it is stated, are made "at GC Sessions and Annual Councils."[11]

This is an interesting perspective, especially in the light of the Roman Catholic Church's usage of that passage and its parallel in Matthew 16 to teach that whatever the church votes on earth is ratified in heaven. But the Greek in the verse actually says that "whatever you bind on the earth will have been bound in heaven" (cf. NASB). *The Seventh-day Adventist Bible Commentary* is correct when it notes that "even here Heaven's ratification of the decision on earth will take place only if the decision is made in harmony with the principles of Heaven."[12]

The *Commentary*'s remark on the parallel passage in Matthew 16:19 is even clearer. Namely, the binding and loosening function of the church is

---

11 Secretariat, "Summary," 6, cf. 4; Secretariat, "A Study," 12.

12 "Matthew," in. *The Seventh-day Adventist Bible Commentary,* 7 vols., ed. Francis D. Nichol, (Washington, DC: Review and Herald, 1953–1957), 5:448.

... to require or to prohibit whatever Inspiration clearly reveals. But to go beyond this is to substitute human authority for the authority of Christ ... a tendency that Heaven will not tolerate in those who have been appointed to the oversight of the citizens of the kingdom of heaven on earth.[13]

Ellen White makes the same point when she notes that "whatever the church does that is in accordance with the directions given in God's word will be ratified in heaven."[14]

What is most interesting about the repeated use of the verses about binding and loosening in the General Conference's documents is that Matthew 18:18 is quoted consistently but Matthew 16:19 is neglected. That is understandable since in Matthew 16:18, 19 not only is the binding function of the church set forth but the passage also contains Christ's remark about Peter and the rock upon which Christ will build his church and the keys of the kingdom, making it the foundation of Roman Catholic ecclesiology. With that in mind, it is easier to see why in the General Conference's documents Matthew 18:18 is emphasized but the parallel passage is avoided. There is not much to be gained in using Catholicism's favorite passage even if it makes the same essential point. But a fascinating aspect of the use of those verses is that both the Adventists in their recent documents and the Roman Catholics have misread the text in the same manner for similar ends.

One interesting point related to the General Conference's use of Matthew 18 is that, according to Ephesians 4:11, it is not the church that calls pastors but God. All the earthly church can do is bind or ratify God's decision through commissioning or ordaining. That is biblical, as is the laying on of hands in recognition of God's call. What is not biblical is ordination as it is now understood. In fact, the English word "ordination" does not derive from "any Greek word used in the New Testament, but from the Latin *ordinare*."[15] As a result, modern

---

13 *Adventist Bible Commentary,* 5:433.

14 Ellen G. White, *Testimonies for the Church,* 9 vols. (Mountain View, CA: Pacific Press, 1948), 7:263.

15 Russell L. Staples, "A Theological Understanding of Ordination," in Nancy Vyhmeister, ed., *Women in Ministry: Biblical and Historical Perspectives* (Berrien Springs, MI: Andrews University Press, 1998), 139; see also Darius Jankiewicz, "The Problem of Ordination: Lessons from Early Christian History," in Graeme J. Humble and Robert K. McKiver, eds., *South Pacific Perspectives on Ordination: Biblical, Theological and Historical Studies in an Adventist Context* (Cooranbong, NSW: Avondale Academic Press, 2015), 101–129.

translations tend to use such words as "appoint" or "consecrate" where the KJV uses "ordain."[16] *The word "ordination" as Adventists use it is not a biblical teaching but one that finds its roots in the early and early-medieval church.*[17] *From that perspective, the distinction between ordaining and commissioning is a word game of no biblical substance.*

Ellen White's Historical Approach to Authority

At the very heart of Ellen White's understanding of religious authority was the place of the Bible. "The Bible," she wrote, "must be our standard for every doctrine and practice ... We are to receive no one's opinion without comparing it with the Scriptures. Here is divine authority which is supreme in matters of faith. It is the word of the living God that is to decide all controversies."[18] That thought undergirded Ellen White's theology throughout her long ministry.

In regard to her own authority, she (as did the other founders of Adventism) regarded it as derived from the authority of Scripture and subservient to it. She pictured her relation to the Bible as "a lesser light to lead men and women to the greater light."[19]

In many ways the most enlightening episode regarding Ellen White's position on authority took place in relation to the 1888 General Conference session.[20] At that event she had to confront those pushing traditional Adventist perspectives at several levels of human authority. One approach was General Conference president G. I. Butler's self-perception of having "the highest position that our people could impose" and his claim of special rights and responsibilities in settling theological issues in the church. Ellen White made short shrift

---

16 See, e. g., Titus 1:5; Mark 3:14; John 15:16; Acts 1:22; 14:23; 16:4.

17 See White, *Acts of the Apostles*, 161–162.

18 E. G. White to Brethren who shall assemble in General Conference, Aug. 5, 1888.

19 Ellen G. White, *Colporteur Ministry* (Mountain View, CA: Pacific Press, 1953), 125. For more on this topic, see George R. Knight, "Visions and the Word: The Authority of Ellen White in Relation to the Authority of Scripture in the Seventh-day Adventist Movement," in Robert L. Millet, ed., *By What Authority? The Vital Question of Religious Authority in Christianity* (Macon, GA: Mercer University Press, 2010), 144–161.

20 For a fuller treatment of the authority crisis in the events surrounding the 1888 General Conference session, see George R. Knight, *Angry Saints* (Nampa, ID: Pacific Press, 2015), 121–140.

of that approach. Soon after the 1888 meetings she wrote that Butler "thinks his position gives him such power that his voice is infallible." "No man is to be authority for us," she penned.[21]

A second approach she had to deal with was the attempt to use Adventist tradition to solve the biblical issues. She responded to that tactic by writing that "as a people we are certainly in great danger, if we are not constantly guarded, of considering our ideas, because long cherished, to be Bible doctrine and in every point infallible, and measuring everyone by the rule of our interpretation of Bible truth. This is our danger, and this would be the greatest evil that could ever come to us as a people."[22]

A third category of human authority she had to face in the 1888 era was the drive at the Minneapolis session to solve the theological and biblical issues by establishing the denomination's official position through a formal vote of the General Conference in session. As usual, Ellen White had words for the denomination on that topic:

> *The church may pass resolution upon resolution to put down all disagreement of opinions, but we cannot force the mind and will, and thus root out disagreement. These resolutions may conceal the discord, but they cannot quench it and establish perfect agreement. Nothing can perfect unity in the church but the spirit of Christlike forbearance.*[23]

W. C. White expressed his view regarding an official vote to settle the disputed issues by declaring to the Minneapolis delegates that he would feel compelled "to preach what he believed, whatever way the conference decided the question" at hand.[24]

Unrelated to the 1888 event, but intimately connected to the problem of churchly authority, is Ellen White's statement in *The Great Controversy* that "the very beginning of the great apostasy was in seeking to supplement the authority of God by that of the church."[25]

---

21 G. I. Butler to E. G. White, Oct. 1, 1888; E. G. White to Mary White, Nov. 4, 1888; E. G. White to M. H. Healey, Dec. 9, 1888; Cf. E. G. White to G. I. Butler, Oct. 14, 1888.

22 E. G. White, "Light in God's Word," MS 37, 1890; italics supplied.

23 E. G. White, "Love, the need of the Church," MS 24, 1892; italics supplied.

24 Minneapolis *Tribune*, Oct 18, 1888, 5; Minneapolis *Journal,* Oct. 18, 1888, 2.

25 E. G. White, *Great Controversy*, 289–290.

A second major topic related to Ellen White's historic view on authority has to do with the General Conference as God's highest authority on earth. That topic will be treated in the next major section of this chapter, in which ecclesiastical authority in Adventism will be examined.

But before moving to that topic, Ellen White's perspective on ordination must be briefly examined. It was noted earlier that ordination as practiced by the church is not a biblical issue. However, according to Ellen White, it did become an important issue in the history of the early church. In discussing the laying of hands on Paul and Barnabas in Acts 13:3, she writes that God

> instructed the church ... to set them apart publicly to the work of the ministry. Their *ordination was a public recognition of their divine appointment* ... [They] *had already received their commission from God Himself,* and *the ceremony* of the laying on of hands *added no new grace or virtual qualification* ... By it the seal of the church was set upon the work of God ... *At a later date the rite of ordination by the laying on of hands was greatly abused; unwarrantable importance was attached to the act*, as if a power came at once upon those who received such ordination."[26]

In speaking of the same event in another place she says much the same thing, but adds that their ordination by the laying-on of hands "was merely setting the seal of the church upon the work of God—an acknowledged form of designation to an appointed office."[27]

By speaking of abuse of the term "ordination" in the church, Ellen White is undoubtedly referring in part to the sacerdotal approach to the authority of the priesthood conferred by ordination that gave them such power as to transform the bread and wine into the actual body and blood of Christ. But more to the point is the hierarchical power of the higher clergy, in which excessive authority has traditionally been granted to bishops with special headship function as fathers of the church. Such power is conferred through the "sacrament of holy orders or ordination."[28]

---

26 White, *Acts of the Apostles*, 161–162; italics supplied.

27 White, *Story of Redemption*, 304.

28 See *Catechism of the Catholic Church: With Modifications from the Editio Typica* (New York: Image, 1995), 433–437; Jaroslav Pelikan, *The Riddle of Roman Catholicism* (Nashville: Abingdon, 1959), 84, 124–125;

Given the amount of heat generated in some Adventist circles on the topic of ordination, one might surmise that somehow it transferred power and authority to the ordained. While that might be the case in Roman Catholic theology, it does not hold true in either the Bible or Ellen White's writings. To the contrary, just as baptism does not erase original sin but is rather an outward symbol of a changed heart, and just as the bread and the wine of the Lord's Supper are not transformed, in some mystical way, into the actual body and blood of Christ in the sacrifice of the Mass but are rather symbols of what Christ accomplished on the cross, so it is that the laying-on of hands in what has come to be called ordination does not confer power but is symbolic in recognition of the power already conferred by God in the calling and empowerment of a pastor. *What counts is not the act of ordination but the calling of God.* The Seventh-day Adventist Church has for many years recognized that God calls both men and women to pastoral ministry, the only difference being that the church has opted to call one ordination and the other commissioning. Such non-biblical verbal gymnastics must lead the angels to scratch their heads in bewilderment. However, it all seems to be clear in Adventist policy.

But at least Ellen White is forthright on the topic. No power or authority is transferred in ordination. That is a product of the history of the church. And, in the words of the Revelator, much of the Christian world seems to be following after the beast (Rev. 13:3, NKJV) on the understanding and importance of ordination.

Historical Issues in Adventism's Approach to Ecclesiology

So far in this chapter Adventism's approach to biblical authority and Ellen White's historical approach to authority have been examined. Thus the stage has been set for an examination of the denomination's struggle to find and be faithful to a balanced and biblical view of ecclesiastical authority.

The Earliest Adventists and Ecclesiastical Authority: 1843–1863

Looking back at early Adventism, no one could have predicted that by mid-twentieth century Seventh-day Adventism would be the most highly structured denomination in the history of Christianity, with

---

Richard P. McBrien, *Catholicism*, study edition (San Francisco, Harper & Row, 1981), 558–559, 846–847.

Catholic or Adventist?

four levels of authority above the local congregation.[29] The plain fact is that the earliest Adventists feared structured churches—and with good reason. That fear was nicely expressed in the October 1861 meeting that saw the establishment of the first local conference. Part of the discussion at that historic meeting had to do with developing a formal statement of belief. John Loughborough took the lead in the discussion and laid out five progressive points that expressed the attitude of most of his audience:

> The first step of apostasy is to get up a creed, telling us what we shall believe. The second is, to make that creed a test of fellowship. The third is to try members by that creed. The fourth to denounce as heretics those who do not believe that creed. And, fifth, to commence persecution against such.[30]

James White also expressed his fears. "Making a creed," he wrote, "is setting the stakes, and barring up the way to all future advancement." Those churches that had set up creeds

> have marked out a course for the Almighty. They say virtually that the Lord must not do anything further than what has been marked out in the creed ... The Bible is our creed. We reject everything in the form of a human creed. We take the Bible and the gifts of the Spirit; embracing the faith that thus the Lord will teach us from time to time. And in this we take a position against the formation of a creed. We are not taking one step, in what we are doing, toward becoming Babylon [as oppression].[31]

Those points are informative to Adventists who live 150 years later. While White feared a backward-looking rigidity that would inhibit the progressive dynamic in what the early Adventist's thought of as an ongoing present truth, Loughborough expressed fear of persecution for those who did not line up with official positions.

The participants in that 1861 meeting had good reasons to fear organized religious bodies. Fresh in their memories was the persecution of Millerites in 1843 and 1844 as pastors lost their pulpits and followers their memberships because of their understanding of the Bible's teaching on the Second Advent. They had come to see

---

29 The Roman Catholic Church, for example, has only two levels of authority above the local congregation.

30 Joseph Bates and Uriah Smith, "Doings of the Battle Creek Conference, Oct. 5 & 6, 1861," *Review and Herald,* Oct. 8, 1861, 148.

31 Bates and Smith, "Doings," 148.

organized religion in terms of the persecuting Babylon of the books of Daniel and Revelation. It was no accident that Millerite George Storrs wrote in early 1844 that "no church can be organized by man's invention but what it becomes Babylon *the moment it is organized.*" In the same article Storrs asserted that Babylon "is the *old mother* and all her children [the Protestant denominations], who are known by the family likeness, a domineering, lordly spirit; a spirit to suppress a free search after truth, and a free expression of our conviction of what is truth."[32] Charles Fitch had been of the same opinion when he preached his famous sermon calling Millerites to come out of Babylon, the fallen denominations.[33]

It was the fear of Babylon as persecuting churches that kept any of the six major groups that came out of the Millerite movement from organizing before the 1850s and 1860s, and none but the Sabbatarian Adventists would ever organize above the congregational level.[34]

The fear of organized denominations as persecuting Babylon stands at the foundation of early Adventist attitudes in regard to organizing as a church. However, in the 1850s James White began to emphasize an alternative biblical meaning of Babylon. In July 1859 he let it be known in the most descriptive language that he was sick and tired of the cry of Babylon every time that anyone mentioned organization. He wrote:

> Bro. Confusion makes a most egregious blunder in calling system, which is in harmony with the Bible and good sense, Babylon. As Babylon signifies confusion, our erring brother has the very word stamped upon his own forehead. And we venture to say that there is not another people under heaven more worthy of the brand of Babylon than those professing the Advent faith who reject Bible order. Is it not high time that we as a people heartily embrace everything that is good and right in the churches?[35]

It is impossible to overestimate the force of White's redirection of the emphasis from Babylon being primarily seen as persecution to its

---

32 George Storrs, "Come Out of Her My People," *The Midnight Cry*, Feb. 15, 1844, 237–238.

33 Charles Fitch, *"Come Out of Her, My People"* (Boston: J. V. Himes, 1843).

34 See George R. Knight, *William Miller and the Rise of Adventism* (Nampa, ID: Pacific Press, 2010), 228–250.

35 James White, "Yearly Meetings," *Review and Herald*, July 21, 1859, 68.

being seen as confusion. That new emphasis went far toward paving the way for the Sabbatarians to organize as a religious body, legally own property, pay pastors on a regular basis, assign pastors to locations where they were needed, and develop a system for transferring membership. In the end, developing church organization had one major purpose, namely, to expedite the mission of the denomination. But the redefinition of Babylon was only one of the transformations that allowed the Sabbatarian Adventists to organize.

A second essential transformation had to do with moving beyond the biblical literalism of White's earlier days when he believed that the Bible must explicitly spell out each aspect of church organization. In 1859 he argued that "we should not be afraid of that system which is not opposed by the Bible, and is approved by sound sense."[36] Thus he had come to a new hermeneutic. *White had moved from a principle of Bible interpretation that held that the only things Scripture allowed were those things it explicitly approved to a hermeneutic that allowed for developments that did not contradict the Bible and were in harmony with common sense. That shift was absolutely essential to moving forward in the creative steps in church organization that he would advocate in the 1860s.*

That revised hermeneutic, however, put White in opposition to those who maintained a literalistic approach to the Bible that demanded that something be spelled out explicitly before the church could accept it. To answer that mentality, White noted that nowhere in the Bible did it say that Christians should have a weekly paper, a steam printing press, build places of worship, or publish books. He went on to argue that the "living church of God" needed to move forward with prayer and common sense.[37]

Without the radical shift in hermeneutical principles there would have been no organization among the Sabbatarians above the level of the local congregation. The new hermeneutic allowed them not only to organize but to create a structure that made it possible to take their unique message to the ends of the earth. Mission was always behind the Adventist mentality as it sought to develop dynamically on the basis of a hermeneutic that allowed those things that did not contradict the Bible and were in harmony with common sense.

---

36 White, "Yearly Meetings," 68.
37 White, "Yearly Meetings," 68.

With the new hermeneutic and the new definition of Babylon in place the Sabbatarians were in position to develop the non-biblical concept of local conferences in 1861 and the equally non-biblical concept of a General Conference in 1863. That last move was "for the purpose of securing unity and efficiency in labor, and promoting the general interests of the cause of present truth, and of perfecting the organization of the Seventh-day Adventists."[38]

Ecclesiastical Tensions and the Creation of Unions: 1863-1903

As might be expected, tensions eventually developed between the authority of the local conferences and that of the General Conference. In August 1873, for example, in the context of a lack of respect for General Conference officers, James White noted that "our General Conference is the highest earthly authority with our people, and is designed to take charge of the entire work in this and all other countries."[39]

Then in 1877 the General Conference in session voted the following:

> the highest authority under God among Seventh-day Adventists is found in the will of the body of that people, as expressed in the decisions of the General Conference *when acting within its proper jurisdiction*; and that such decisions should be submitted to by all without exception, *unless they can be shown to conflict with the word of God and the rights of individual conscience.*[40]

That vote seems clear enough and both of the Whites accepted it. It must be noted, however, that it left unspecified the "proper jurisdiction" of the General Conference and "the rights of individual conscience."

Interestingly, Ellen White on several occasions questioned whether the rulings of the General Conference were always the voice of God. In 1891, for example, she wrote that

> I was obliged to take the position that there was not the voice of God in the General Conference management and decisions ... Many of the positions taken, going forth as the voice of the

---

38 John Byington and Uriah Smith, "Report of General Conference of Seventh-day Adventists" *Review and Herald*, May 26, 1863, 204–206.

39 James White, "Organization," *Review and Herald*, Aug. 5, 1873, 60.

40 "Sixteenth Annual Session of the General Conference of S. D. Adventists," *Review and Herald*, Oct. 4, 1877, 106 (italics supplied).

General Conference, have been the voice of one, two, or three men who were misleading the Conference.[41]

In 1896 she noted that the General Conference "is no longer the voice of God,"[42] and in 1901 she wrote:

> the people have lost confidence in those who have management of the work. Yet we hear that the voice of the [General Conference] is the voice of God. Every time I have heard this, I have thought that it was almost blasphemy. The voice of the conference ought to be the voice of God, but it is not.[43]

An analysis of those negative statements indicates that they refer to occasions when the General Conference did not act as a representative body, when its decision-making authority was centralized in a person or a few people, or when the General Conference had not been following sound principles.[44]

That conclusion lines up with Ellen White's statements across time. In fact, she specifically spoke to the point in a manuscript read before the delegates of the 1909 General Conference session in which she responded to the schismatic activities of A. T. Jones and others. She told the delegates:

> At times, when a small group of men entrusted with the general management of the work have, in the name of the General Conference, sought to carry out unwise plans and to restrict God's work, I have said that I could no longer regard the voice of the General Conference, represented by these few men, as the voice of God. But this is not saying that the decisions of a General Conference composed of an assembly of duly appointed, representative men from all parts of the field should not be respected. God has ordained that the representatives of His church from all parts of the earth, when assembled in a General Conference, shall have authority.[45]

The second round of organizational refinement took place between 1901 and 1903,[46] when several major changes were made. The two most important ones were the replacement of the autonomous auxiliary

---

41 E. G. White, "Board and Council Meetings," MS 33, [no date] 1891.

42 E. G. White to Men Who Occupy Responsible Positions, July 1, 1896.

43 E. G. White, "Regarding the Southern Work," MS 37, April 1901.

44 Barry David Oliver, *SDA Organizational Structure: Past, Present and Future* (Berrien Springs, MI: Andrews University Press, 1989), 98–99.

45 E. G. White, *Testimonies*, 9:260–261.

46 For the best treatment on this reorganization, see Oliver, *SDA Organizational Structure*.

organizations (such as those that controlled education, publishing, medical, Sabbath school, and so on) with the departmental system, and the development of union conferences to stand as intermediary administrative units between the General Conference and the local conferences. There had been experimentation with both of those innovations in South Africa and Australia before the 1901 session. Both of them had been developed in response to regional mission needs and both were developed in opposition to General Conference pronouncements and procedures.

General Conference President O. A. Olsen thought he saw "elements of danger" in the departmental systems and told A. T. Robinson in South Africa not to develop departments.[47] But it was too late. Because of the large amount of time it took to communicate from North America, Robinson had instituted the program and found that it worked.

It is of interest that the General Conference leadership also opposed the creation of union conferences.[48] But in the period preceding the 1901 General Conference Session, W. C. White and A. G. Daniells, president and secretary respectively of the Australian field acted in spite of counsel from headquarters. Years later Daniells reported that not everyone was happy with the union conference idea. "Some of our brethren thought then that the work was going to be wrecked, that we were going to tear the organization all to pieces, and get up secession out there in the South Sea islands." But in actuality, he observed, the result was quite the opposite. The new organizational approach greatly facilitated the mission of the church in the South Pacific while the new Australasian Union Conference remained a loyal and integral part of the General Conference system.[49]

Here an important lesson in the history of Adventist organization must be remembered: namely, that both of the major innovations adopted by the 1901 General Conference session were made in response to regional mission and both were developed in opposition to General Conference counsel. But they worked. The major lesson is

---

47 O. A. Olsen to A. T. Robinson, Oct. 25, 1892; see George R. Knight, *Organizing for Mission and Growth: The Development of Adventist Church Structure* (Hagerstown, MD: Review and Herald, 2006), 78–80 for the sequence of events.

48 General Conference Committee Minutes, Jan. 25, 1893.

49 *General Conference Bulletin*, 1913, 108.

that without the freedom to experiment Adventism would not have its present system of organization.

Ellen White was overjoyed with the development of union conferences. In calling for reform on the first day of the 1901 session she said to the delegates:

> God has not put any kingly power in our ranks to control this or that branch of the work. The work has been greatly restricted by the efforts to control it in every line ... If the work had not been so restricted by an impediment here, and an impediment there, and on the other side an impediment, it would have gone forward in its majesty.[50]

At the 1903 session she declared that *"it has been a necessity to organize union conferences, that the General Conference shall not exercise dictation over all the separate conferences."*[51]

On the basis of those and other comments, the late Gerry Chudleigh has argued that the unions "were created to act as *firewalls* between the GC and the conferences, making 'dictation' impossible." He buttressed his firewall image with two major points. First, "each union had its own constitution and bylaws and was to be governed by its own constituency." Second, "the officers of each union were to be elected by their own union constituency, and, therefore, could not be controlled, replaced or disciplined by the GC."[52]

Chudleigh wrote:

> To put it as bluntly as possible, after 1901, the General Conference could vote whatever it wanted unions and conferences to do, or not do, but the unions and conferences were autonomous and could do what they believed would best advance the work of God in their fields. The GC executive committee, or the General Conference in business session, could vote to fire a union president or conference president, or vote to merge a union or conference with another one, but their vote would change nothing: the union or conference would still exist and the member delegates could elect whoever they wanted as president.[53]

---

50 *General Conference Bulletin*, 1901, 26.

51 E. G. White, "Regarding Work of General Conference," MS 26, Apr. 3, 1903; italics supplied.

52 Gerry Chudleigh, *Who Runs the Church? Understanding the Unity, Structure and Authority of the Seventh-day Adventist Church* (n.p.: AdventSource, 2013), 18; italics supplied.

53 Chudleigh, *Who Runs the Church?* 18.

A case in point in contemporary Adventism is the Southeastern California Conference, which has an ordained female president, in spite of the wishes of the General Conference.

The situation looked good in 1901 with the union conferences in place, but over time the push for both unity and uniformity by the General Conference would erode the accomplishments of 1901. The most significant move along that line took place at the 1995 General Conference session.

The erosion of the ideal of unity in diversity had, unfortunately, already begun soon after the 1901 session. The following two years witnessed a major struggle for the control of Adventism between General Conference president A. G. Daniells and J. H. Kellogg, the powerful leader of the denomination's medical work.

In 1894 Ellen White had set forth "unity in diversity" as "God's plan," with unity being achieved by each aspect of the work being connected to Christ the vine.[54] In 1901 and 1902 Daniells had championed that ideal, noting in 1902 to the European Union Conference that just "because a thing is done a certain way in one place is not reason why it should be done in the same way in another place, or even in the same place at the same time."[55]

But that ideal began to give way by late 1902 as the Kellogg forces sought to unseat Daniells and replace him with A. T. Jones, who was by that time in the doctor's camp. In that struggle the Kellogg/Jones forces pushed for diversity. That dynamic impelled Daniells to emphasize unity as he moved toward a more authoritative stance. Thus the delicate balance of unity in diversity was lost soon after the 1901 session. As Barry Oliver points out, unity at the expense of diversity has been the focus of the General Conference leadership ever since the 1902 crisis.[56]

The only significant development in Adventist church structure since the period 1901–1903 took place in 1918 with the creation of world divisions of the General Conference. But it should be noted that the divisions are not conferences with their own constituencies

---

54 E. G. White to the General Conference Committee and the Publishing Boards of the Review and Herald and Pacific Press, Apr. 8, 1894; see also E. G. White, *Testimonies*, 9:259–260.

55 A. G. Daniells, *European Conference Bulletin*, 2, cited in Oliver, 320.

56 Oliver, 317 n. 2, 341.

but parts of the General Conference administration that represent the central body in various parts of the world.⁵⁷

An ongoing temptation of the General Conference throughout its history has been to overstep the bounds of its authority. General Conference president George I. Butler generated one of the boldest moves in that direction in 1873. On the first page of his little book titled *Leadership,* he wrote:

> Never [was there a] great movement in this world without a leader ... As nature bestows upon men a variety of gifts, it follows that some have clearer views than others of what best advances the interests of any cause. And the best good of all interested in any given object will be attained by intelligently following the counsels of those best qualified to guide.

Butler had no doubt that James White had played a role akin to that of Moses, and that in all matters of expediency in the Adventist cause it was right "to give his [White's] judgment the preference."⁵⁸ The 1873 General Conference session officially adopted Butler's ideas. But both of the Whites eventually felt uncomfortable with the document and wrote against many of its principles.⁵⁹ As a result, the 1875 and 1877 sessions rescinded the endorsement, especially those sections dealing with leadership being "confined to any one man."⁶⁰

In his recent MA thesis on Butler's *Leadership,* Kevin Burton did an excellent job of demonstrating that Butler wrote with James White as the leader he had in mind. But the self- imposed scope of Burton's research did not allow for the demonstration that Butler's style and claims in the 1873 document mirror his own style and claims in the 1888 conflict.⁶¹ On October 1, 1888, Butler wrote a long letter

---

57 See Knight, *Organizing,* 133–140.

58 George I. Butler, *Leadership* [Battle Creek, MI: Steam Press, 1873], 1, 8, 11, 13.

59 See, e. g., [James White] in a series entitled "Leadership" that ran in the *Signs of the Times* from June 4, 1874-July 9, 1874; E. G. White, *Testimonies,* 3:492–509.

60 James White and Uriah Smith, "Proceedings of the Fourteenth Annual Session of the S. D. Adventist General Conference," *Review and Herald,* Aug. 26, 1875, 59; James White and A. B. Oyen, "Sixteenth Annual Session of the General Conference of S. D. Adventists," *Review and Herald,* Oct. 4, 1877, 106.

61 Kevin M. Burton, "Centralized for Protection: George I. Butler and His Philosophy of One-Person Leadership," MA Thesis, Andrews University, 2015.

to Ellen White repeatedly emphasizing that he had "the highest position" in the denomination and should have the rights that go with that position. She replied to him on October 14 that he did "not understand [his] true position," that he had "false ideas of what belonged to [his] position," that he had turned his "mind into wrong channels," that he had "not kept pace with the opening providence of God," and that he had mingled his "natural traits of character" with his work. *Most serious of all the charges was that he was seeking to manipulate the information that would come before the 1888 General Conference session.* Speaking to the General Conference president and Uriah Smith (the secretary), she wrote that "you must not think that the Lord has placed you in the position that you now occupy as the only men who are to decide as to whether any more light and truth shall come to God's people." She noted in this letter and others that Butler's influence had led other session delegates to also "disregard light."[62]

A broad study of the 1888 crisis indicates that the most serious problem troubling the Minneapolis meeting was the high-handed assertions of position and manipulation of data by the president and his colleagues.[63] It should be noted in passing that the theme of Butler's 1873 *Leadership* was "union" and "order."[64] Unity was Butler's goal in that document and the same preservation of unity would be Butler's goal in his manipulation of data in the 1888 period.

Butler, as we know, lost the struggle in 1888. He had sought to impose not only unity but theological uniformity on the denomination, but Ellen White pushed against him with the alternative ideal of unity in diversity. She was, the General Conference's newly elected secretary reported in 1890, not so much interested in theological unity as she was in the unity of having a Christ-like spirit built on brotherly love.[65]

The major lesson to flow out of the 1888 crisis is unity in diversity. That same principle would undergird the reform of church structures

---

62 G. I. Butler to E. G. White, Oct. 1, 1888; E. G. White to G. I. Butler, Oct. 14, 1888.

63 See Knight, *Angry Saints*, passim.

64 See Burton, "Centralized for Protection," 60.

65 E. G. White to the General Conference Committee and the Publishing Boards of the Review and Herald and Pacific Press, Apr. 8, 1894; D. T. Jones to J. D. Pegg, Mar. 17, 1890; D. T. Jones to W. C. White, Mar. 18, 1890.

in 1901. This ideal of unity in diversity began to run into major difficulties in 1902 when Daniells began to assert his authority as General Conference president in his struggle with Kellogg. At that point, diversity began to take a back seat to unity and in 1903 Ellen White had to warn the reforming General Conference president that he could not "exercise a kingly power over [his] brethren."[66]

Removal of the Union Conference Firewall: 1980–2016

In spite of Daniells' temptation to abuse the power of his office, the balance between unity and diversity institutionalized by the creation of union conferences fared tolerably well for most of the twentieth century. In his summary of that period, Gerry Chudleigh notes that the constitutions and bylaws for the first unions created and voted at the 1901 session "contained no requirement that the unions adopt or follow GC policies, procedures, programs, initiatives, etc."[67]

However, in the legal documents of the denomination that would begin to change in the 1980s and come to a climax in the 1990s and the first two decades of the twenty-first century. The 1980s witnessed the development by the General Conference of a "Model Union Conference Constitution and Bylaws." In 1985 the *Working Policy* stated that the model should be "followed as closely as possible." But by 1995 the same section would note that the model "shall be followed by all union conferences ... Those sections of the model bylaws that appear in bold print are essential to the unity of the Church worldwide, and shall be included in the bylaws as adopted by each union conference. Other sections of the model may be modified." In 1985 the model stipulated that all **"purposes and procedures"** of the unions would be in harmony with the **"working policies and procedures"** of the General Conference. By 1995 General Conference **"programs and initiatives"** had been added and in 2000 all **"policies"** was included. All of those additions were in bold print.[68] Thus between 1985 and 2000 the *Working Policy* not only erased the 1901 model of unity in diversity set forth for unions in the drive for decentralization led by

---

66 E. G. White to Elder Daniells and His Fellow Workers, Apr. 12, 1903.

67 Chudleigh, *Who Runs the Church?* 31.

68 Stanley E. Patterson, "Kingly Power: Is It Finding a Place in the Adventist Church?" *Adventist Today*, Sept–Oct. 2012, 5; Chudleigh, *Who Runs the Church?* 32–33; *Working Policy of the General Conference of Seventh-day Adventists*, 1999-2000 edition (Hagerstown, MD: Review and Herald, 2000), 125–126.

Ellen White, but had become progressively more engineered toward centralization of authority in a drive for unity with progressively less diversity.

The challenge for the General Conference in the mid-eighties was to get existing union conferences to adopt the new model. The General Conference succeeded in that objective in some unions and failed in others. The case of the North Pacific Union opens a window into the dynamics. In September 1986 it rejected the model, but perhaps the most significant event connected to that rejection was the reading of General Conference president Neal Wilson's letter to the delegates. Wilson made it clear that the General Conference was the "highest authority in the church" and that it had the authority to create subordinate organizations. He then chastised the North Pacific Union for having two years before created a constitution of its own that was not in harmony with the model. He also threatened the noncompliant union, claiming that he saw "the only other option" to be an investigation "to determine whether [the] union ... is operating within the spirit and guidelines established for union conferences, with the understanding that appropriate action will be taken in the case of organizations that do not measure up to the standard."[69]

That unvarnished threat indicates that the type of actions threatened by the General Conference in 2016 have a history and that history is solidly rooted in the tightening up of the relationship between union conferences and the General Conference in the modified *Working Policy*.

The 1990s would witness the move by the General Conference leadership to centralize its authority shift into high gear. Robert Folkenberg, the new General Conference president, faced with the important but daunting task of maintaining order in a massive world church, established in 1991 the Commission on World Church Organization, which met several times until its work was completed in 1994. The successful aspects of the Commission's work went to the 1995 General Conference session. Others fell by the wayside. All of them were aimed at the centralization of authority.

Among those that fell by the wayside was an attempt to take away the exclusive right of local congregations to disfellowship

---

69   Rosmary Watts, "North Pacific Reasserts Constitutional Independence," *Spectrum*, February 1987, 29–33. Wilson's letter is found as an appendix on pages 31–33.

members. The stimulus for the move was the fact that Des Ford of Glacier View fame and John Osborne of Prophecy Countdown still held church membership in sympathetic congregations that would not disfellowship them. Osborne's case is interesting since, although he lived in Florida, his membership, being threatened there, had been rescued by the church at Troy, Montana, where he had never lived. At that point those in the General Conference who wanted action threatened to disband the church.[70] The congregation was disbanded, but Osborne's membership had been rescued by the Village Church in Angwin, California. Interestingly enough, it was the Pacific Union College Church in the same city that held Ford's membership. Neither congregation responded to the call to disfellowship the men, but the solution seemed obvious—give higher levels of the church structure the prerogative to disfellowship local church members.[71] Ideally, the idea ran, the same sort of logic could be used to remove ministerial credentials and disband congregations. Thus the "higher" levels would have more control over situations that they believed the lower levels were not handling correctly.

Bert Haloviak, General Conference archivist at the time, notes that he, Paul Gordon of the White Estate, and a member of the Biblical Research Institute were summoned to Folkenberg's office where each was asked to write a paper with the "hidden agenda" of supporting some of the General Conference's initiatives. The Institute's paper was written by Raoul Dederen of Andrews University. All three papers, although written independently and from different perspectives, concluded that the General Conference did not have grounding to do such things as to disfellowship members. Dederen, a colleague of mine at the time with specialties in ecclesiology and Roman Catholic theology, remarked at the Cohutta Springs meeting in March 1993 that some of the proposed initiatives were in essence the revival of medieval Catholicism.[72]

---

70 I still remember getting a late evening phone call from one of the congregation's leaders telling me that they had an ultimatum: either disfellowship Osborne or face dissolution as an Adventist church.

71 "Church Leaders Favor Model Constitutions," *Adventist Today*, May–June 1995, 19; "Administration Seeks Greater Control," *Adventist Today*, Nov–Dec. 1994, 23, 26.

72 Susan S. Sickler to George R. Knight, Feb. 27, 2017; Bert Haloviak to George R. Knight, Mar. 7, 2017; "Administration Seeks Greater Control," 26.

The most successful aspects of the Commission's recommendations saw passage at the 1995 General Conference session. That session not only endorsed a further tightening of the control measures embedded in the model constitutions, but also passed legislation that allowed for noncompliant unions, conferences and missions to be disbanded if they did not come into line with General Conference policies and initiatives. Since 1995 the *General Conference Working Policy* has contained a new section titled "Discontinuation of Conferences, Missions, Unions, and Unions of Churches by Dissolution and/or Expulsion."[73] Utilizing the ever-more centralizing requirements of the model constitution, the new section (B 95) proclaims the power to disband any union, conference, or mission that is out of harmony with General Conference policy. With what has become policy B 95 in place, the General Conference had arrived at the point where it could threaten the existence of two North American Division unions in September and October 2016.

Meanwhile, the measures attempted in the early nineties had met a fair amount of resistance both in committees and at Annual Council meetings. Susan Sickler, as a member of the Governance Commission, saw it as a "huge power grab", while Herman Bauman, Arizona Conference president, said that the essence of the commission report could be spelled "with the letters C-O-N-T-R-O-L." One General Conference staffer quipped in a private conversation that "What the Catholic Church took 300 years to achieve, we are doing in 150."[74]

Folkenberg, on the other hand, "kept saying this was in no way a centralization of power." In response, one union president in the North American Division noted to the Commission that "if it walks like a duck and it quacks like a duck, it probably is a duck." Neal Wilson, who had his own issues with his successor, aggressively supported those who saw the issue as centralization.[75]

Ted Wilson, then president of the division encompassing Russia, was reported to have said at a commission meeting that he would have difficulty getting some of the recommendations accepted in a

---

73 Designated in the *Working Policy* as B 45 in earlier post-1995 editions but now as B 95.

74 Susan S. Sickler to George R. Knight, Feb. 27, 2017; "Administration Seeks Greater Control," 23, 26.

75 Susan S. Sickler to George R. Knight, Feb. 27, 2017; "Administration Seeks Greater Control," 23, 26.

country that had just exited communism.[76] That, needless to say, was a pertinent insight that might have meaning in 2017 for those who understand the significance of the Protestant Reformation.

One final point needs to be made in regard to the Governance Commission. Namely, that some person or persons "high up" in the General Conference apparently manipulated the data so that the final form of the commission report was not in accordance with what was voted. Folkenberg did not indicate "how and why it came into final form without discussion and a vote from the commission."[77] The manipulation of data reappeared in 2015.

The 2015 General Conference session can be seen as a final building block that led up to the noncompliance threat issued at the 2016 Annual Council. The major event of the 2015 session, of course, was the vote not to allow divisions the option of ordaining female pastors. That action is clear enough. However, the way it took place leaves open the question of whether the action represents a "voice of God" vote enacted by the General Conference in session.

To grasp the significance of that issue it is necessary to go to the early presidency of Ted Wilson when he established the Theology of Ordination Study Committee (TOSC). This worldwide panel of over 100 scholars and non-scholars who had a burden on the topic met in 2013 and 2014 with the aim of informing the church on ordination issues at a scholarly level so that an informed vote could take place in 2015.[78] The study cost the denomination hundreds of thousands of dollars. As the General Conference Secretariat noted, "voices from around the world from all sides were heard; the arguments and supporting documents of all perspectives were made freely available online … The process was unmatched in both breadth and depth."[79] All those points are true and were included in a document that suggested penalties for those unions that had not come into line with the 2015 vote. All of this is forcefully outlined in a document

---

76 See "Administration Seeks Greater Control," 26.

77 "Administration Seeks Greater Control," 23; Susan S. Sickler to George R. Knight, Feb. 27, 2017.

78 "General Conference Theology of Ordination Study Committee Report, June 2014," 3–7. An examination of the committee membership list reveals that a large portion, if not the majority, were not scholars.

79 Secretariat, "A Study of Church Governance," 41; Secretariat, "Summary of *A Study*," 14.

entitled "A Study of Church Governance and Unity" developed by the General Conference Secretariat in September 2016.

Unfortunately, in actuality the "Study" set the stage for disunity in that it inflated the document's value for its own purposes, but did not report the findings of TOSC. That maneuver is merely the tip of a nasty iceberg. As impossible as it seems, after having spent so much money and time on the project the results of TOSC were never clearly presented to the General Conference session at the time of the vote—and for good reason. Apparently, TOSC's consensus did not support the conclusions desired by certain individuals at the top of the denominational power structure.[80] Thus the 2015 delegates were not informed that a super majority of 2/3 (62 for and 32 opposed) of the members of TOSC was in favor of allowing divisions to make the choice on whether to ordain female pastors.[81] In addition, the delegates were not informed that at least nine[82] of the 13 Divisions of the church in their TOSC reports were favorable toward letting each division make its own decision on female ordination. Nor did the final TOSC report present that data. It did, however, present the positions of three distinct groupings of delegates that developed during TOSC's two-year journey. But the delegates at the 2015 session were not explicitly informed that two of those groupings were in favor of each division making its own choice.[83]

Had the actual findings of TOSC been reported, the vote, in all probability, would have been different. After all, a 10% shift in the vote would have changed the outcome. The final tally at the General Conference session in San Antonio was 977 (42%) in favor of flexibility in ordination to 1,381 against, which was a remarkably close vote considering how the process was handled.

Not the least of the problems associated with the vote was the non-neutrality of the General Conference president, who reminded

---

80 As will be noted below, many of the TOSC participants were disillusioned when the General Conference president reversed his opinion on the importance of the committee between the time of its first meeting, when it looked as if it would come up with the "proper" answer, and its last, in which the majority voted against his position.

81 TOSC "Report," 12.

82 This point needs further investigation into the 13 division reports. Nine divisions in favor of diversity is the lowest number I have come across. Some sources report 11 and others 12 divisions in favor of flexibility.

83 TOSC "Report," 122, 123.

Catholic or Adventist?   237

the session delegates on voting day that they knew his position on the topic (which was clearly understood to be against the ordination of women). This was stated with the full knowledge that a significant majority of TOSC, a committee that he had authorized to solve the problem, had concluded to recommend that divisions should have the right to ordain females if they chose to do so.[84] And in a world church in which the vast majority of the delegates come from tribal and Roman Catholic cultures, a word from the denomination's top administrator has significance. The Norwegian Union Conference made an important point when it suggested that if unity was high on the agenda of the General Conference president he could have clearly reported the findings of TOSC and called for a solution in line with its results.[85]

At this point the widespread "disgust" expressed by a significant number of the TOSC membership at the about-face by the General Conference president should be noted for the record. At the beginning of the meetings, when it apparently looked like the carefully selected participants would come up with the "correct" conclusion, he spoke to the committee on the importance of their work, saying that it was not merely another investigation into a much-studied topic but that their findings would make a difference. But when the majority recommendation went against his personal viewpoint, he intimated at the final meeting that it was largely a North American committee and that if it had been a world committee the decision would have been different. He was reminded publicly that although many of the members were working in North America, they were in fact from around the world, but to no avail. The findings of the committee seemed at that point to have become not so important and were marginalized at the 2015 session.[86]

There were also serious irregularities in the 2015 voting, but this is not the place to discuss them.[87] On the other hand, it should be

---

84 TOSC, "Report," 12, 122, 123.

85 Norwegian Union Conference, "A Response to 'A Study of Church Governance and Unity,'" Oct. 4, 2016; See William G. Johnsson, *Where Are We Headed? Adventism after San Antonio* (Westlake Village, CA: Oak and Acorn Publishing, 2017), 153–161 for a published version of the document.

86 Recollections of several participants who wish to remain anonymous.

87 See, e.g., George R. Knight, "The Role of Union Conferences in Relation to Higher Authorities," *Spectrum* (44:4, 2016), 40.

pointed out that no matter how the vote turned out or how it could have turned out, the procedure itself suffered from the suppression and manipulation of data. This is a serious charge to make, but there is no alternative in the face of the handling of the TOSC findings and the ongoing misuse of them in General Conference documents, which trumpet the importance of the study without reporting its results.[88]

William Johnsson, retired editor of the *Adventist Review*, has pointed out that 2015 will go down in history as the most divisive General Conference session since 1888.[89] And he is correct. What is interesting is that in both sessions, people in high positions in the General Conference manipulated data. In the 1888 era it was President G. I. Butler, who Ellen White faulted for his desire to decide what information came to the delegates.[90] One can only guess who decided to suppress and manipulate the reporting of the findings of TOSC in 2015, but the only possibility is that they were a few people near the top of the General Conference structure.

The significance of the manipulation and suppression of crucial data that had been produced at immense expense for the purpose of informing the church has vast implications, especially since Ellen White, as noted earlier, repeatedly claimed in the 1890s that she no longer held that the General Conference was the voice of God because its decisions were really the decisions of a few men. That is exactly what is found in the events leading up to the vote in San Antonio. A few people decided what information went to the delegates. Even the General Conference's document, "Study of Church Governance and Unity", pointed out that Ellen White was upset when "two or three men" tried to control the church's mission or when "merely a half a dozen' at the world headquarters" sought "to be a ruling and controlling power." The "Study" document was correct in its use of that inspired material. But it was completely wrong when it claimed that what happened in the late 1800s "is a world away from the situation today."[91] It was actually the same situation and dynamic, with a few people in their decision-making capacity controlling information and events. As a result, from the perspective of Ellen

---

88 Secretariat, "Summary of *A Study*," 14; Secretariat, "A Study," 40, 41; see also Barry Oliver to George R. Knight, Feb. 20, 2017.

89 Johnsson, *Where Are We Headed?* 1.

90 E. G. White to G. I. Butler, Oct. 14, 1888.

91 Secretariat, "A Study," 34.

White's writings, there was no "voice of God vote" from the world church in 2015. Instead, it was the same old manipulation and kingly power approaches that she detested in 1888 and the 1890s.

The manipulation was not merely of the data, but also of the process. Here one example must suffice. The General Conference documents uplift the Jerusalem council of Acts 15 "almost as much for its *process* as for the theological decision that resulted," but that appreciation was not evident in San Antonio. For one thing, the General Conference documents do not describe the process of the Jerusalem council. Rather, they infer that the process consisted of a vote, to be followed by mandatory obedience.[92] However in Acts 15 not only is the actual process outlined but also the essential tipping point in that process is identified. The breakthrough, according to Acts 15, truly was based on process and came when Peter was able to demonstrate that the Holy Spirit made no distinction between Jews and Gentiles but came in the same way to both groups (Acts 15:8, 9). Without that evidence there would have been nothing but ongoing divisiveness, but with it there was healing and unity. What would have happened in San Antonio if the process adopted in Jerusalem had been used on the day of the vote? There would have been put on the program testimonies from people that demonstrated that the Holy Spirit fell upon the pastoral/evangelistic ministries of women in the same way as for men. Such testimonies were important in the final TOSC meeting and helped lead a significant majority of the participants, despite their personal position on women's ordination, to approve flexibility in the practice of ordaining women.[93] However, the few people who set up the procedure in San Antonio chose not to follow the model of Acts 15 even though the "Study of Church Governance" documents cite that passage to bolster the General Conference's authoritative position.

Much more could be said about the manipulation of data and process in the events related to the 2015 vote, but the illustrations are many and my space is limited. The final conclusion is that the vote settled nothing, but it did divide the denomination in ways that are tragic. Here some wisdom from James and Ellen White would have helped. James wrote in 1874:

---

92 Secretariat, "Summary of *A Study*," 5; Secretariat, "A Study," 13; italics supplied. See also Mark A. Finley, "United in Message, Mission, and Organization," *Ministry,* April 2017, 14.

93 Recollections of several participants who wish to remain anonymous.

creed power has been called to the rescue [of church unity] in vain. It has been truly said that 'The American people are a nation of lords.' In a land of boasted freedom of thought and of conscience, like ours, *church force cannot produce unity; but has caused divisions*, and has given rise to religious sects and parties almost innumerable.[94]

His wife was of the same opinion. "The church may pass resolution upon resolution to put down all disagreement of opinions," she penned in 1892, "but we cannot force the mind and will, and thus root out disagreement. These resolutions may conceal the discord, but they cannot quench it and establish perfect agreement."[95] From her perspective, only the clear word of Scripture could bring true unity.

Christ made a pertinent point when he proclaimed that he who has ears needs to "hear what the Spirit says to the churches" (Rev. 3:22, RSV). In order to do this, those who like to quote Ellen White must listen to all she has to say and not just use her to get across their own goals. Here are two selections that have been relevant throughout Adventism's ongoing struggle over authority. In 1895 she wrote:

> *the high-handed power that has been developed, as though position has made men gods, makes me afraid*, and ought to cause fear. *It is a curse* wherever and by whomsoever it is exercised. *This lording it over God's heritage will create such a disgust of man's jurisdiction that a state of insubordination will result.*

She went on to recommend that the "only safe course is to remove" such leaders since "all ye are brethren," lest "great harm be done."[96]

Another fascinating insight comes from the *Testimonies*.

> One man's mind and judgment are not to be considered capable of controlling and molding a conference ... The president of a conference must not consider that his individual judgment is to control the judgment of all. *Many, very many matters have been taken up and carried by vote, that have involved far more than was anticipated and far more than those who voted would have been willing to assent to had they taken the time to consider the question from all sides.*[97]

---

94 James White, "Leadership," *Signs of the Times*, June 4, 1874; italics supplied.

95 E. G. White, "Love, the need of the Church," MS 24, 1892.

96 Ellen G. White, *Special Testimonies: Series A* (Payson AZ: Leaves-of-Autumn, n.d.), 299–300; italics supplied.

97 E. G. White, *Testimonies*, 9:277-278; italics supplied.

This quotation contains some excellent advice for Adventist decision-makers as they approach the 2017 Annual Council.

Where is the Church in 2017?

Since the problem that has developed in the past few years is about women's ordination, some brief comments on that topic are necessary here. First, women's ordination is not prohibited in the Bible.[98] Nor is it prohibited in Ellen White's writings. Not only so, but the General Conference *Working Policy* does not stipulate a gender requirement.[99]

The issue is not settled, in large part, because of the suppression of information and the manipulation of the process in 2015. Nevertheless, the practice of women's ordination will not stop because there is no biblical evidence for doing so. Neither can its prohibition be settled by a vote alone. Adventist leaders also need to refrain from seeking to use policy as if it were Catholicism's Canon Law. And it must be remembered that Adventism is a post-Reformation religious community.

It is true that in 1990 the denomination officially voted not to ordain women to the gospel ministry because of "the possible risk of disunity, dissension, and diversion from the mission of the church."[100] That vote, it must be noted, did not claim that the practice was wrong. It was not a theological vote, but one based on the practical grounds that it might cause disunity. That was 27 years ago and the denomination has discovered that unity can be fractured in more than

---

98 This point has been made repeatedly with Adventism. See, e.g., Gordon Hyde, ed., *The Role of Women in the Church* (Washington, DC: General Conference of Seventh-day Adventists, 1984); Nancy Vyhmeister, ed. *Women in Ministry: Biblical and Historical Perspectives* (Berrien Springs, MI: Andrews University Press, 1998); John Reeve, ed, *Women and Ordination: Biblical and Historical Studies* (Nampa, ID: Pacific Press, 2015); Graeme J. Humble and Robert K McIver, eds, *South Pacific Perspectives on Ordination: Biblical, Theological and Historical Studies in an Adventist Context* (Cooranbong, Avondale Academic Press, 2015); Bertil Wiklander, *Ordination Reconsidered: The Biblical Vision of Men and Women as Servants of God* (Bracknell: Newbold Academic Press, 2015).

99 See *Working Policy*, L 35, L 50. The sexist language in these sections is not a voted policy, but an editorial decision made in the 1980s. See Knight, "The Role of Unions," 41; Gary Patterson, untitled critique of the Secretariat's paper on "Unions and Ordination," 1.

100 "Session Actions," *Adventist Review*, July 13, 1990, 15.

one direction. The plain fact in 2017 is that the church is seriously divided on women's ordination. But it probably would not be so if the conclusions generated by the TOSC committee had not been suppressed at San Antonio, if the process described in Acts 15 had been utilized at the session, and if the General Conference leadership had used the findings of TOSC as a tool to bring unity and healing to the church.

But that healing approach did not take place. As a result, a small group at denominational headquarters decided to exert what it believed to be its authority in September and October of 2016, months that witnessed the apex of the evolution of Adventist ecclesiological authority and the continuation of the problematic results that both James and Ellen White had predicted from the use of such authority. The initial recommendation was made in September, was formulated in the presidential offices, and utilized the *Working Policy* rulings developed in the 1980s and 1990s to centralize authority. Especially important was B 95, voted into policy at the 1995 session, which authorized the "dissolution" of noncompliant union conferences that were not in harmony with General Conference policy. That initial document, the basic content of which was leaked to *Spectrum*, urged the disbanding of the offending unions and their reconstitution as missions attached to the General Conference. By that means the union leaders could be removed and replaced and constituency meetings could be called to reverse the ordination votes.[101] A number of people, many of whom requested confidentiality in the present intimidating and threatening denominational climate,[102] relate that the initial proposal, which did not have widespread input, was withdrawn and all copies were collected by the General Conference president.

---

101   See, e.g., Bonnie Dwyer, "General Conference Leadership Considers Takeover of Unions that Ordain Women," Sept. 29, 2016, http://spectrummagazine.org/print/7661.

102   Most of my sources have requested confidentiality, given the intimidating atmosphere in the General Conference building, in General Conference institutions, and among other denominational employees who have hopes for a future in the upper realms of the denomination. In fact, intimidation and threats in matters related to finances and funding have been in the "air" emanating from Silver Spring. It is no accident that no professors from Andrews University or its theological seminary are participating in this conference. "Kingly power" is alive and well. It is fortunate that those of us who are retired are beyond that intimidating authority.

What eventually came out of a complex process was the document generated by the Secretariat entitled "A Study of Church Governance and Unity." This is not the place to critique that document,[103] but its existence points to an interesting paradox, namely, that the move by General Conference headquarters in Silver Spring to correct the noncompliant unions is out of harmony with the General Conference's own policy. Mitchell Tyner, retired Associate General Counsel to the General Conference, points out that the denomination's top administrators in September and October 2016 set about to approve a policy for dealing with noncompliant union conferences in spite of the fact that such a policy already existed. According to B 95 15, all such moves in regard to noncompliant unions are to be initiated by the division and "if" the division executive committee determines that a union conference/union of churches with conference status is in apostasy or rebellion and should be expelled from the world sisterhood of unions, the division shall refer the matter to the General Conference Executive Committee.[104]

With a clear procedure already in the *Working Policy*, Tyner, with his legal training, wondered out loud why anybody would want to create a new policy. The most likely answer, he points out, "would seem to be that B 95 wasn't exactly what the initiator(s) of this episode wanted to do."[105]

To put it bluntly, the General Conference presidential officers had to step outside of policy to make its case for punishing those it deemed to be outside of policy. After all, the *Working Policy* spells out in unmistakable language that dissolution of unions must begin at the division level. But if the division is not likely to come to the "proper" answer, alternatives must be used. The selected alternative, in this case, was for the president to step outside of policy to accomplish the task. So *here is a case of blatant noncompliance with the Working Policy to punish noncompliance.*

It is obvious that what is needed is a new policy that allows the General Conference president to initiate actions against anybody

---

103 For one perceptive critique, see Norwegian Union Conference, "A Response to 'A Study of Church Governance and Unity,'" Oct. 4, 2016.

104 Mitchell Tyner, http://spectrummagazine.org/article/2016/10/10/analysis-use-general-conference-working-policy-case-unions-ordain-women.

105 Tyner, "general-conference-working-policy".

deemed deserving of such attention. Such a policy, of course, would be a major step toward papalism and unrestricted kingly power.

Tyner points out that General Conference officers "more than once have chosen to ignore policy if it seems the best thing to do, as though policy is optional, not mandatory. *This is a bit like Richard Nixon's position that if the president does it, it isn't illegal.*"[106]

With that rather pregnant thought attention must turn to 2017, during which the Annual Council is to act on the fate of those lower rungs in the organization that have been noncompliant in regard to women's ordination. To put it mildly, the leadership of the General Conference has backed itself into an extraordinary situation in the evolution (or revolution) of Adventist authority.

Perhaps at this point it might be beneficial to hear—and heed—a word from the originator of Adventist church structure, who claimed in 1874 that "organization was designed to secure unity of action, and as a protection from imposture. It was never intended as a scourge to compel obedience, but, rather, for the protection of the people of God." Interestingly, James White published that exact statement at least twice, but with different comments each time. In 1874 he added that "church force cannot press the church into one body. This has been tried, and has proved a failure."[107] In 1880 he added:

> those who drew the plan of our church, Conferences, and General Conference organizations, labored to guard the precious flock of God against the influence of those who might, in a greater or less degree, assume the leadership. They were not ignorant of the evils and abuses which had existed in many of the churches of the past, where men had assumed the position which belongs to Jesus Christ, or had accepted it at the hands of their short sighted brethren.[108]

Ellen White's statement that the church should think through all the possible consequences of any voted action before legislation is enacted, should also be recalled.[109]

It must also be remembered that the medieval Catholic Church never viewed itself as persecuting anybody. It was just making sure that people were in line with Canon Law, its version of the *Working Policy*.

---

106 Tyner, "general-conference-working-policy," italics supplied.
107 James White, "Leadership," *Signs of the Times*, July 9, 1874, 28.
108 James White, "Leadership," *Review and Herald*, June 17, 1880, 392.
109 E. G. White, *Testimonies*, 9:278.

A little bit of history demonstrates that Adventism's ideas on church authority have come a long way in 150 years. James Standish, formerly of the religious liberty department of the General Conference, has written that "as a movement, we are drifting very dangerously into the hierarchicalism, formalism and dogmatism that our pioneers explicitly rejected."[110]

It needs to be remembered that part of James White's strategy in getting Adventists to organize in the first place was to help them to see that the biblical use of the word "Babylon" not only signified persecution but also confusion. White convinced them on the second meaning, but it appears that the denomination is now intent on resurrecting the first. Of course, given the noncompliance of the General Conference with its own policy, perhaps both meanings are in evidence in 2017.

In the spirit of Luther Year and the General Conference president's call to be faithful to the principles of the Reformation, I am offering my own 9.5 Theses (I do not have time for 95). There are times for soft words, but there comes a time, as Martin Luther discovered, for firm ones. Like Luther, I love my church and hope for its reformation. Luther wrote his propositions with love in his heart, and I do the same, with a real desire to see healing. Here are my 9.5 theses:

9.5 Theses[111]

1. The only basis for Christian unity is Scripture, mutual trust, and the love of God.

2. The *Church Manual* makes it clear that the General Conference is the "highest authority" for the world church, "*under God.*"[112]

3. It is God who calls pastors. All the church can do is to recognize God's call by the laying-on of hands

4. Ordination is not a biblical topic. (The passages using the word in the KJV generally mean to appoint or consecrate.) Therefore, it is absolutely impossible to use the Bible to differentiate between ordaining and commissioning.

---

110 Quoted in Johnsson, *Where Are We Headed?* 74.

111 Even a casual reader will discover that, like Luther, I have had a bit of a challenge keeping the number of theses from expanding--thus the 9.1 and 9.2 maneuver, so that I could maintain the 9.5 symbolism.

112 *Seventh-day Adventist Church Manual*, 16th ed. (Hagerstown, MD: Review and Herald, 2000), 27; italics added.

5. For Adventists the Bible is the only source for doctrine and practice. An appeal to policy is not an appeal to the Bible. A vote by a General Conference session is not equivalent to Bible evidence.

6. On issues not definitively settled in the Bible, James White utilized the only possible way forward in unity of mission when he moved from a hermeneutic that stipulated that practices must be expressly spelled out in the Bible to a hermeneutic that held that practices were permissible if they did not contradict Scripture and were in harmony with common sense. (The new hermeneutic made it possible for the Sabbatarian Adventists to organize as a denomination.)[113]

7. The so-called noncompliant unions are not out of harmony with the Bible.

8. Adventism has moved at times from being a church based on Scripture to one based on tradition and ecclesiastical pronouncements.

9. The General Conference leadership in 2017 is coming dangerously close to replicating the medieval church in its call for the serious discipline of large sectors of the church on the basis of a non-biblical issue.

9.1. The recent General Conference documents and procedures do not reflect faithfulness to the Bible's teachings in Acts 15 or Matthew 18.

9.2. Because data were suppressed and events surrounding the voting process were manipulated, the 2015 vote on women's ordination did not indicate the voice of God.

9.3. One of the important functions of the ancient Hebrew prophets was to confront priests and kings over their abuse of authority. One of the functions of Ellen White was to confront conference presidents for similar reasons. If there were a prophet in modern Adventism, that prophet should find plenty to do.

---

113 See George R. Knight, "Ecclesiastical Deadlock: James White Solves a Problem that Had No Answer," *Ministry*, July 2014, 9–13; George R. Knight, "James White Finds the Answer," in John W. Reeve, ed., *Women and Ordination: Biblical and Historical Studies* (Nampa, ID: Pacific Press, 2015), 113–120.

9.4. The current atmosphere of confrontation in Adventism has not been brought about by the unions, but by the General Conference leadership and its non-biblical, manipulative tactics.

9.45. The October 2017 meetings may help the worldwide Adventist Church decide whether it wants to move toward an Adventist Ecclesiology or more toward a Roman Catholic style.

9.5. The so-called nonconforming unions must stand together, come into line with General Conference demands, or go down one by one. Martin Niemöller, a leading German Protestant pastor during World War II, has written these thought-provoking lines: "First they came for the Socialists, and I did not speak out—because I was not a Socialist. Then they came for the Trade Unionists, and I didn't speak out—because I was not a Trade Unionist. Then they came for the Jews, and I didn't speak out—because I was not a Jew. Then they came for me—and there was no one left to speak out."

Two historical recollections are relevant. First, Peter's words in Acts 5:39: "We must obey God rather than men" (RSV). Second, Luther's words at the Diet of Worms: "I cannot submit my faith either to the pope or to the councils, because it is clear as the day that they have frequently erred and contradicted each other. Unless therefore I am convinced by the testimony of Scripture ... *I cannot and I will not retract*, for it is unsafe for a Christian to speak against his conscience. Here I stand, I can do no other; may God help me. Amen."[114]

---

114 E. G. White, *The Great Controversy*, 160.

www.ingramcontent.com/pod-product-compliance
Lightning Source LLC
Chambersburg PA
CBHW061636040426
42446CB00010B/1450